The GIANT Encyclopedia of Math Activities

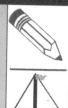

The
GIANT
Encyclopedia of
Math
Activities
For Children 3 to 6

*Written by Teachers
for Teachers*

*Edited by Kathy Charner,
Maureen Murphy, and Charlie Clark*

gryphon house
Beltsville, MD

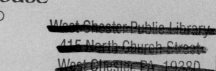

© 2007 Gryphon House
Published by Gryphon House, Inc.
10726 Tucker Street, Beltsville, MD 20705
800.638.0928; 301.595.9500; 301.595.0051 (fax)

Visit us on the web at www.ghbooks.com

Illustrations: Kathi Whelan Dery
Cover Art: Beverly Hightshoe

Library of Congress Cataloging-in-Publication Data

The giant encyclopedia of math activities / edited by Kathy Charner, Maureen
Murphy, and Charlie Clark.

    p. cm.
 ISBN 978-0-87659-044-7
 1. Mathematical recreations--Encyclopedias. 2. Mathematics--Study and
teaching (Primary)--Activity programs--Encyclopedias. I. Charner, Kathy.
II. Murphy, Maureen. III. Clark, Charlie.
 QA95.G469 2007
 793.74--dc22

                  2007002489

Gryphon House is a member
of the Green Press Initiative, a
nonprofit program dedicated
to supporting publishers in
their efforts to reduce their
use of fiber-sourced forests.
For further information visit
www. greenpressinitiative.org

Bulk purchase

Gryphon House books are available for special premiums and sales promotions as
well as for fund-raising use. Special editions or book excerpts also can be created to
specification. For details, contact the Director of Marketing at Gryphon House.

Disclaimer

Gryphon House, Inc. and the authors cannot be held responsible for damage,
mishap, or injury incurred during the use of or because of activities in this book.
Appropriate and reasonable caution and adult supervision of children involved in
activities and corresponding to the age and capability of each child involved, is
recommended at all times. Do not leave children unattended at any time.
Observe safety and caution at all times.

Table of Contents

Table of Contents

Table of Contents

Table of Contents

General Tips

Group or Circle Time

Table of Contents

Table of Contents

Science

Sensory

Snack & Cooking

Table of Contents

Introduction

"Emily, what is math for?" Four-year-old Emily sat at the kitchen table with her chin resting on her clasped hands. She listened to this easy question, rolled her eyes, and gave the only answer she knew: "Math is for making cakes!"

Emily loves helping her mother bake moist, tender cakes with sweet frosting on top. When her mother lets her spoon the sugar into the measuring cup, Emily grins, remembering how soft and good the cake tastes, warm from the oven. So, through measuring, spooning, counting, and mixing, Emily has learned that "math is for making cakes."

Most preschoolers, just like Emily, learn best about math concepts when they touch, move, build, and experiment with things in their everyday world. And, as Emily and her preschool friends will discover along the journey, math is definitely for making cakes...plus a whole lot more!

Just What Are Preschoolers Made of?

Curious and Assertive

Three-year-olds are interested in everything they find: measuring tapes, shape puzzles, sets of blocks, and mixing bowls that nest together. These little learners explore with all their senses and imitate whatever they see, ready to make the jump from toddler to preschooler.

Friendly and Imaginative

Four-year-olds expand on the curiosity they had as three-year-olds, discovering new ideas and predicting what comes next. Working with others is important to this age group: even shy four-year-olds enjoy helping a buddy draw rectangles at the art table or park trucks in order on the rug.

Involved and Hardworking

When children are five and six, they build higher towers and spend time painting more details than their four-year-old friends. Not only can they listen to longer, more complex stories, they can also begin to imagine living in castles far away across the sea, and brainstorm ways to find out more about them.

Unique and Extraordinary

Every preschool child (and every preschool teacher) is a rare and unique collection of the attributes listed above: curious, friendly, imaginative, hardworking. The wise adult gets to know each child in his or her classroom,

discovering a child who grins after dropping all the shapes into the right bin, but hesitates about drawing a circle to make a snowman. And another child who cuts out a purple frog quickly for the color chart, but fidgets when asked to count the cutouts. Understanding math concepts is developmental; and thankfully, our imaginative preschoolers don't fit into any rigid educational slots.

What Math Concepts Do Preschoolers Want to Learn About?

Children want to know about everything they see. How do clocks work? What comes next in a pattern? How many sides does a triangle have? Teachers take this curiosity and build on it to capture the imaginations of their children.

Curious preschoolers want to explore:
- shapes of balls, dishes, blocks, and tools;
- numbers used to count and measure, and the numerals that represent them;
- groups of crayons and sets of pipe cleaners by counting, sorting, and ordering them;
- patterns of stripes and bugs and glittering stars;
- charts and graphs about favorite colors, birthdays, and wiggly pets;
- clocks for telling time;
- coins to know how much something costs; and
- stories about numbers, counting, and everything else mathematical.

How Do Teachers Help Young Children Learn?

Authentic Work
Young children need real world activities that tie in to their everyday lives. Put away the worksheets with line drawings of measuring cups for the children to circle. Instead, put out some flour, salt, water, and a big red mixing bowl so the children can make playdough.

Concrete Objects
Young children need real items they can touch and move and handle. Work in small groups so each child can measure a cup of flour and pour it into a big bowl, then blend it with salt and water.

Sensory Learning
The more senses involved, the more knowledge constructed. Give all the children a small amount of flour to rub in their hands. Have them drop in food coloring and peppermint extract for color and fragrance.

Integrated experiences

Write a paragraph, as a group, about making the playdough together. Read "The Gingerbread Boy" and make gingerbread. Let the children measure and mix the ingredients. Talk about the sizes of the spoons and cups and the temperature of the oven. Dramatize the story outside. Compare the recipes.

More Practice

Wait a few days and make playdough again, asking the children to choose the color and extract for fragrance. Send small bags of playdough home to the children's families at the end of the day, along with the recipe and the story the children wrote together.

Here are the six levels of questions, taken from Benjamin Bloom's *Taxonomy of Educational Objectives*, followed by examples. Avoid the trap of asking questions from only the top two types. Deepen your questioning techniques and watch children's understanding grow!

> **Bloom's Taxonomy**
>
> *One of the strongest ways to help young children learn is talking with them about what they think. Benjamin Bloom in* Taxonomy of Educational Objectives *(New York: Longman, Inc., 1956) stresses the importance of asking good questions. Ask the children questions that help them make connections and use the information they are learning.*

- Knowledge: recall information. What kind of shape is round?
- Comprehension: understand information. How did we measure the flour?
- Application: use new information. Name something like a clock.
- Analysis: break a whole into parts. What would happen if we couldn't count things?
- Synthesis: put parts together to make a new whole. What other ways can we use to sort the bugs?
- Evaluation: give an opinion and a reason. Is "Our Pet Graph" a good name for this activity? Why or why not?

Six Tips for Getting the Most from This Book

There are 18 chapters in this book. Some of them have math activities for specific classroom centers (block center, or sand and water table, for example), and others have activities for different classroom routines (transitions). Each activity identifies the math concept, the materials needed, and the steps involved. To get the most from this book, read the following tips:

1. Use the math skills index. When you begin teaching the skill of classifying, for example, review the sorting activities from the index and choose the ones that meet the needs of the children in your class. Each activity in this book has at least one math concept that the activity teaches.

2. Create a unit of learning. How will you introduce the classifying skills you want the children to learn? You could group the learning activities around a theme, such as a jungle unit, asking the children to sort types of animals and place them into their natural habitats. Or you could then spend two weeks helping the children classify everything in sight, such as the color of their eyes, the kinds of fruits they'll eat for snack that week, and the types of vehicles parked in the block area.

3. Fit the activities into your unit plan. Be flexible and creative. Which learning experiences should you start with? You might want to begin a new unit with a simple counting activity and get more involved as you go along. Or you might try adding a related art activity. Customize the sequence of lessons in your unit until you have the right mix of math activities bursting with colorful graphs, jazzy music, rhyming fingerplays, and tasty snacks, all designed to enrich the learning.

4. Map out the materials. Collect the supplies for the activities, noting that you might need to get some things ready before the lesson, such as creating a large graph or collecting paper towel tubes. These do-ahead items are clearly spelled out for you, along with everything else you will need to make the learning enterprise successful and fun for all.

5. Add integrated learning and sensory activities into the mix. Many of the activities have a "more to do" and/or "related books" sections. These sections contain enriching and creative ways to extend the learning with art ideas, cooking, music, science activities, and of course, books. Take advantage of these ideas to make your unit plan full of experiences that appeal to young learners.

6. Save the best for last: Plan a culmination activity. Save one of your favorite activities from this book for last. Use this final learning experience of the unit to review with the children what they have learned, and to give them a sense of completion. What would this look like? The closing activity could be something as simple as drawings of "My Favorite Habitat" arranged in a graph on the bulletin board, or as involved as a parent participation day to present what they children have learned. Reminding the children of this special ending activity as they work through the unit's math activities gives them additional purpose for their learning, as well as something to look forward to.

Ask the children in your class to complete this sentence: Math is for _____.

✚ *Susan Oldham Hill, Lakeland, FL*

A-Weigh We Go!

comparison, estimation, observation, weight

Materials
bathroom and kitchen scale
objects to weigh, such as bags of sugar, flour, potatoes, or onions; boxes of
    detergent and cookies; shoes of different sizes; and so on
chart or graph paper and pencil
small re-sealable bag filled with sugar
large re-sealable bag filled with corn flakes
suitcase

What to do
1. Show the children two of the objects, such as a five-pound bag of sugar and a 10-pound bag of potatoes. Ask the children to guess which one weighs more.
2. Show the children how to use a bathroom scale to weigh the objects. Let one child weigh the items to see if they guessed correctly.
3. Next, show the children several items and ask them to guess how much each weighs. Record the children's guesses on a chart.
4. Weigh each object (using the appropriate scale) and write the correct weight on the chart or graph. Discuss whether the children's guesses were correct.
5. Have each child estimate how much she weighs. Record the estimations on a chart.
6. Weigh each child and record the child's weight on the chart. Discuss how close the children came to guessing their own weight accurately.
7. Show the children a small plastic bag filled with sugar and a larger plastic bag filled with corn flakes. Ask them which one weighs more, the smaller bag or the larger bag. Keep track of their answers. Weigh the bags. Afterward, point out that bigger does not always mean heavier.
8. Ask older children to figure out how to weigh a suitcase that is too large for the scale. Listen carefully to their suggestions and try some out. If necessary, suggest that one way to weigh the suitcase is to have one child stand on the scale while holding the suitcase and note the total weight. Then subtract the weight of the child from the total weight to determine the weight of the suitcase.

✚ *Virginia Jean Herrod, Columbia, SC*

Alternative Measuring

measurement

Materials
paper
scissors
markers

What to do
1. Help the children trace objects and cut them out to use for measuring. They might trace their arm, a classroom object, or their whole body.

2. Ask the children questions about the measurements: "How many arms long is the table? How many children do we need to be as tall as a dinosaur? How many crayons did it take to measure the chair?" This method is meaningful to children and is a great preparation for using standard measuring devices, such as a ruler.

TAPE

PAPER

TRACE AROUND HAND and ARM

10"

ARM CUTOUT

Related book
Inch by Inch by Leo Lionni

✚ *Phyllis Esch, Export, PA*

Apple Picking Time!

counting, sorting

Materials
green, red, and yellow construction paper
scissors
laminator
hole punch
yarn

large cutout tree

pushpins (not thumbtacks)

bulletin board

3 envelopes or baskets (one for each color apple)

What to do

1. Cut out apples from green, red, and yellow paper. Laminate for durability.
2. Punch a hole in the top of each apple. Loop a piece of yarn through the hole and tie a knot.
3. Put a large cutout tree on a bulletin board that the children can reach. Put pushpins all over the tree.
4. Hang apples on the tree by hanging the yarn loops on the pushpins.
5. Place baskets on the floor under the board, or attach envelopes (you can make them out of colored construction paper). Glue an apple to each one to identify which apples go in which basket or envelope.
6. Invite the children to "pick" the apples out of the tree and place them in the appropriate baskets or envelopes.
7. Have the children place their apples on the floor and count them. Ask the children questions: *Which color has more? Less? Are they the same amount?*
8. Hang the apples back up on the tree for the next apple pickers!

✚ *Shelley F. Hoster, Norcross, GA*

Bow Fun

counting, sorting

Materials

3 sturdy gift or shoeboxes

large package of bows in assorted colors and sizes

What to do

1. Cut a hole in the lid of each box, big enough to fit the bows. Make a small hole in one lid, a medium hole in another lid, and a large hole in the last lid.
2. Invite the children to sort the bows so they fit in the corresponding openings in the boxes. Label the holes *small*, *medium*, and *large* so the children can see the written instructions.
3. An alternative is to color code the boxes with colored tape and invite the children to sort the bows by color.

✚ *Maxine Della Fave, Raleigh, NC*

Button Patterns

patterns

Materials
buttons
marker
sentence strips

What to do

1. Before doing this activity with the children, trace around buttons to make patterns on the sentence strips. For example, trace one large button, one small button, and so on, or a button with two holes, one with four holes, one with two holes, one with four holes, and so on.

2. Give each child a sentence strip with a button pattern on it, and invite all of the children to match buttons to the patterns, continuing the pattern to the end of the paper.

   Safety Note: Supervise this activity closely to make sure no children put buttons into their mouths. If any of the children tend to put items in their mouths, use larger items to make the patterns.

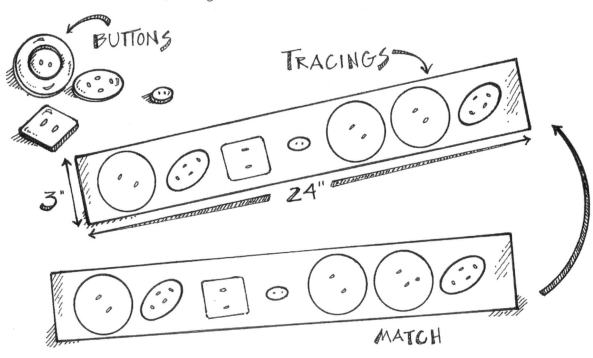

Barbara Saul, Eureka, CA

Calendar Numerals

counting, writing numerals

Materials   old calendar pages
markers
paper

What to do   1. Place markers and old calendar pages with the squares and numerals on them in the writing center or art center.
2. Encourage the children to copy and count the numerals on the calendar squares.

✚ *Holly Dzierzanowski, Brenham, TX*

Car Dealership

sorting

Materials   small toy cars (such as Hot Wheels™ and Matchbox Cars™) or paper cutouts of cars
construction paper
markers

What to do   1. Explain to the children that they are going to divide up the big group of cars into smaller groups. **Note:** If you do not have a lot of toy cars, cut out a variety of car shapes in different colors.
2. Ask for ideas about making smaller groups of cars. If no one comes up with a way, suggest sorting the cars by color.
3. Choose a child to pick up a car of any color. Ask the other children to find colors that match (have them do this one child at a time).
4. Continue until all the cars of that color have been chosen.
5. Use a marker to make a label for the color of that set of cars.
6. Continue with a different color until all the cars have been sorted by color.

7. Ask for another sorting idea. Give the children hints if they need some help. Suggest they try convertibles and hardtops, those with doors that open and those that don't, trucks and cars, those made of metal and those made of plastic, and so on.

✚ *Susan Oldham Hill, Lakeland, FL*

Charting Inch by Inch

measurement, sorting

Materials
25 classroom objects measuring 12" or less
chart paper
marker
rulers

What to do

1. Ahead of time, measure 12" across and 12" down on chart paper to make a 12" x 12" square. Make a grid with 1" squares so that there are 12 squares in each row and 12 squares in each column.
2. Number the grid 1 through 12 in the first column. Place the grid on the rug so the children can see it easily.
3. Choose a child to measure one of the classroom objects from the collection, such as a crayon.
4. Demonstrate how to put one end of a ruler at the end of the crayon to measure it correctly, making sure both edges are on an equal line.
5. Ask the child to look at where the end of the crayon is on the ruler. Help the child identify the length of the crayon in inches.
6. Show how to place the crayon on the grid next to the correct number of inches. For example, a 3" crayon would be placed next to the numeral 3.
7. Continue measuring all the objects and placing them on the grid. Discuss with the children which measurement had more, fewer, and equal numbers of objects.

More to do

Language and Literacy: Give each child a ruler to measure objects. Ask them to trace the outline of each object onto a piece of paper, help them label it in inches, and use the pictures to create a class booklet.

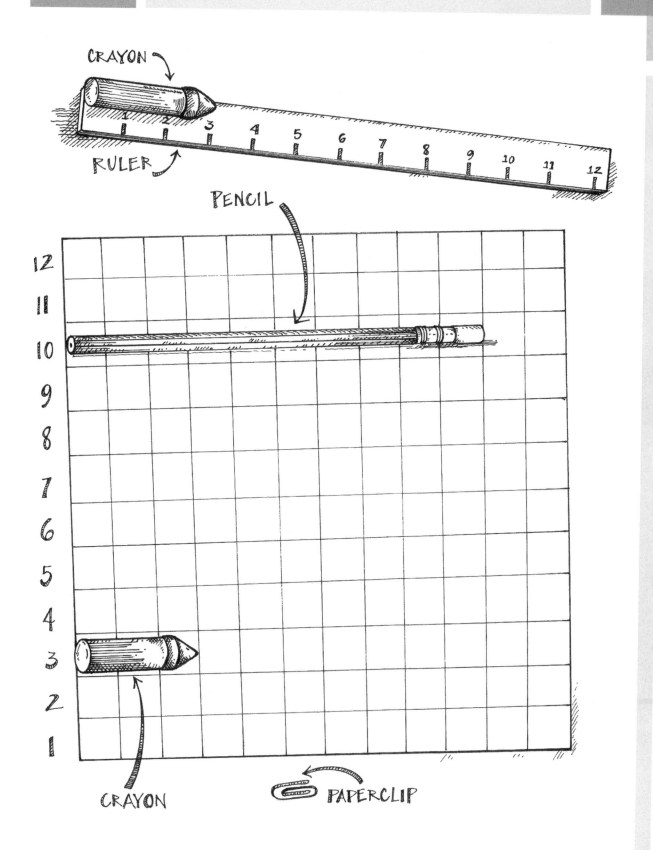

CRAYON

RULER

PENCIL

CRAYON

PAPERCLIP

✚ *Susan Oldham Hill, Lakeland, FL*

Classification

classification, counting

Materials
poster board or chart paper
marker
magazines
scissors
construction paper
glue

What to do

1. Beforehand, choose a few categories such as transportation, animals, clothing, foods, tools, and so on. Write each category on a large piece of poster board and include a couple of example pictures for each (such as a bike and car for transportation, and a hammer and nails for tools).
2. Provide magazines and invite the children to cut out a few pictures for each category.
3. Show each picture to the group and ask the children to tell you which category it belongs in. Glue the pictures to the poster board where they belong.
4. For younger children, precut pictures and glue them to construction paper so that children do only the classifying. Ask the child to choose one of the pictures you made and add it to the classification sheet.

Related books
Growing Vegetable Soup by Lois Ehlert
Millions of Cats by Wanda Gag
Pancakes, Pancakes! by Eric Carle

✚ *Sandy L. Scott, Meridian, ID*

Counting Watermelon Seeds

counting

Materials
10 sheets of white construction paper
red, yellow, and green crayons
black marker
55 pompoms

What to do

1. Before doing this activity, draw outlines of watermelon slices on the sheets of construction paper and color them to look like watermelon slices. Color the bottom arc green, add a small strip of yellow-green, then leave a small strip of white. Color the rest red.

   WHITE   RED   YELLOW-GREEN

   GREEN

2. On the first watermelon, draw one watermelon seed and write "1 seed" under the watermelon drawing. On the second watermelon, draw two seed and write "2 seeds" under it. Continue in this manner with the remaining watermelon drawings.

   POMPOMS

3. Put pompoms ("watermelon seeds") next to the paper watermelon slices and challenge the children to put the correct number of pompoms on each slice of watermelon.

2 seeds

✚ *Mary Brehm, Aurora, OH*

Cube Caterpillars

counting

Materials
1" snap-together cubes
index cards
marker

What to do
1. Create number cards by writing one numeral from 1–10 on an index card.
2. Hold up a card and invite the children to count the correct number of cubes and snap them together. Encourage them to use several different variations of colors to make their "caterpillars."
3. Put all the caterpillars beside one another and see how many the children made altogether.

Related book
The Very Hungry Caterpillar by Eric Carle

✚ *Barbara Saul, Eureka, CA*

Cut and Carry

numeral recognition, sequencing

Materials
copy paper in various colors
marker
scissors
hole punch
card-size envelopes
3' strands of yarn
rubber stamp numerals and stamp pads, or numeral stickers

What to do
1. Create a number grid by drawing a 10-square grid on a sheet of copy paper. Write 1–10 in the spaces on the page, with a large bold marker. (For older children, make a 20-square grid and number from 1 to 20.) Make copies of the number page on various colors of paper.

2. Give each child a number grid. Help them cut apart the number grid and practice sequencing the numerals in order from 1 to 10. **Note**: For younger children, you may need to cut out the squares for them.

3. Invite the children to make a fun pouch to carry their number cards in. Help them punch two holes in the top of an envelope, beneath the flap, one hole on each side.

4. Guide the children in stringing the yarn through the two holes and tying it at the top.

5. Invite them to decorate the "pouch" with numeral stamps or stickers.

6. The children can wear their pouch at home or in the classroom so they can practice placing the numerals in order from 1 to 10 when time permits.

+ Mary J. Murray, Mazomanie, WI

Dot to Dot

number sequence, problem solving

Materials

crayons
paper
pencils

What to do

1. On a piece of paper, create a dot-to-dot page. Use a few dots for younger children (no more than 10), and more for older children (1 to 20).
2. Place dots to create a form the children will recognize after they have connected the dots. You can begin with simple items, such as a ball, a star, a doll, a dog, and so on.
3. Place numbers in sequential order beside the dots.
4. Have the children connect the dots in sequential order to find out what the item is.
5. Invite the children to make their own dot-to-dot pictures.

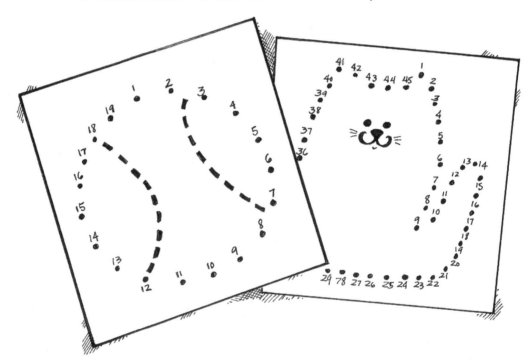

More to do

Language and Literacy: You can make a dot-to-dot page using the letters of the alphabet instead of numbers.

✚ *Monica Hay Cook, Tucson, AZ*

Easy Shapes Clown

shape awareness

Materials
felt in various colors
scissors
glue
flannel board

What to do
1. Use felt shapes of various colors to construct a clown face for flannel board use.

2. Cut out the following shapes from felt:
   - a 6" circle from cream-colored felt for the face
   - two purple triangles for the eyes
   - a larger blue triangle for the hat
   - a yellow circle to go on top of the hat for a tassel
   - two medium-sized orange triangles for the hair on each side of the face
   - a red circle for the nose
   - two smaller pink circles for cheeks
   - a green crescent moon shape for the mouth

3. Make a smaller (approximately half the size) version of the clown as a model. Glue this one together as a single unit to display on the flannel board for the child to duplicate. Discuss each shape with the children.

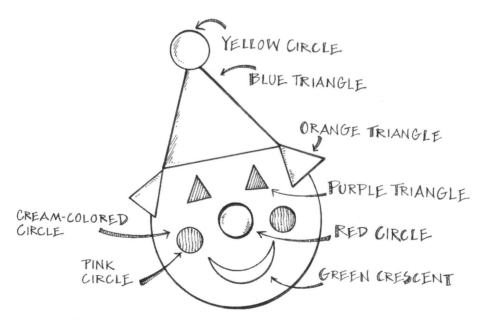

4. The child first puts the example on the flannel board. She then uses the larger pieces to construct a clown face to match the example. After admiring her clown, she removes the felt pieces and continues using them to make the clown face any way she desires.

✚ *Jackie Wright, Enid, OK*

Flag Fun

patterns, sorting

Materials index cards
printout or photocopy of state flags
scissors
glue

What to do 1. Find a copy of all of the state flags and make a color photocopy of the pages.
2. Let the children help cut out all of the flags.
3. Glue one flag onto each index card.
4. Have the children sort the flags into categories. They can sort by colors, stripes, and symbols.
5. The children can do this over and over again, each time sorting by different criteria.

Related books *Celebrate the 50 States!* by Loreen Leedy
Scrambled States of America by Laurie Keller

✚ *Monica Hay Cook, Tucson, AZ*

Four Square

coin identification, money value

Materials
coins (pennies, nickels, dimes, quarters), one of each coin for each child
black felt
small cloth bag
white copy paper
crayons

What to do
1. Have the children sit quietly in a circle. Join the children and place a penny, nickel, dime, and quarter on a piece of black felt.
2. Point to each coin and ask the children if they know the name of each. Talk about the value of each coin. For example, a penny is one cent, a nickel is five cents, and so on.
3. Place a penny into a child's hand for her to explore and pass on. Repeat with the other coins.
4. Give each child a piece of white paper and a crayon. Fold the paper twice, so that there are four sections.
5. Ask the children to place a penny, nickel, dime, and quarter under each section of the paper and rub the crayon over each coin.
6. Place the coins in a cloth bag. The children take turns reaching into the cloth bag, pulling out one coin, and matching the coins with the coin rubbing on their paper.

Related book
Bunny Money by Rosemary Wells

✚ *Randi Lynn Mrvos, Lexington, KY*

Grab Bag Color Match

classifying, counting, quantity

Materials
10 sheets of 9" × 12" construction paper, each a different color
masking tape
75-100 objects that are different solid colors (red cup, blue crayon, black comb)
bags to hold items

What to do
1. Laminate the construction paper and tape the pieces together to form a long rectangle, using two rows of five sheets.
2. Fill the grab bags with miscellaneous items.
3. Invite the children to pull objects from the grab bags, name the colors, and place them on the correct sheets of paper in the multi-colored rectangle.
4. When all the bags are empty, help the children count the total number of objects in each color square. Record these numbers on a piece of paper.
5. Ask the children which colors have the most and least objects on their squares.

Related books
Cat's Colors by Jane Cabrera
The Color Box by Dayle Ann Dodds
Mouse Paint by Ellen Stoll Walsh

✚ *Sheila Dandeneau, Riverside, RI*

Guess My Rule

reasoning, sorting

Materials
10–20 different objects, including blocks, toys, play foods or empty food containers, writing implements (chalk, pencils, markers, crayons), and so on

What to do
1. Without telling the children, choose one characteristic that is the same for some of the items. For example, if some are made of wood, and some are plush, sort the items by those characteristics. You could also sort them by use

if some are play food items and some are writing implements, or you could sort by color if some are red and some are blue.

2. Put all the items together that have the same characteristic. Invite the children to figure out your rule for sorting them.

3. Find another way to group these items. Let them figure this one out.

4. Let the children take turns sorting the items, with the rest of the group working on the rule. Find as many different ways to group the items as you can. Ask the children to find more items with the same characteristics from their surroundings to place in one of the groups.

5. Put everything away, and ask the children to collect a new group of items to sort.

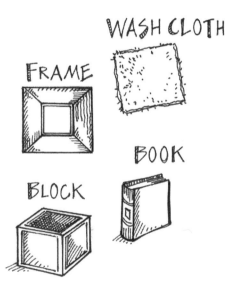

✚ *Sandra K. Bynum, Blackfoot, ID*

Heart to Heart

counting, numeral recognition, one-to-one correspondence

Materials
old Valentine cards
scissors
markers
tagboard
glue

What to do
1. Make a counting chart out of old Valentine cards.
2. Help the children cut out the hearts or the whole card and glue them on a large piece of tagboard. Write the numerals 1 through 10 on the tagboard across the top.
3. The children put one heart under the numeral 1, two under the numeral 2, and so on.
4. Choose a child to point to the chart as the other children identify the number of hearts and count them. This can also be one of the "helper" jobs each day.
5. Children can make a counting chart of their own with a heart stamp or heart stickers.

Related books
Valentine Cats by Jean Marzollo
Valentine Mice by Bethany Roberts and Doug Cushman

✚ *Laura Durbrow, Lake Oswego, OR*

Horsin' Around

counting, measurement

Materials
chart paper
marker

What to do
1. Horses are measured by hands. Have the children use this method of measurement to measure one another.
2. Let each child choose a partner (or assign partners).

3. Begin with one of the partners placing the flat side of her hand at the side of her friend's shoe. Then she keeps placing one hand above the other, counting hands until she gets to her partner's head.

4. Ask the children how many hands tall their partners are.

5. Now the partners switch places and the other partner does the measuring. Write down each child's measurement on a piece of chart paper.

6. When all the children are finished, they can compare results.

Related books   *Cowboys* by Lucille Recht Penner
Kickin' Up Some Cowboy Fun by Monica Hay Cook

✚ *Monica Hay Cook, Tucson, AZ*

How Much Food?

comparison, weight

Materials   packages of food weighing different amounts
food scale

What to do

1. Do this activity with a very small group. Begin with an item that weighs one pound, such as a box of pasta, and a lighter weight item, such as a box of gelatin mix.

2. Ask the children to pick up one item in each hand.

3. Ask the children which item is heavier and which one is lighter.

4. One at a time, add other items that have weights in between the first two items. By picking up the items and comparing them, see if the children can put them in order from lightest to heaviest, then from heaviest to lightest.

5. Next, show the children how to weigh the items on a food scale to see if they arranged them in the correct order.

6. Another way for them to check their work is to have them check the weights on the packages. Older children may be able to do this step, but younger children will need your help.

✚ *Monica Hay Cook, Tucson, AZ*

Human Shapes

counting, shape recognition

Materials   pictures or cutouts of different shapes

What to do
1. Gather the children in a large, open area.
2. Show them a shape, such as a triangle. Ask how many sides it has.
3. Call for three children to each be one side of the triangle. Ask them to lie down on the floor to create a human triangle.
4. Have the rest of the class divide into groups of three and create triangles with their bodies.
5. Repeat above process with other shapes, according to the children's experience or developmental level.
6. For a variation, put children into groups of different numbers and encourage them to make different shapes. They can also try to make individual shapes on their own.

✚ *Shelley F. Hoster, Norcross, GA*

I Spot It

counting, number concepts

Materials   books or pictures
paper
markers

What to do
1. Choose a picture or book to use when playing "I Spot It."
2. Name an item in the picture or in the book and tell the children how many of each item they are to find in the picture or book.
3. Make a checklist of items in the picture with the number of each item the children are to find. Use pictures on the checklist instead of words for children who cannot read.
4. The children search the picture to find the items listed.
5. When the children find the items, they check them off the list.

Related book   *I Spy Two Eyes* by Lucy Micklethwait

✚ *Monica Hay Cook, Tucson, AZ*

Inches and Feet

measurement

Materials   wall growth chart
ruler
butcher paper

What to do   1. Talk to children about 1" measurements. Explain that 12 inches equals 1 foot. Show them a ruler and point out the inch marks.
2. Measure all the children using a wall chart. Mark each child's name and height on the wall next to the chart. You can put a large piece of butcher paper next to the chart to write on.
3. For older children, measure their height in feet, and help them convert their height measurements to inches.
4. If a child is 3'6", ask the children if she is taller in inches because she is 42". Use words such as *taller, shorter, tallest,* and *shortest*.

✚ *Sandy L. Scott, Meridian, ID*

It's All in the Box

counting

Materials
boxes that are the same size
assorted items to fill boxes (blocks, pencils, erasers, paper, shoes, Styrofoam
    pieces)
paper
pencil

What to do
1. Invite each of the children to select a box.
2. The children choose one type of item to put in their box (for example, all
   erasers).
3. When their boxes are full, the children count how many items they put in
   their box.
4. Have the children chart their results by drawing pictures of their boxes and
   writing the results beside their drawing.
5. Discuss the results. "It takes *more* erasers to fill the box." "It takes the *same
   amount* of pencils and pens to fill the box."

Related books
How Many Bugs in a Box? by David A. Carter
More Bugs in Boxes by David A. Carter

✚ *Monica Hay Cook, Tucson, AZ*

Jewelry Chart

counting

Materials
magazines and catalogs containing pictures of jewelry including bracelets, rings,
    necklaces, and earrings
large butcher paper
marker
scissors
glue

What to do
1. Make a chart of the various types of jewelry. Draw columns on the paper and write the name of one type of jewelry (bracelet, ring, and so on) at the top of each column.
2. Have the children cut out pictures and glue them in the appropriate column of the chart.
3. Help the children count the number of items in each column.

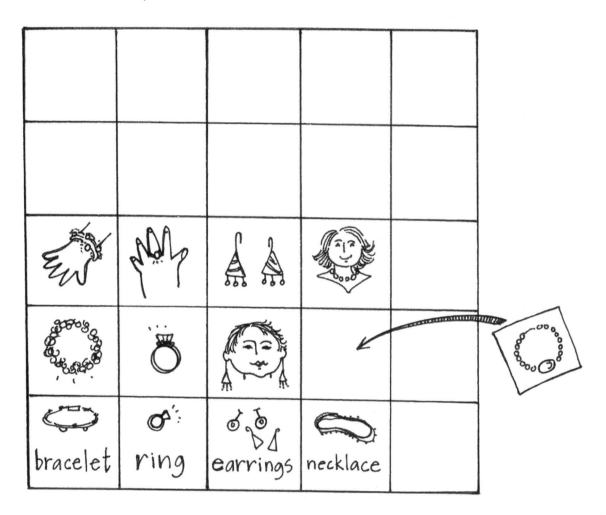

✚ *Sandy L. Scott, Meridian, ID*

Let's Get a Bang Out of This!

counting

Materials

tagboard or medium card stock
die-cut balloons
pocket chart
computer or marker
glue stick
scissors or paper cutter
laminator

What to do

1. Print the following four lines of the song on a piece of 8 ½" × 11" tagboard turned sideways:

   Skip count, skip count, count by fives.
   Skip count, skip count, count by fives.
   Skip count, skip count, count by fives.
   We can count to 50.

2. Label 10 die-cut balloons by fives, each with a different numeral from 5 to 50 (5, 10, 15, and so on).
3. Glue each balloon to a piece of 3 ½" × 3 ½" tagboard, laminate, and cut out the balloons.
4. Cut the four lines of the song into sentence strips and laminate them.
5. Hang a pocket chart at children's eye level. Place the four lines of the song in a separate pocket in the pocket chart.
6. Talk about counting by fives. Count to 50 with the children by fives (5, 10, 15, 20, and so on).
7. Have partners work together to arrange the numbered balloons in sequential order in the rows underneath the song.
8. Enjoy singing the song together using any tune. Then everyone chants the numbers 5 to 50 on each balloon.

✚ *Jackie Wright, Enid, OK*

Make a Fraction Pie

fractions

Materials

cardboard
felt in light blue, brown, purple, dark blue, yellow, and red
scissors
glue

What to do

1. First make a flannel board by cutting a piece of cardboard into a 9" square. Cut out a 9" square from light blue felt and glue it onto the cardboard square.
2. Cut out an 8" circle from brown felt. This will be the crust.
3. Cut out one 7 ½" circle from each of the other colors of felt. These will be the fillings (purple for grape, blue for blueberry, yellow for lemon, and red for cherry).
4. Cut the purple circle in half, the blue circle into quarters, the yellow circle into eighths, and the red circle into thirds.
5. Use the fraction pie to help the children learn fractions. For example, if you ask them to make one half, they might show you the purple piece, two blue pieces, or four yellow pieces. Older children can also use the pie to add the fractions together to make a whole pie.

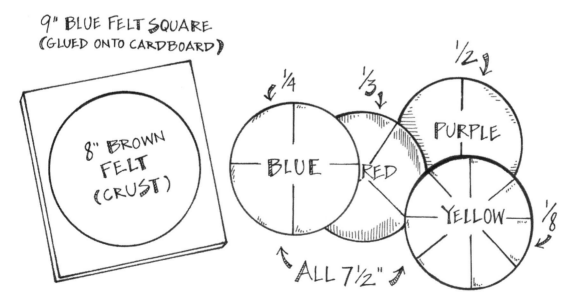

9" BLUE FELT SQUARE
(GLUED ONTO CARDBOARD)

8" BROWN FELT (CRUST)

BLUE ¼

RED ⅓

PURPLE ½

YELLOW ⅛

ALL 7½"

✚ *Jennifer Galvin, Stafford, VA*

Many Hands, Many Feet

counting

Materials
construction paper
butcher paper
glue
markers

What to do
1. On construction paper, help the children trace and cut out their hands and feet.
2. Glue all the hands in a long line onto the butcher paper.
3. Have the children count how many hands are in their classroom.
4. Repeat the steps with the children's feet.

✚ *Monica Hay Cook, Tucson, AZ*

Measure Me!

measurement

Materials
several tape measures
chart paper
marker

What to do
1. The children work in pairs with a tape measure to measure each other's height.
2. They can continue the experience by measuring other parts of their partner's body, such as arms, legs, waist, wrists, feet, hands, and so on.
3. Keep track of the results and make a chart of the entire class's height or arm lengths. Compare the results. Who has the longest arm?

Related book
Inch by Inch by Leo Lionni

✚ *Barbara Saul, Eureka, CA*

Measurement Fun

length, measurement

Materials
6" ruler
12" ruler
yardstick
tape measure
wall height chart
classroom items to measure
pictures of classroom items, one copy for each child

What to do
1. Talk about the tools used to take measurements, including a ruler, yardstick, tape measure, and height chart.
2. Let the children use the tools to take measurements around the class.
3. Give each child a sheet of paper with different classroom items pictured on it. During the day, the children measure the different items pictured on their sheet and write down the numbers.
4. Talk about which doll is the *longest*, which truck is the *widest*, which car is *shorter*, and so on. This will introduce a variety of new measurement words into the children's vocabulary.

✚ *Sandy L. Scott, Meridian, ID*

My Foot Ruler

measurement

Materials
light card stock
pencil
scissors
paper

What to do
1. The children place one foot on a piece of card stock and trace around it.
2. Help the children cut out their footprints.

3. Invite the children to use this "ruler" to measure items. Ask the children "how many feet tall" the various objects are.

4. Have the children record the measurements of the objects on a piece of paper.

More to do   **Outdoor Play:** Have the children do long jumps in the sand and measure how many feet they can jump.

Related books   *How Big Is a Foot?* by Rolf Myller
How Big Is a Pig? by Clare Beaton
How Big Were the Dinosaurs? by Bernard Most

✚ *Monica Hay Cook, Tucson, AZ*

Nest the Boxes

counting, subtraction

Materials   boxes of different sizes and shapes

What to do   1. Provide the children with a variety of boxes.
2. Count the boxes with the children.
3. Ask the children to nest as many of the boxes inside other boxes as they can.
4. When they are finished, have them count the visible boxes (some of the boxes will be nested inside other boxes).
5. Talk about subtraction. If they started with 10 boxes, and nested six of the boxes inside other boxes, they would now see four boxes. Explain that 10 - 6 = 4. This may be a difficult concept, so focus on introducing the general idea of subtraction.

Related books   *How Many Bugs in a Box?* by David A. Carter
More Bugs in Boxes by David A. Carter

✚ *Monica Hay Cook, Tucson, AZ*

Number Cards

counting, numeral recognition

Materials   index cards
marker

What to do   1. Make number cards for the children.
2. On the first card, draw one circle and write the numeral 1.
3. On the second card draw two circles, and write the numeral 2. Continue until you have 10 cards.
4. Give the children the group of index cards to put in numerical order, beginning with numeral 1.
5. As the children get more practice at ordering the number cards, add more cards (through 15 and eventually through 20).

✦ *Sandy L. Scott, Meridian, ID*

Numeral Fun

numeral recognition, sorting

Materials   magnetic numerals or small plastic numerals from 1 to 10 (10 of each number)
tray
magnet board or table
10 small boxes

What to do   1. Place all the numerals in a tray and place the tray on a large table.
2. Ask the children to sort the numerals. Ask, "Which ones are the same? Which ones are different?"
3. The children place all the ones together, the twos together, and so on, and then put them into boxes of ones, twos, and so on.
4. Ask them to show you where numerals 1, 2, and so on are located.

✦ *Lily Erlic, Victoria, BC, Canada*

Number Hunt

counting

Materials   large pieces of construction paper
magazines or catalogs
marker
glue sticks

What to do   1. Prepare several large pieces of construction paper by writing a numeral in the center of each sheet. Start with 1–4, and make the activity more difficult as the children become more adept at it.
2. Collect an assortment of pictures of objects from catalogs, making sure they are all in groups of between 1 and 4.
3. Place the pictures in the center of the table.
4. Seat four children around the table with different numerals in front of them, and encourage each child to find pictures that include the same number of objects as the numerals on their paper.
5. Ask the children to glue the images to their paper.
6. When a child glues one image with the correct number of items to her paper, she passes the paper to the next child, and waits to get another numbered sheet of paper from the child on her other side.
7. Continue until all the children have put several images on each sheet of paper.

✚ *Iris Rothstein, New Hyde Park, NY*

Observation Glasses

observation

Materials   plastic rings from a beverage six-pack (1 for every 3 children)
scissors
chenille stems
colored cellophane (optional)

What to do
The ability to observe and notice things is fundamental to developing math skills. Only through this process can we receive information about the world.

1. Tell the children that they are going to make a pair of glasses that will help them see amazing things.
2. Cut the plastic six-pack rings apart to make three sets of two. These will be the "eyeglasses."
3. Give each child a set of eyeglasses and two chenille stems.
4. Show the children how to wind the end of the chenille stems around the outside edge of the glasses to form earpieces.
5. Show the children how to bend the other end of the chenille stems to fit over the ears. If desired, have them add colored cellophane lenses to the glasses by gluing colored cellophane circles to the rings after adding the earpieces.
6. Have the children put on their glasses and go on a walk around the school or playground.
7. Stop occasionally to look carefully at an interesting item such as a fish tank.
8. Ask questions to encourage them to carefully observe what they are seeing:
   - Which fish is spending more time at the bottom of the tank?
   - What happens when one fish swims in front of another?
   - Which fish are swimming together?
9. Encourage the children to wear their observation glasses when playing in centers. Occasionally join them in play and ask questions about what they are seeing. Remember to ask more than just, "What do you see?" If a child says she sees the dishes, ask questions about them. For example:
   - What color are the dishes?
   - How many dishes are there?
   - Are the dishes the same size or different sizes?

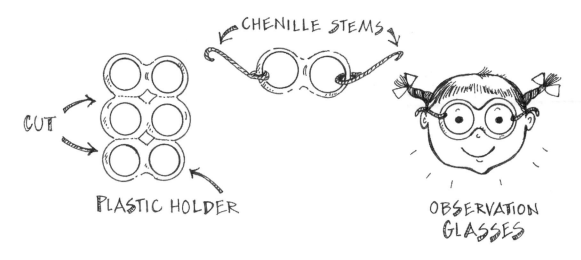

CHENILLE STEMS

CUT

PLASTIC HOLDER

OBSERVATION GLASSES

✚ *Virginia Jean Herrod, Columbia, SC*

One Dozen Equals 12

counting

Materials

muffin tins
egg cartons
cookie sheets
playdough
items to use with playdough, such as plastic knives, rolling pins, measuring spoons, and cookie cutters
plastic eggs
pretend cupcakes

What to do

1. Discuss the idea of a dozen with the children, and tell them that 12 items make a dozen. Ask the children if they have ever seen a dozen eggs or a dozen muffins in a muffin tin.
2. Count (out loud) 12 plastic eggs and place them in an egg carton. Do the same with 12 pretend cupcakes, placing them in a muffin tin.
3. Then, encourage children to mold playdough shapes in groups of 12.

✚ *Judy Fujawa, The Villages, FL*

Penny Practice

counting, number sense, one-to-one correspondence, shape awareness

Materials

poster board
pennies
small cutout pictures of various products (from magazines or catalogues)

What to do

1. Divide the poster board into four equal squares and label each section with one of the following titles: Balancing, Shapes, Counting, and Buying.
2. Trace four or five pennies in the Balancing section.
3. Trace small circles, squares, and triangles in the Shapes section.
4. Write 1 to 5 in the Counting section, with a corresponding number of dots next to each numeral.

5. Glue magazine pictures in the Buying section. Write a price next to each picture. (For example, next to a picture of a candy bar, write 5¢.)

6. Provide pennies for children to do the following activities:
   - ■ In the Balancing section, children stack pennies on top of the traced pennies.
   - ■ In the Shapes section, children match the pennies to the circles (not the triangles and squares).
   - ■ In the Counting section, children place their pennies on the dots next to each numeral.
   - ■ In the Buying section, children put the correct number of pennies beside each indicated price.

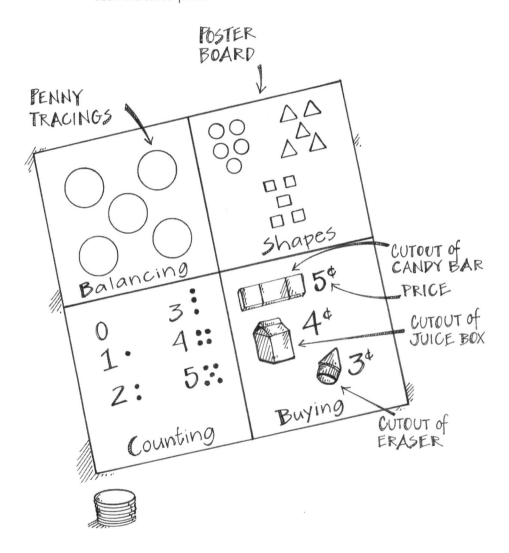

Related book   *Benny's Pennies* by Pat Brisson

✚ *Diane Shatto, Kansas City, MO*

Photograph Box

counting, matching

Materials

digital or 35mm camera
small classroom objects
large shallow tray or plastic tub
re-sealable plastic bags
decorative photograph or recipe box

What to do

1. Take photographs of various sets of objects in your classroom (for example, four pinecones, six wooden blocks, 10 crayons, and one ball). You can invite parent helpers to gather the objects and take the photographs for this activity. If desired, let each child find one set of objects for this activity. This allows children to be a part of creating the game.
2. Place the objects in a tray or tub.
3. Place each photograph inside a re-sealable plastic bag to protect it from fingerprints.
4. Place all the photographs in the photo or recipe box.
5. Set the tray and the photograph box at a table or learning center.
6. Invite individual children or pairs of children to work at this counting activity.
7. The child chooses a photo from the photo box, and then finds the same number of objects from the tray and places them on the table.
8. Instruct the child to continue selecting photographs and counting out a matching set of objects until all the photos are removed from the box.

More to do

Working with Families: Store the materials for this activity in a backpack. Invite one child to take the backpack home each night and play the counting game with family members.

✚ *Mary J. Murray, Mazomanie, WI*

Pumpkin Patch Math

comparison, measurement

Materials

pumpkins of all shapes and sizes
yarn
bathroom scale
yardstick
chart paper
math cubes
large note cards or card stock
markers

What to do

1. During the month of October, have each child bring in a pumpkin. Label each pumpkin with a child's name. If cost is an issue, see if you can borrow pumpkins from a garden center or grocery store or even friends.
2. Set up a "pumpkin patch" area in the room.
3. Do the activities below, and after you finish all three pumpkin measurements, hang the cards that you write results on together for the children to compare.

Weight

1. During center time, the children can weigh their pumpkins using the bathroom scale.
2. Help the children write the weight on a note card: "My pumpkin weighs ____ pounds!"
3. Make a chart, comparing the weights.
4. Let the children guess just by looking which pumpkin they think weighs the most.
5. Older children can try to pick up the pumpkins (with assistance) so they can see if they can feel which pumpkin is the heaviest.

Circumference

1. Show the children how to use yarn to measure the circumference of their pumpkins by wrapping the yarn around the pumpkin and cutting a length that is equal to the circumference of the pumpkin.
2. Have the children guess which pumpkin one is the fattest, skinniest, and so on.
3. Have the children take their yarn pieces and place them against the yardstick to see how large the circumference is in inches. Help the children write it down on the card: "My pumpkin is ____ inches around."
4. Make a chart comparing the circumferences of the pumpkins.

Height

1. Have the children use the math cubes to measure the height of their pumpkins.
2. They can stack the cubes beside the pumpkin and see how many math cubes tall their pumpkin is. They can also take a ruler and measure the height.
3. Help the children write the results on the card: "My pumpkin is _____ cubes tall." or "My pumpkin is ____ inches tall!"
4. Children can also guess by looking at the pumpkins which is the tallest, shortest, and so on.

✚ *Shelley F. Hoster, Norcross, GA*

Rebus Counting

counting, writing numerals

Materials

art prints
note cards
paper
pencils

What to do

1. Set up 10 stations, placing a copy of a famous painting or photograph at each station. Stations should not be in numerical order.
2. Beside each picture, place a rebus note card that asks, "How many _____?" For instance, the question for a painting with children in it might be "How many children?" Because children are probably not reading yet, make rebus note cards with pictures of the items instead of words. In the above example, draw children.
3. Have the children go from station to station, counting the items in the pictures. Ask them to write the answers on a piece of paper.

Related books

Anno's Counting Book by Mitsumasa Anno
Chicka Chicka 1, 2, 3 by Bill Martin, Jr. and Michael Sampson
Each Orange Had 8 Slices by Paul Giganti
From One to One Hundred by Teri Sloat

✚ *Randi Lynn Mrvos, Lexington, KY*

Shape Match

matching

Materials   colored construction paper
marker
scissors

What to do
1. Draw different shapes on different colors of paper. Cut out the different shapes.
2. Give each child a shape (for example, a red triangle or brown square).
3. The children take their shapes around the room and find an object that is the same color and shape.

✚ *Jean Potter, Charleston, WV*

Shoebag Counting

counting, sorting

Materials   hanging shoe holder
permanent marker
variety of objects that will fit in the pockets of the shoe holder (1 of one item, 2 of another item, three of another item, and so on up to 12 of the final item)

What to do
1. Label each pocket on the shoe holder with a numeral from 1 to 12.
2. Hang the shoe holder at a level where the children can reach all the pockets.
3. Put out the various objects, and invite the children to place the collections of objects in the pocket by matching numeral (three of one item in the #3 pocket).

✚ *Audrey Kanoff, Allentown, PA*

Size Box

* *

estimation, spatial awareness

Materials
boxes in a variety of sizes
paint
classroom items of various sizes

What to do
1. Remove lids of boxes and paint or decorate the boxes.
2. Have the children find the biggest item that will fit in each box.
3. This activity is self-correcting because if the item doesn't fit inside the box the child chose, she can find a box that it will fit into.
4. Children could do this same activity in the house area using pots and pans.

✚ *Phylis Esch, Export, PA*

Spool Counting

* *

one-to-one correspondence

Materials
empty sewing spools
poster board
markers

What to do
1. On the sheets of poster board, trace the outlines of a different number of spools of varying sizes. Write the number of outlines at the bottom of each poster board. **Note**: If spools are not available, use other circular items such as buttons, blocks, or bottles tops.

2. Set out the spools and the different sheets of poster board, and invite the children to match the spools to their outlines on the poster boards.

✚ *Cookie Zingarelli, Columbus, OH*

Ten Green Bottles

counting backwards, subtraction

Materials
10 green, plastic soda bottles
sand
tape
table or bench

What to do
1. Fill 10 green plastic bottles with a little bit of sand. Tape the lid on securely.
2. Place the 10 green bottles in a row along the edge of a table.
3. Choose a child to be the one to make the bottle "accidentally" fall each time. It will be a very popular job!
4. Sing the song, "Ten Green Bottles," knocking off one bottle each time.
5. With very young children, count the remaining bottles between each verse.

Ten Green Bottles
Ten green bottles standing on a wall,
Ten green bottles standing on a wall,
And if one green bottle should accidentally fall,
  CRASH!
There'd be nine green bottles standing on a wall.

Nine green bottles standing on a wall,
Nine green bottles standing on a wall,
And if one green bottle should accidentally fall,
  CRASH!
There'd be eight green bottles standing on a wall.

6. Repeat the verse, reducing it by one bottle each time, until there are no bottles on the wall.

✚ *Anne Adeney, Plymouth, United Kingdom*

Tracing Numerals

printing numerals

Materials   paper with dotted numerals
yellow highlighter
blue highlighter

What to do   1. Have the child first trace over the dotted numerals with a yellow highlighter.
2. Then have the child use a blue highlighter to trace over the yellow numerals.
3. Watch the numerals change color!

Related book   *Little Blue and Little Yellow* by Leo Lionni

✚ *Jackie Wright, Enid, OK*

Transportation Chart

counting

Materials   butcher paper
marker
scissors
magazines and newspapers with pictures of planes, cars, trains, boats, bikes,
trucks, and so on
glue

What to do   1. Draw a column chart and label with a variety of transportation vehicles (use
words and pictures).
2. Have children cut out pictures of transportation vehicles.
3. Ask them to glue the pictures in the appropriate column.
4. With the children, count the number of items in each column.

Related book   *Trains* by Gail Gibbons

✚ *Sandy L. Scott, Meridian, ID*

Treasure Hunt

classification, comparison, counting, sorting

Materials   small objects, such as buttons, old keys, washers, beads, seashells, bottle caps, pebbles, or pennies
container

BOTTLE CAPS

BUTTONS

PENNIES

BEADS

WASHERS

SCREWS

What to do

1. Beforehand, collect an assortment of small objects and find a special container to hold them. There is a lot of math the children can do with these "treasures."

   ■ Sort and classify the treasures. Ask, "Are all of the seashells the same size? What about the keys? How are they alike? How are they different?"

   ■ Use the treasures to ask addition, subtraction, multiplication, and division questions. For example, "If we share three buttons among three friends, how many will we each one get?" Or, "If we have three shirts that need two buttons on each, how many buttons do we need?" Even young children can visualize these types of problems by manipulating, counting, and sorting the items.

   ■ Organize the treasures by one characteristic and place them end to end. Compare and contrast the different numbers of each type of treasure. For example, "There are three short keys, seven long keys, and 11 medium keys. There are four more medium keys than long ones."

2. Keep the treasures in a special container that is readily available for counting and sorting to provide practice in problem solving. The treasures will be there when needed to help you to explain the concepts of addition, subtraction, multiplication, and division because they can be manipulated and grouped together so the children can count the items and visualize the mathematical concept.

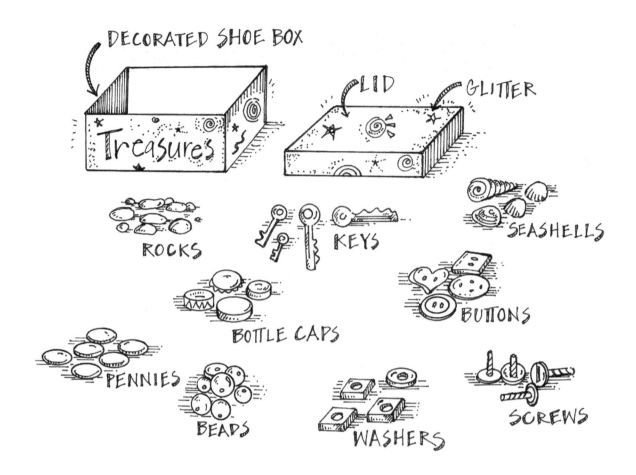

Related books   *Smart Kids Play and Learn: Sorting* by Roger Priddy
Superskills Shapes and Patterns: Plus Sorting, Classifying, Measuring, Counting by
   Ellen Booth Church

✚ *Sandra K. Bynum, Blackfoot, ID*

Treasure Hunt Binoculars

counting

Materials

paper towel rolls
scissors
paintbrushes
tempera paint
paper
pencil
string
hole punch

What to do

1. Cut the paper towels rolls in half. Make a pair of treasure-hunting binoculars for each child by gluing two halves of a paper towel roll together side by side.
2. After the glue dries, the children can paint their binoculars. When the paint is dry, punch a hole toward the outside top edge of each of the two rolls.
3. Lace string through the holes and tie a knot so the children can wear the binoculars around their necks. The children are ready to use their binoculars on a treasure hunt walk.
4. Have the children look through their binoculars and look for "treasures" (flowers, rocks, leaves, and so on).
5. Ask the children how many treasures they can see. Take notes on your paper.
6. When you get back to the classroom, chart what you saw.
7. Talk about whether you could count everything you found. Were there too many rocks, trees, and so on to count?

Related books

I Spy Little Animals by Jean Marzollo
I Spy Treasure Hunt by Jean Marzollo
I Went Walking by Sue Williams

✚ *Monica Hay Cook, Tucson, AZ*

Walk the Shape!

geometry

Materials   masking tape (white or colored)

What to do
1. Using masking tape, draw a large shape on the floor.
2. Gather the children and talk about the shape on the floor, such as the size, number of sides, other shapes it resembles, and what objects are that shape.
3. Show them how to "balance" along the tape line and walk the shape.

✚ *Shelley F. Hoster, Norcross, GA*

What Am I Drawing?

shapes

Materials   none

What to do
1. Have the children split up into pairs.
2. Ask one partner to use her finger to draw a shape on her partner's back.
3. Encourage the child being drawn on to guess what her partner drew on her back.
4. After several turns, have the children switch places and do it again.

✚ *Monica Hay Cook, Tucson, AZ*

What's Different?

comparison

Materials

2 strips of paper (1" × 6" and 1" × 12")
2 ribbons (one 6" and one 12")
2 coffee cans
sand
masking tape
shoeboxes
cereal boxes

What to do

The Long and Short of It

1. Place the two strips of paper in front of a child. Ask the children what is different about them. It's okay if they mention characteristics other than length, but eventually, you want them to notice the length.
2. If there is no response, ask, "Are they the same length or are they different lengths?" If the child does not answer say, "Show me which one is longer."
3. If the child is unable to respond, hold the two papers together and point out that one is longer and one is shorter.
4. Do the activity again, using two different lengths of ribbon or string, a ruler and a meter stick, or small plastic snakes and small plastic worms.

Heavy and Light

1. Fill one coffee can with sand and leave the other empty. Tape both shut so the children cannot see inside them.
2. Place the coffee cans on a low table in front of a child. Ask her to pick up each can and say what is different about them.
3. If the child guesses incorrectly, ask her to hold one in each hand.
4. Point to the heavy can and say, "This can is heavy." Point to the light can and say, "This can is light." Ask her to show you the heavy can and the light can.
5. Repeat the activity using other items that are the same size but different weights (shoeboxes, cereal boxes, cookie tins, and so on). With each set, leave one empty and fill the other with sand or another heavy material.

✚ *Virginia Jean Herrod, Columbia, SC*

What's Your Name?

comparison, counting

Materials   1" graph paper
                  pens

What to do   1. Write each child's name on 1" graph paper, putting one letter in each square.
                  2. Cut out each name.
                  3. Give the children their names and have them count how many letters are in their names.
                  4. Encourage them to compare the lengths of their strips with other children to find out if their names are longer, shorter, or the same length.

Related book   *Cat Up a Tree* by Ann Hassett

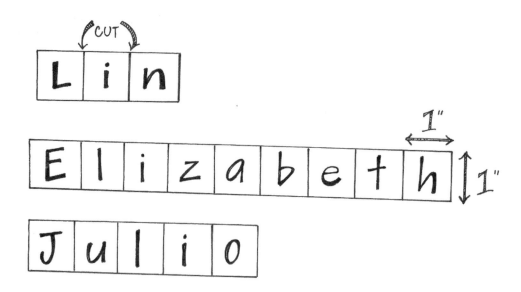

✚ *Barbara Saul, Eureka, CA*

What's Your Number?

numeral recognition

Materials   large chart of numerals from 1 to 10

What to do   Set out the chart and invite the children to trace the numerals on each other (backs, legs, arms, and so on) and guess the number.

Related book   *Moja Means One* by Muriel Feeling

✚ *Barbara Saul, Eureka, CA*

Who Made that Sound?

number recall

Materials   none

What to do
1. Have the children stand in a line.
2. Go down the line and tell each child a number. More than one child can have the same number.
3. Now match the numbers with an animal sound. For example, tell them that one is a "moo" sound, two is a "meow" sound, and so on.
4. Call out numbers and the children with that number call out their sound. If number two is a "meow," for example, the child meows twice.

✚ *Monica Hay Cook, Tucson, AZ*

Who's Got the Button?

sorting

Materials   buttons

What to do
1. Collect a large number of buttons. Ask parents to donate old buttons.
2. Give each child a handful of assorted buttons. Ask them to sort the buttons. You may want to have them sort the buttons according to specific attributes (size, color, and so on), depending on the children's ability. Older children can sort the buttons as desired.
3. When they are done, ask the children to talk about how they sorted the buttons (size, color, and so on).
4. Ask the children to think of a different way to sort the buttons.

Related book   *Corduroy* by Don Freeman

➕ *Barbara Saul, Eureka, CA*

Writing in Space

numeral recognition, writing numerals

Materials   none

What to do
1. Gather the children in a group and ask them to choose their favorite number.
2. When each child picks a number, encourage her to practice writing it in air with her fingers.

➕ *Margery Kranyik Fermino, West Roxbury, MA*

3-D Art in a Shape

sequencing, shapes

Materials

9" × 12" construction paper in assorted colors
scissors
¾" × 3" paper strips
glue

What to do

1. Beforehand, cut out 9", 6", and 3" squares, circles, and triangles from assorted colors of construction paper to make an assortment of large, medium, and small shapes.
2. Ask the children to choose a 9" × 12" piece of paper for the background.
3. Ask each child to choose his favorite shape (circle, square, or triangle) and pick out a large shape, a medium one, and a small one. Remind them that the colors can be different, but shapes should be the same.
4. Invite the children to glue the largest shape on the background paper and then glue the medium shape on top of the large shape.
5. Help the children make a small loop with the paper strip by gluing the two ends together, holding it with their fingers until it holds.
6. Demonstrate how to put glue on one side of the loop and glue it to the center of the medium shape, holding it in place for a moment.

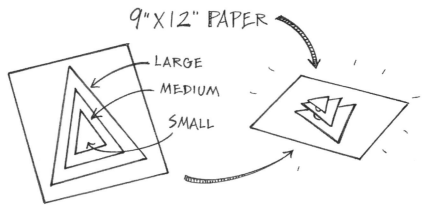

9" X 12" PAPER

LARGE
MEDIUM
SMALL

① GLUE LARGE SHAPE DOWN
② GLUE a PAPER LOOP ON the BACK of the MEDIUM SHAPE and ATTACH to LARGE SHAPE
③ REPEAT ON the SMALL SHAPE and ATTACH IT to the MEDIUM SHAPE

7. Next, show the children how to put glue on the top of the loop and place the small shape on top, so that there is a space created by the loop separating the small and medium shapes. Allow to dry.

✦ *Susan Oldham Hill, Lakeland, FL*

3-D Numerals

numeral recognition and formation

Materials
air putty (available at discount school supply stores)
number flash cards
Liquid Watercolor
blotter bottles
paintbrushes

What to do
1. Provide air putty. Demonstrate how to make snakes with the putty.
2. Show the children how to shape their snakes to make different numerals. If necessary, they can use flash cards to copy the formation of the numeral.
3. Let them make as many numerals as they want.
4. Children can paint their numeral shapes using the blotter bottles or paintbrushes to dab on Liquid Watercolor.
5. Let dry, then talk with the children about the numbers they created. "What number did you make?" "Why did you choose those numbers?"

✦ *Shelley F. Hoster, Norcross, GA*

Apple Headband

counting

Materials

Ten Apples Up on Top by Dr. Seuss
red, yellow, and green construction paper
apple pattern (the size of a real apple)
3" wide paper strips, long enough to fit around
   children's heads
stapler
glue
scissors

GLUE IN A VERTICAL ROW

What to do

1. Read *Ten Apples Up on Top* by Dr. Seuss.
2. In advance, prepare 3" wide paper strips for each child, making them long enough to fit as headbands.
3. Encourage the children to trace the apple patterns on green, red, and yellow paper, making a total of 10 apples per child. You may need to do this step for younger children.
4. Help them cut out the apples. (If children have trouble cutting, provide precut apples.) Demonstrate how to glue the apples together in a vertical row. If desired, children can make an apple pattern (green, red, green, red, and so on).
5. Allow the glue to dry and then help them staple the row of apples on their paper strips.
6. Fit the strips around each child's head and staple in place.

APPLE PATTERN

 Quazonia J. Quarles, Newark, DE

Big Day Countdown

counting backwards, subtraction

Materials   construction paper in colors associated with the chosen "big day"
bell pattern
pencils or markers
scissors
glue or stapler
glitter

What to do   1. Give each child a piece of construction paper in colors associated with the upcoming special day or holiday (for example, orange and black for Halloween).
2. Help the children trace the bell pattern on their paper and cut it out. You may need to provide precut bells for younger children.
3. Attach the following rhyme to each bell:

How many days 'til (holiday/special day)?
It's mighty hard to tell.
Take a link off every night
When the sandman casts his spell,
And (holiday/special day) will be here
By the time you reach the bell.

4. Encourage the children to decorate the bell using glitter and markers.
5. Cut 1" strips of construction paper in holiday colors.
6. Children make a paper chain (with enough loops for however many days until the special day) by looping the strips of paper through each previous loop.
7. Have the children glue the loops as they link them, and encourage them to count to 10 while holding the loop for the glue to dry. (You can also use a stapler to speed the process.)
8. Attach the chain to the bottom of the bell.
9. For younger children, you may want to complete half of the loops of the chain first.

✛ *Sandy L. Scott, Meridian, ID*

Art

Birthday Chart

comparison, counting

Materials
large piece of poster board
marker
small card stock circles or small paper plates
craft materials (yarn, wiggle eyes)
crayons, markers, and colored pencils

What to do

1. Use a marker to divide the large poster board into 12 equal columns, one for each month of the year. Write the names of the months across the top of the chart, one in each column. Draw a black line under the names.

2. Give each child a circle of paper or a paper plate. Let them use the craft materials, crayons, markers, and colored pencils to create a self portrait.

3. Ask each child when his birthday is. Have the correct information close at hand so you can give hints as needed.

4. Invite the children to place their self-portrait in the appropriate column. Start at the top of the chart and work toward the bottom.

5. When all of the children have had a chance to participate, ask them what the results of the chart are:

   ■ Which month has the most birthdays?
   ■ Which month has the fewest birthdays?
   ■ Which months have no (or zero) birthdays?
   ■ Which months have the same amount of birthdays?

6. Print these interpretations on a piece of paper and post them under the chart.

More to do

Language and Literacy: Create a class birthday book by making one page for each month using card stock paper. Encourage the children to draw a small self-portrait on their birth-month page. Create a front and back cover, punch three holes in each page on the left-hand side, and bind the pages using heavy yarn.

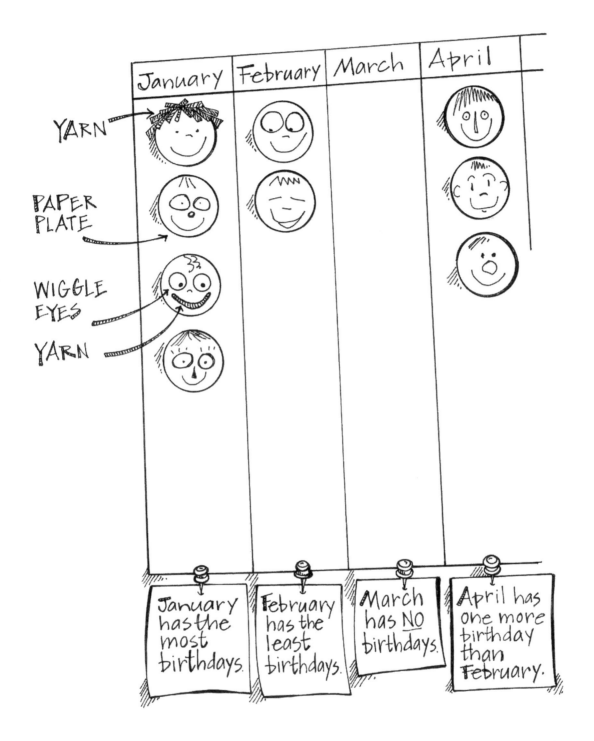

YARN

PAPER PLATE

WIGGLE EYES

YARN

January	February	March	April

January has the most birthdays.

February has the least birthdays.

March has NO birthdays.

April has one more birthday than February.

Virgina Jean Herrod, Columbia, SC

Body Outlines

graphing, comparison

Materials
large sheets of paper
black pen
paints or crayons
roll of display paper
glue

What to do
This is a good activity for small groups of about five children.
1. Have each child lie down on a large piece of paper, and trace their outlines.
2. Encourage the children to paint or color their outlines as desired.
3. Cut out the body outlines and have the children write their names on them.
4. Place all of them (four or five) on the floor.
5. Ask the children which is the *tallest* and which is the *shortest*. Ask them which is the middle-sized one in the group.
6. Ask them to point out three outlines that show *tall, taller,* and *tallest*. Then ask them to point out three outlines that show *small, smaller,* and *smallest*.
7. Let them take turns putting the outlines in order by size.
8. Explain that one can learn facts from pictures as well as from words. Explain that a pictogram of their sizes is called a *graph*.
9. Let the children help glue the body outlines, in the right order, to a contrasting roll of paper to make a graph and hang it on the wall.

✚ *Anne Adeney, Plymouth, United Kingdom*

Caterpillar Patterning

patterns

Materials
paper or card stock circles in various colors
paper
glue
markers
wiggle eyes

What to do

1. Talk about patterns and creating an AB pattern (or a more difficult pattern depending on children's level).
2. Give each child a piece of paper. Ask them to create an AB pattern on their paper (or other pattern) using the paper or card stock circles.
3. The children glue the circles to the paper to form a caterpillar body.
4. Encourage them to use markers to create antennae and glue on wiggle eyes.

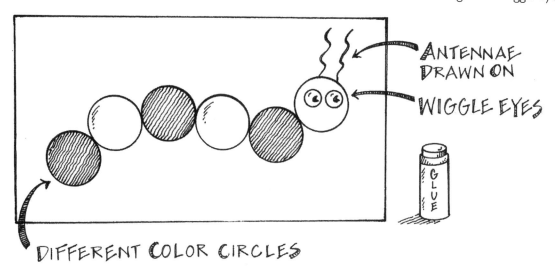

ANTENNAE DRAWN ON

WIGGLE EYES

GLUE

DIFFERENT COLOR CIRCLES

Related books   *Charlie the Caterpillar* by Dom Deluise
The Very Hungry Caterpillar by Eric Carle

✚ *Kristi Larson, Spirit Lake, IA*

Counting Cows

addition, counting, subtraction

Materials

white socks
pink felt circles
black felt ovals, triangles, and small circles
glue

What to do

1. Help the children make cow puppets using white socks. Each child glues on a pink felt circle for the nose, black felt ovals for eyes, black triangles for ears, and small black circles for body spots.
   Note: You can also make puppets using white paper plates; pink paper circles; black paper ovals, triangles, and circles; and craft sticks to make handles.

2. Review counting to the target number you have chosen for this lesson.

3. Children stand in two designated areas with their puppets—one area on the right and one on the left—with an empty common area in the middle.

4. Children count to add or subtract the number of cows as you call out children's names to come to the common area. For example, Susie is on the right side. When you call her to common area the class counts "one." Then call two more children. The class counts "two, three" for the total number in the center. You can also make large +, −, and = signs for the children to hold to illustrate the process.

5. This activity provides a visual portrayal of 1 + 2 = 3.

6. Children in the center can also illustrate subtraction. For example, after the class counts to three in the above example, Susie might return to her original spot, and 3 − 1 = 2 is shown.

TRIANGLES (EARS)

PINK OVAL (NOSE)

BLACK OVALS (EYES)

BLACK CIRCLES (SPOTS)

PAPER PLATE

CRAFT STICK

Related fingerplay

Invite the children to hold up fingers to show the numbers mentioned in the following original rhyme:

How many cows do I see?
I see one, two, three!
Wait! There's a tail; here comes one more.
That makes one, two, three, four!
Here come four more, just a little late.
They're numbers five, six, seven, eight!
Two are missing; where have they been?
Here they come, numbers nine and ten!

Related book   *Sixteen Cows* by Lisa Wheeler

✚ *Theresa Callahan, Easton, MD*

Dinosaur Shapes

shape recognition, spatial relationships

Materials pattern templates
paper in a variety of colors and shapes
glue

What to do
1. Invite the children to create dinosaur shapes using the different shapes and colored pieces of paper.
2. As the children make their dinosaur shapes, occasionally ask them to identify the shapes they used to make them.

✚ *Kristi Larson, Spirit Lake, IA*

Falling Leaves Banner

counting, number order, writing numerals

Materials   9" × 12" construction paper in brown and green
4" construction paper squares in assorted colors
3" wide tagboard leaf patterns
crayons
scissors
number cards (1–5)
glue
hole punch
yarn

What to do

1. Ahead of time, position the 9" × 12" paper vertically and cut the lower ends to make a point like the tip of an arrow pointing down. Make one for each child.

2. Ask each child to trace and cut out five leaves from the 4" paper squares. (Younger children will need a lot of help with this step. You may need to provide precut leaves.)

3. Show them the number cards and help them write the numeral 1 on one leaf, numeral 2 on the second leaf, and so on.

4. Ask the children to choose banner papers in green or brown. Show them how to put the leaf marked 1 near the top of the banner, and then put the leaf marked 2 slightly below the first one.

5. The children place the rest of the leaves in order on the banner, each one below the previous one as though they were falling from the trees.

6. Encourage them to spread the leaves out rather than placing them in a straight vertical line from top to bottom. When they are in place, ask the children to glue them on. Allow to dry.

7. Help them punch two holes near the top of the banner. Show them how to thread the yarn through and tie for hanging the banner.

8. Punch an additional hole near the pointed end and tie a tassel on, if desired.

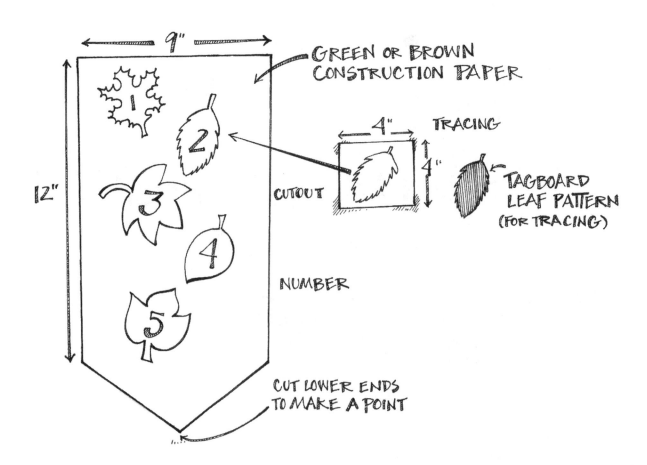

Related books   *School* by Emily Arnold McCully
The Seasons of Arnold's Apple Tree by Gail Gibbons
A Tree Is Nice by Janice May Udry
Why Do Leaves Change Color? by Betsy Maestro

✚ *Susan Oldham Hill, Lakeland, FL*

Foot Creature

measurement

Materials   paper
pencils
ruler
scissors
crayons

What to do   1. Have each child trace his bare foot on a piece of paper.
2. Demonstrate how to measure the length of their foot from the big toe to the heel using the ruler.
3. After they cut out their foot outlines, ask them to turn their foot outline around and create a creature using crayons. Encourage them to name their creatures. For example, if the child's foot is 4" long, the caption for the picture will be "My 4-Inch Creature."
4. Discuss the following:
   - the need for measuring feet for buying footwear
   - the need for measuring other body parts, such as height, waist size, and arm size for buying clothes; and circumference of the fingers for buying rings
   - accessories that fit everyone, such as earrings, buttons, and belts

✚ *Shyamala Shanmugasundaram, Nerul, Navi Mumbai, India*

Glittery Geometric Mobile

shape identification

Materials
sandpaper
scissors
colored construction paper
pencils
hole punch
glue
glitter
paper plates
yarn
coat hangers

What to do

1. From sandpaper, cut the following geometric shapes: circle, triangle, square, rectangle, pentagon, and hexagon. Each shape should be about 3".
2. Tell the children the names of the geometric shapes. Pass them around so the children can feel the difference in the shapes.

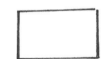

SANDPAPER SHAPES

3. Have the children trace the shapes onto colored construction paper.
4. Ask them to cut out the shapes and punch a hole at the top of each shape.
5. Pour glitter on paper plates. Have the children spread glue on their shapes and dip them into the glitter. Shake off the excess glitter.
6. Cut different lengths of yarn. When the glitter has dried, tie the yarn through the shapes and tie to a coat hanger. Hang the mobiles on doorknobs, dresser pulls, or curtain rods.

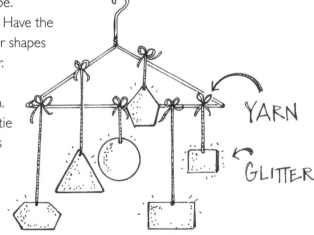

YARN

GLITTER

More to do   Add more geometric shapes to the mobiles such as a rhombus, parallelogram, trapezoid, and octagon.

Related books   *The Greedy Triangle* by Marilyn Burns
The Shape of Things by Dayle Dodds
Shape Space by Cathryn Falwell
Shapes, Shapes, Shapes by Tana Hoban

✚ *Randi Lynn Mrvos, Lexington, KY*

A Handful of Buttons

comparison, estimation, number sense

Materials
paper
pencil
copy machine
different types of buttons
bowl

What to do

1. In advance, draw 20 paper button counters on a piece of paper (make them actual button size if possible). Make a copy for each child.

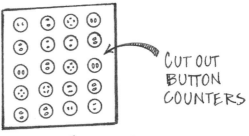

PAPER of BUTTON COUNTERS

CUT OUT BUTTON COUNTERS

2. Give each child a piece of plain paper and a copy of the button sheet.

3. Encourage the children to trace their hand on one side of the plain paper. This is the estimation side.

4. After they trace their hands, ask them to draw how many buttons they think will fit in the palm of their handprint. Show them a bowl containing one type of buttons so they can see the size.

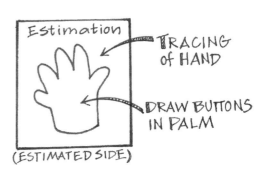

Estimation

TRACING of HAND

DRAW BUTTONS IN PALM

(ESTIMATED SIDE)

GLUE BUTTON
COUNTERS ON
PALM

BOWL OF
BUTTONS

(OTHER SIDE)

5. After they have estimated, they turn over their paper and trace their hand again.
6. Ask the children to take a handful of buttons and count how many fit in the palms of their hands.
7. Have the children cut out the button counters from the button sheet and glue them on their hand outline.

✚ *Quazonia J. Quarles, Newark, DE*

Hang Up Your Shirt!

number sequence

Materials
T-shirt pattern on white paper
decorative items, such as ribbon, glitter, confetti, wallpaper scraps, and felt
clothesline
clothespins (one per child)
crayons
glue

What to do
1. Give each child a T-shirt pattern.
2. Invite them to use crayons, ribbon, felt, and so on to decorate their T-shirts.
3. Write a different numeral on each child's T-shirt, starting with 1 and going up to however many children are in the class.
4. Hang a clothesline across the room and give each child a clothespin.
5. Have the children hang their shirts in numerical order. Younger children may only be able to order them from 1 to 5 or 1 to 10, so help them as needed.

Related book
Mrs. McNosh Hangs Up Her Wash! by Sara Weeks

✚ *Quazonia J. Quarles, Newark, DE*

How Many Hands?

measurement

Materials   art paper
markers
scissors

What to do   1. Trace around each child's hands and cut them out.
2. Invite the children to measure objects and distances in the room using their hand cutouts.
3. Discuss differences in units of measurement with the children.

 *Barbara Saul, Eureka, CA*

Insect Shapes

shape recognition, spatial relationships

Materials   paper in a variety of colors and shapes
glue

What to do   1. Talk about different shapes with the children. Explain that they will be making different insects using cutout shapes.
2. Invite the children to create insect shapes using the different pieces of cut paper, like those on the following page.

✚ Kristi Larson, Spirit Lake, IA

Jingle Doorknob Counters

counting, numeral recognition

Materials

tagboard
9" squares of sturdy poster board in assorted colors
crayons
scissors
hole punch
5" lengths of yarn or string
small jingle bells (or small lightweight craft items with holes for tying)

What to do

1. Beforehand, cut out 8" numeral patterns from tagboard (1–9).
2. Ask the children to choose a numeral pattern. Make sure they have the correct side of the numeral facing up. Demonstrate how to trace the shape of the numeral onto a poster board square.
3. Have the children cut out the numerals.
4. Help the children punch the correct number of holes to match the numeral they chose. Show them how to punch the holes near the lower end of each numeral.
5. Tie one end of a piece of yarn securely to a jingle bell, and the other end to the hole punched in the numeral.
6. Punch two more holes near the top of the numeral and thread yarn through for hanging.

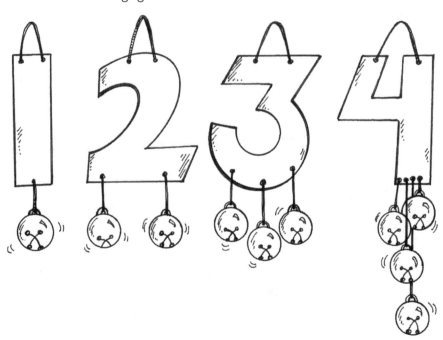

Related books   *Moja Means One* by Muriel Feelings
Ten Black Dots by Donald Crews

✚ *Susan Oldham Hill, Lakeland, FL*

Magic Numbers

number formation

Materials   8 ½" × 11" pieces of card stock
scissors
white glue
newsprint paper
crayons

What to do   1. Cut the card stock in half.
2. Write a large numeral with glue on each piece of cardstock.
3. When the glue is dry, put a piece of newsprint over it and invite the children to rub over the paper with crayons, making the numeral appear like "magic."

✚ *Barbara Saul, Eureka, CA*

Making a Number Page

numeral recognition

Materials   paper
glue
various small objects (buttons, cotton balls, beads, confetti, and so on)

What to do   1. Divide a piece of paper by the numbers you want the child to learn. You can make columns or divide the paper in thirds one way and in half the other way.
2. Write a numeral in each box or column (use as many numbers as desired).

3. Invite the children to glue one object beside the numeral 1, two objects beside the numeral 2, and so on.
4. Encourage the children to say the number and count the objects as they work.

✚ *Phyllis Esch, Export, PA*

Math Symmetry

matching

Materials

paper
paint
paintbrushes

What to do

1. Have the children fold a piece of paper in half and then open it back up.
2. Invite them to paint a design on half of the paper.
3. Before the paint dries, they fold the blank half of paper over the painted half. Show them how to smooth the paper over so that picture copies onto the other half of the paper.
4. Open the folded paper and allow it to dry.
5. Repeat this process. Compare the pictures.

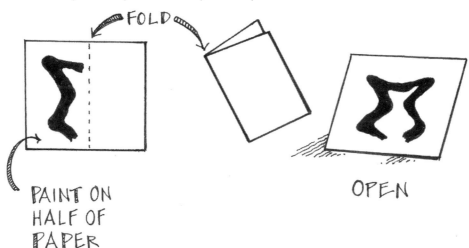

FOLD

PAINT ON HALF OF PAPER

OPEN

✚ *Jean Potter, Charleston, WV*

Mitten Math

matching, odd and even, pairs

Materials
drawing paper
crayons
scissors

What to do
1. To make mitten shapes, children trace the outline of their hands (fingers together) or trace a cardboard pattern.
2. Encourage the children to color their mittens in bright patterns and designs (make sure the child colors both mittens the same way).
3. Cut out the mittens and scramble them together.
4. Have children work in small groups to match the mittens. Encourage them to count the mittens one by one and use the pairs to identify even and odd numbers.

More to do
Have the children pin their mittens on a bulletin board display in color groups or pattern groups, for example, red, blue, and green or stripes, dots, and swirls.

Related books
Missing Mittens by Stuart J. Murphy
The Mitten by Jan Brett

✚ *Barbara Hershberger, Watertown, WI*

Number-Symbol Art

addition, shape identification, symbolic number representations

Materials
colored construction paper
scissors
paste or glue
white paper
markers or crayons
pencil

What to do

1. Before beginning the activity, select three simple shapes (or symbols) to represent the numerals 1, 5, and 10.
2. Using a different color for each shape, trace several of each shape on the construction paper. For example: green squares for the numeral 1, red hearts for 5, and blue circles for 10.
3. Cut out all the shapes and label with the correct numeral.
4. Give each child a sheet of white paper and a few of each shape (they will need more squares than circles), or place all the shapes in piles for the children to draw from as needed.
5. Say a number and have the children depict it by maneuvering the shapes on their papers. For example, the numeral 8 would be eight squares or one heart and three squares.
6. Help the children count out the shapes and find ways to depict each of the numerals. For example, 12 would be one circle (10) and two squares (1 + 1) or two hearts (5 + 5) and two squares (1 + 1). Encourage the children to think of other combinations.
7. Help the children understand that five squares equal one heart, and two hearts or 10 squares equal one circle, and so on by manipulating and substituting shapes to show equalities.
8. Once the children have grasped the idea that the shapes symbolize numbers and quantities, invite them to select one or more numbers of their own to depict.
9. Have them glue their shapes on the paper, and write the number represented next to the shapes.

✚ *Sandra K. Bynum, Blackfoot, ID*

One, Two, Buckle My Shoe

counting, numeral recognition

Materials

large colored paper
scissors
magazines and catalogs
construction paper
glue sticks

What to do

1. Precut large numerals out of colored paper.
2. Read or recite "One, Two, Buckle My Shoe."
3. Invite the children to help make a wall display of the nursery rhyme.
4. Invite the children to cut out and glue a corresponding number of pictures of shoes to the numerals. For example, for 1, they can cut and glue a picture of one shoe. For 2, they can glue two shoes, and so on.
5. For 9 and 10, say, "Start all over again," and help the children glue arrow shapes pointing back to the beginning.
6. Display the numerals on the wall, next to the words of the rhyme.

More to do

Draw around the children's shoes with chalk on the carpet or cut out the outlines from paper to tape to the floor. Write the numerals from 1 to 10 on the outlines. Invite the children to walk on the footprints as they say the rhyme.

✚ *Laura Durbrow, Lake Oswego, OR*

Pattern Chain

patterns

Materials

construction paper cut into strips of different colors
staplers

What to do

1. Put the strips of construction paper and staplers in the art center.

2. Model for the children how to make a chain by making the strip into a circle and stapling it together. Then demonstrate how to thread another strip through the circle and staple it.
3. Do a few to show the children how to make a chain. Make sure to use different colors to make a pattern.
4. After stapling together about five or six circles of alternating colors, point out to the children the specific pattern you made (red, orange, red, orange, and so on).
5. Ask the children to come to the center and add to the pattern. Leave it out for a few weeks and measure it each day.

6. As a group, make a goal to construct a chain that will reach across the room or down a hall. The children will get excited watching it grow longer and reaching their goal.

7. When done, the chain makes a great decoration for your room.

8. If desired, make a chain to count down to a particular event. For example, make a red, pink, and white chain and remove a circle each day to count down to Valentine's Day.

✚ *Gail Morris, Kemah, TX*

Pattern Mural

patterns

Materials

large paper
paint
colored paper or markers in at least 2 different colors
butcher paper (optional)

What to do

1. Divide the class into two (or more) groups (group A and group B, or more).

2. Assign group A one color (for example, blue) and group B another color (for example, yellow). Group A makes all blue pictures and group B makes all yellow pictures. For older children, you may want to have more groups and more colors, so they can make more complex patterns.

3. Give the children the option of making their pictures independently and then mounting them on butcher paper, positioning themselves by standing in a particular order, such as ABABAB, or creating their murals directly on butcher paper.

Related books

A Mural for Mamita by Alecia Alexander Greene
When Pigasso Met Mootisse by Nina Laden

✚ *Kristi Larson, Spirit Lake, IA*

Picture Clues for Recognizing Numerals

numeral recognition

Materials

index cards
markers
pencils

What to do

1. Write the numerals 1–10 on index cards, one numeral per card.
2. Add drawings to each numeral, making them into pictures the children can recall (see the following page). Be sure to outline these drawings in lighter colors than the numeral itself, so they stand out from one another.

   - 1 becomes a tree (draw a bunch of branches at the top of the numeral).
   - 2 becomes a swan (draw a body connected to the bottom line of the numeral).
   - 3 becomes a snake (add eyes and a mouth to one end of the numeral).
   - 4 becomes a cactus (add thorns and a shrub at the bottom of the numeral).
   - 5 becomes a planet with a flag (draw a light line connecting the bottom of the circle to the top, and color the top as though a flag).
   - 6 becomes a monkey head and arm (put a paw at the top of the numeral and a face in the center of the circle).
   - 7 becomes a running leg (add a foot at the bottom).
   - 8 becomes a snowman (add stick arms to the bottom circle and coal eyes and mouth to the top circle).
   - 9 becomes a flower (the top of the numeral becomes the head of the flower, draw petals around it, dots in the circles, and two leaves at the base).
   - 10 becomes a fork and plate.

3. Give the children their own cards with numerals written on them. Encourage them to turn the numerals into any picture they want.

 one

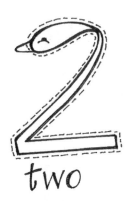 two

 three

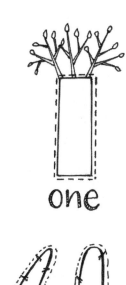 four

 five

 six

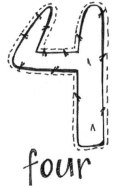 seven

 eight

 nine

 ten

Mary Brehm, Aurora, OH

Art

Shamrock Ladder

counting, patterns

Materials
green and yellow construction paper
scissors
hole punch
yarn
straws
masking tape

HOLE

½" PIECE of STRAW

What to do

1. Cut out shamrock shapes from green and yellow construction paper. Punch a hole in the top of each.
2. Cut straws into ½" pieces.
3. Give each child a 2' piece of yarn.
4. Demonstrate attaching a small piece of tape to the end of the yarn, and then string alternating straw pieces and shamrocks.
5. Hang the "ladders" from the ceiling for "leprechauns" to climb.
6. Help the children count how many shamrocks are on their ladders.

SHAMROCK SHAPE

TAPE

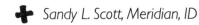

2' PIECE of YARN

Related book
St. Patrick's Day in the Morning by Eve Bunting

✚ *Sandy L. Scott, Meridian, ID*

Shape Collages

patterns, shapes, spatial relationships

Materials black construction paper
precut shapes in bright colors and different sizes
glue sticks

What to do 1. Give each child a piece of black construction paper and an assortment of paper shapes.
2. Encourage them to experiment with using shapes to make a design by gluing shapes to their paper.
3. Invite them to make patterns with their shapes, if they are interested.

Related book *Shapes and Colors* by Tana Hoban

✚ *Barbara Saul, Eureka, CA*

Silvery Falling Snowflakes

counting

Materials newspaper
smocks
12" x 18" construction paper in dark colors
crayons
number cards, 4–7
bag
silver paint
snowflake cookie cutters

What to do

1. Teach the children the following original song to the tune of "Twinkle, Twinkle, Little Star."

    Snowflakes falling from the sky.
    I can see you up so high!
    Little snowflake, falling fast,
    How I wonder if you'll last…
    Snowflakes falling from the sky,
    I can catch you if I try!

2. Ahead of time, cover the work surface with newspapers and have the children put on smocks.
3. Give the children sheets of dark colored paper, and ask them to position the paper vertically.
4. Invite the children to use crayons to draw a small picture of themselves in one of the bottom corners of the paper.
5. Let each child choose a number card from the bag. Have them write that numeral on the paper in the other lower corner of their paper.

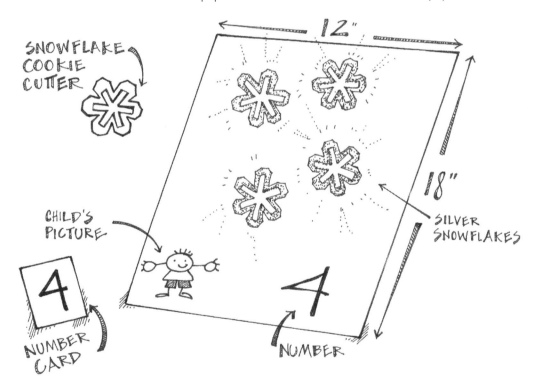

SNOWFLAKE COOKIE CUTTER

12"

18"

SILVER SNOWFLAKES

CHILD'S PICTURE

4

NUMBER CARD

4

NUMBER

6. Demonstrate how to dip the cookie cutter into the silvery paint and count the correct number of snowflakes to print on the paper. Explain that it only takes a small amount of paint, and ask the children to try to keep printing until they reach the correct number without dipping the cutter into the paint again.

✦ *Susan Oldham Hill, Lakeland, FL*

Sponge-Painted Schools

counting, printing numerals

Materials
number cards, 7–10 (or higher depending on children's counting ability)
bag
newspapers
pictures of schools of fish
markers
9" x 12" construction paper in turquoise or dark blue
bright-colored paint
shallow containers
sponges cut in the shape of small fish

What to do
1. Ahead of time, cover the work surface with newspapers and place the number cards in a small bag.
2. Discuss the pictures of fish swimming in schools.
3. Ask the children to choose a number card from the bag, explaining that this will be the number of fish they will paint. Have them draw the numeral on their blue paper.
4. Show the children how to dip the sponge gently into the paint and wipe off the excess paint.
5. Ask them to count carefully and print the correct number of fish, dipping in the paint again only if all the paint is gone from the sponge before they reach the correct number of fish.
6. Allow the paintings to dry.
7. Provide plenty of additional paper for the children to make more paintings, because the number of fish they will print will be very small.
8. When the number pages are dry, invite the children to look again at the pictures of the fish and add features such as eyes, scales, dots, stripes, and gills.

Related books
Blue Sea by Robert Kalan
Fish Is Fish by Leo Lionni
Jump, Frog, Jump! by Robert Kalan
Lovable Lyle by Bernard Waber

✚ *Susan Oldham Hill, Lakeland, FL*

Stars on Parade

shapes

Materials

7" construction paper squares in red, white, and blue
6" tagboard star patterns
crayons
scissors
shiny star stickers in red, blue, and silver
glue
craft sticks
marching music

What to do

1. Let each child choose a red, white, or blue square.
2. Children trace the star pattern with a crayon and cut it out.
3. Provide an assortment of shiny star stickers to decorate the larger paper star.
4. Encourage the children to count the number of star stickers they add to their large star and write the numeral on the back of the large star.
5. Demonstrate how to glue the large stars to a craft stick.
6. Play marching music and invite the children to march around in a parade, holding their stars high.

Related song

Teach the children this original verse to the tune of "This Land Is Your Land:"

I hold my star high
As I go marching by.
It shines out red and blue
And shiny silver, too.
While I am on parade,
I love to march and say,
"This land was made for you and me!"

Related book

The Planets by Gail Gibbons

 *Susan Oldham Hill, Lakeland, FL*

What Makes a Pair?

pairs

Materials

gingerbread-type person cut from construction paper (one for each child)
markers

What to do

1. Ask the children to think about their faces and heads. "What features come in twos?" (eyes, ears, nostrils)
2. Explain what a pair is. Now ask them to think of the rest of their body. "What else comes in pairs?"
3. Give each child an outline of a person. Ask them to draw facial features on their outlines.
4. Ask them what articles go on various body pairs, such as glasses on eyes, earphones on ears, and so on.
5. Discuss pair coverings for arms (elbow pads), feet (socks, shoes, boots, skates, and so on), legs (pants, shorts, knee pads), and hands (gloves, mittens).
6. Invite the children to draw clothing and accessories on their outlines.

✚ *Theresa Callahan, Easton, MD*

What's in a Name?

counting, ordinal numbers

Materials

1" graph papers
pens
crayons

What to do

1. Help the children write their names on the 1" graph paper, putting one letter in each square, and repeat the name all the way down the paper until each square is full.
2. Invite the children to find the first letters in their names and color them red, then color the second letter another color, and so on, until all the letters are filled with particular colors.
3. Ask the children to count how many red letters they have on their pages, or how many blue, and so on.

Related book *Fish Eyes: A Book You Can Count On* by Lois Ehlert

✚ *Barbara Saul, Eureka, CA*

What's My Line?

numeral recognition

Materials
9" × 12" yellow paper
yellow crayons
smocks
paintbrushes
thinned black paint
shallow paint containers
number stencils
newspaper

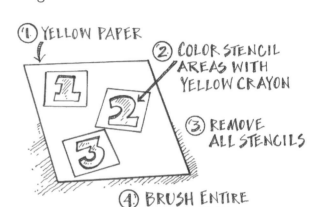

① YELLOW PAPER

② COLOR STENCIL AREAS WITH YELLOW CRAYON

③ REMOVE ALL STENCILS

④ BRUSH ENTIRE PAPER WITH THINNED BLACK PAINT

What to do

1. Ahead of time, experiment by coloring with yellow crayon on the yellow paper and painting over it with black paint thinned with water. Make sure the paint is thinned enough to reveal the crayoned area.
2. Ask the children to place a stencil on the yellow paper and color in the area completely, pressing firmly with the yellow crayons.
3. Show them how to place several stencils on one sheet of paper.
4. Demonstrate how to remove the final stencil and paint over the yellow paper, brushing across from left to right without brushing over the same area twice.
5. Ask the children to start at the top and work down the paper, revealing the crayoned numerals as the colored portion resists the paint.

Related books *Count and See* by Tana Hoban
One Fish, Two Fish by Dr. Seuss

✚ *Susan Oldham Hill, Lakeland, FL*

As Tall as the Doll

length, measurement

Materials   50–100 uniform rectangular blocks
several dolls or stuffed animals, each a different height
camera

What to do
1. Invite the children to bring a favorite doll or stuffed animal to class.
2. Stand one of the dolls (or animals) on the floor or a table. Explain that they should stack blocks as tall as the doll. Count together how many blocks are needed.
3. Repeat with a couple more dolls. Invite the children to guess the number of blocks needed prior to the count.
4. Invite children to measure the doll or animal they brought to class using bocks.
5. Photograph each doll with corresponding blocks. Display the photographs, and label the height of each.

✚ *Karyn F. Everham, Fort Myers, FL*

Block Measuring

measurement

Materials   1" blocks
ruler
glue

What to do
1. Glue 1" blocks onto a ruler.
2. When dry, encourage the children to use the block ruler to measure different items in the classroom.
3. By gluing the blocks onto the ruler, the children have a three-dimensional model of what they are measuring, giving the measurements a sense of proportion.

✚ *Jean Potter, Charleston, WV*

Block Sorting

size relationships, sorting

Materials
blocks
colored paper
colored masking tape

What to do
1. Cover the blocks with colored paper using colored masking tape.
2. Invite the children to sort and stack the blocks by color.
3. Encourage the children to sort them however they want, from shortest to longest, biggest to smallest, and so on.
4. Add colored shapes to the blocks so the children can sort by shapes and colors.

✚ *Sandy L. Scott, Meridian, ID*

Blocks Counting Song

counting

Materials
many colored blocks of the same size
3" x 5" file cards
pen

What to do
1. Copy the verses of the "Blocks Counting Song" (see the following page) on the file cards.
2. Choose two children, and give them several blocks to make a tower.
3. As the two children build, the other children sing the first verse of the song.
4. When the two children use their last block, choose two new children, give them more blocks, and have those children build the road going to the tower. The rest of the children sing the second verse of the song.
5. Choose two more children to count the number of different blocks of each color used to build the tower and road as the other children sing the third verse.
6. Choose two children to take the tower apart and count the total number of blocks used, while the other children sing the fourth verse of the song.

Copy Cats

patterns

Materials   shape pictures
parquetry circles

What to do
1. Make pictures of objects using shapes. For example, draw a caterpillar using only circles.
2. Provide parquetry circles and invite the children to make a caterpillar by copying the design.

✚ *Jean Potter, Charleston, WV*

The Even/Odd Train

comparison, length, odd and even

Materials   blocks

What to do
1. Give the child six blocks to make into a train.
2. Now ask her to make two trains of equal length using the same six blocks. Ask her how many blocks are in each train. Explain that six is an even number.
3. Take one block away. Now ask the child to make two trains the same length. Can she? Talk about odd and even numbers.

Related book   *Even Steven and Odd Todd* by Kathryn Cristaldi

✚ *Monica Hay Cook, Tucson, AZ*

How Many Blocks Make a Body?

length, measurement

Materials
50–100 uniform rectangular blocks
wood glue and marker (optional)

What to do
1. Ask one of the children to lie on the floor.
2. Ask the children to estimate how many blocks tall the child is.
3. Arrange blocks in a line, from the child's head to toe, counting aloud.
4. Repeat for each child and invite the children to measure each other.
5. If desired, glue blocks into a permanent tower, using a marker to number each block. Display the tower and invite the children to check their "block height" as time passes.

✚ *Karyn F. Everham, Fort Myers, FL*

How Many Blocks in the Box?

counting

Materials
5 shoeboxes with lids
craft knife (adult only)
rubber bands (2 per shoebox)
15 wooden blocks
wood glue

What to do

1. On the inside bottom of a shoebox, glue one wood block. Cut a 3" circle into the lid of the box (adult only). Cover the box with the lid and use two rubber bands to hold the lid in place.

2. Glue two blocks to the bottom of another box and cut a 3" circle in the lid. Repeat again, gluing three, four, and five blocks to the remaining three boxes.

3. Invite the children to place a hand inside a box, and determine how many blocks are inside using their sense of touch.

✚ *Karyn F. Everham, Fort Myers, FL*

How Tall Am I? Towers

counting, measurement

Materials

large cardboard blocks

What to do

1. Divide children into pairs. Have them take turns stacking blocks to reach the height of their partner.

2. Have them count the blocks in each tower.

3. Ask them to decide which of them is taller and which is shorter.

4. Encourage older children to figure out the difference in the two numbers.

✚ *Wanda Guidroz, Santa Fe, TX*

Lots of Blocks

counting

Materials   several colored blocks

What to do   1. Provide several blocks, and invite the children to recite the following original poem, holding up the correct number and color of blocks as they are mentioned:

Blocks
White blocks, I have none.
Orange, though, I have one.

Blocks that are blue,
I have two.

Blocks green like the leaf of a tree,
Of these, I have three.

Yellow blocks, I have even more:
I have four.

2. Count the blocks with the children, first one at a time, and then by color group.
3. Consider making up more rhymes for different colors of blocks, and increasing the numbers for children able to work with larger numbers.

✚ *Ingelore Mix, Gainesville, VA*

Measuring Perimeters with Blocks

counting, measurement

Materials
rectangular blocks (same size)
classroom objects including a table

What to do
1. Gather a large number of identical rectangular blocks and use them to measure the perimeter of a classroom object.
2. Explain to the children what the word *perimeter* means (the boundary of a closed plane object).
3. Turn a table upside down on the floor and measure its perimeter by placing blocks end to end around the entire table.
4. Together count the total number of blocks.
5. Ask the children what other perimeters they could measure and invite them to take measurements.

✛ *Karyn F. Everham, Fort Myers, FL*

Number Names

number sense

Materials
small blocks
small toy animals

What to do
1. Place the blocks in a row on a table. Put out an assortment of toy animals.
2. Ask a child to find two blocks.
3. Then ask her to find two cats and put them next to the two blocks. Then ask her to find three blocks and three cows.
4. Repeat the method with all the numbers up to 10.

More to do Ask the children to find things around the room that represent each numeral from 1–10. Ask the children to find two pieces of chalk, three books, four cars, and so on.

✚ *Lily Erlic, Victoria, BC, Canada*

Number Roads

numeral recognition

Materials black poster board
large numeral stencils
marker
scissors
yellow paint
laminator
toy cars and vehicles

What to do 1. Trace large numerals (0–9) on black poster board and cut them out.
2. Paint the middle of each numeral to make a road design. Laminate for durability.
3. Place the "number roads" in the block area with some toy vehicles and invite the children to drive their cars on them.
4. Talk about the numbers as the children drive their cars on them. Point out that driving the cars on the numerals is similar to writing the numerals.
5. Talk about how some of the number roads are straight and some are curvy.

Related book *Truck* by Donald Crews

✚ *Shelley F. Hoster, Norcross, GA*

Road Sign Shapes

shape recognition

Materials
clip art of road signs of various shapes
card stock
marker
scissors
craft sticks
glue
clay
small toy vehicles

What to do
1. Copy road sign shapes on card stock and cut out. Include yield (triangle), stop (octagon), school crossing (pentagon), pedestrians or curve (diamond or rhombus), permit/handicapped parking (square), railroad or do not enter (circle).
2. Attach each sign to a craft stick using glue.
3. Put the other end of the stick into a ball of clay, which will serve as a base (so it stands up).
4. Before placing the signs in the block area, discuss the different shapes.
5. Add cars or other vehicles to the block area.

More to do
Group Time: Show the signs to the children and ask them to identify the shapes.
Language and Literacy: Use the signs as an example and have the children create books by drawing pictures of each sign. Help the children write the shape names on their pictures. Ask them if they can tell by looking at each sign what it is used for.

Related books   *The Shape of Things* by Dayle Ann Dodds
Shapes, Shapes, Shapes by Tana Hoban
When a Line Bends…A Shape Begins by Rhonda Gowler Greene

✚ *Kristi Larson, Spirit Lake, IA*

Road Trip

• •

distance, measurement

Materials   butcher paper
marker
ruler
laminator
tape
toy cars

What to do   1. Using the butcher paper, measure 10 lines about 6" apart.
2. Write the numerals 1–10 on each line, one numeral per line. Laminate for durability.
3. Secure to the floor in the block area with tape.
4. Give the children small toy cars to roll on the mat. Tell them that you want to see how far their cars will go, with each numeral on the paper representing a mile. Ask them to predict how many "miles" their cars will go.

5. Encourage the children to roll their cars down the mat and see where they stop. *How many miles will your car go?*
6. Have each child roll their car down the mat one at a time. Make sure they "roll it off" and let go.
7. Record the number line that it stops closest to.
8. See which cars drive the farthest and shortest distances.
9. Make a chart to hang on the wall. Use die-cut cars with the children's names on them and place them next to the number of miles they went that day. For example, write "Ryan's car drove three miles! Beth's car drove 10 miles! Beth's car drove the farthest!"

✚ *Shelley F. Hoster, Norcross, GA*

Rulers and Tape Measures

measurement, numeral recognition

Materials
rulers
tape measures
yard sticks
blocks

What to do
1. Bring measuring tools to the block center and show the children how to use them.
2. Invite the children to create objects and shapes with the blocks, and talk about the height, size, and length of the objects they build.
3. Leave the measuring tools in the block center for several days for the children to explore at their own pace.

More to do
Art: Put rulers in the art center and invite the children to measure the size of their artwork, or to practice drawing lines and copying the numbers from the ruler onto the lines.

✚ *Holly Dzierzanowski, Brenham, TX*

Sorting and Grouping Blocks

counting, estimation, labeling, shape recognition, sorting

Materials
large and small cards
marker
large, plain wooden blocks
tub or basket
hoops (circles of yarn will also work)

What to do
1. Beforehand, make labels by drawing block shapes on large cards.
2. Set out a tub of wooden blocks in a variety of sizes and shapes.
3. Put the hoops on the floor (or make circles using yarn) and place the block shape labels inside the hoops.
4. Discuss the outlines on the cards. Look for similarities and differences.
5. Ask the children to sort the blocks into hoops according to the block label (for example, square blocks go in the hoop with the square shape).
6. When finished sorting, ask the children if everyone agrees on how the blocks are sorted. If not, discuss the reasoning.
7. Once everyone agrees on the sorting, invite the children to estimate how many blocks are in each hoop. Print the estimations on the small cards. Discuss which hoops the children think have more or fewer blocks than the others.
8. Assign children to count the blocks in the hoops, then place the appropriate number card next to each hoop.
9. Discuss the children's estimations, and ask them which hoops had more or fewer blocks than they thought.

✚ *Sandra Nagel, White Lake, MI*

Tall, Tall Tower

counting, estimation, measurement, spatial relationships

Materials
masking tape
blocks
ruler or measuring tape

What to do
1. Make masking tape squares of the floor in the block area.
2. Have the children use the same number of blocks, but in a variety of sizes, to build towers in each taped section (ask them ahead of time to predict which tower will be the tallest).
3. After building the towers, measure them to see which one was actually the tallest.

More to do   **Outdoor Play:** Use large boxes to build towers outside.

Related book   *Alphabet Under Construction* by Denise Fleming

✚ *Kristi Larson, Spirit Lake, IA*

Tower of Numerals

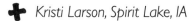

counting, numeral recognition, patterns, sorting

Materials   two sets of blocks that show both numerals and letters

What to do
1. Give the child the blocks and ask her to sort them so that one set shows numerals and one set shows letters.
2. Ask the child to look at the number blocks and choose the block with the numeral 1.
3. Have the child build a tower by choosing and placing the remaining blocks in the correct numerical order.
4. Ask the child to say the name of each numeral as she places the blocks in order.
5. Ask the child to build a second tower beside the first using only the letter blocks (beginning with "A") and placing them in alphabetical order.
6. Have the child say the name of each letter as she places the blocks.
7. Let the child knock over the towers and scatter them. Ask her to build a big tower using all the blocks.
8. When she is finished, ask her to find and point to numerals and letters as you say the names.

More to do   Ask the children to use the blocks to make patterns like the following: one numeral, two letters; one letter, one numeral, two letters, and so on.

✚ *Virginia Jean Herrod, Columbia, SC*

Trucks Rule

measurement

Materials

toy trucks
rulers
paper
crayons or markers
tape (optional)

What to do

1. Gather all the toy trucks from the classroom.
2. Ask the children to measure the length of one of the trucks, showing them how to put one edge of the ruler at one edge of a truck to measure accurately.
3. Ask another child to write the number of inches on a slip of paper and place the paper near the truck. (Optional: tape the measurement to the truck.)
4. Continue until all the trucks are measured.
5. Discuss the results with the children. Ask them to identify the longest truck and the shortest truck. "Were any the same number of inches?"
6. Put the trucks in order from longest to shortest. Then mix them up and ask a child to put them in order again.

Related books

Freight Train by Donald Crews
Harbor by Donald Crews
Mike Mulligan and His Steam Shovel by Virginia Lee Burton
Planes by Anne Rockwell

 *Susan Oldham Hill, Lakeland FL*

Doctor's Physical

measurement, writing numerals

Materials
bathroom scale
height chart
clipboard with paper and pencil
white lab coat
stethoscope

What to do
1. Separate the children into pairs.
2. Invite the children to pretend they are going to the doctor for a physical or checkup. Explain that one child will be the doctor and the other the patient.
3. The "doctor" weighs the patient and records his weight, measures and records his height, and listens to the patient's heart and records how many times the heart beats for 10 seconds. Help them by calling out the time.
4. When the doctor is finished, invite the children to switch roles.

✚ *Wanda Guidroz, Santa Fe, TX*

The Doorbell Rang

counting, one-to-one correspondence

Materials
die-cut cookies from foam or felt
magnets
large cookie sheet
The Doorbell Rang by Pat Hutchins
small paper plates
napkins
small bell

What to do
1. Make "chocolate chip cookies" from brown felt or foam sheets, one for each child. Attach a small magnet to the back of each cookie so they will stick to the cookie sheet.

2. Place the cookies on the cookie sheet and hide it nearby.
3. Gather the children and read *The Doorbell Rang* by Pat Hutchins.
4. After the story, show the children the felt cookies on the cookie sheet. Ask them if they think if there are enough cookies for everyone.
5. Act out the story by having two children start out with all of the cookies and then have more children ring the bell and come over for cookies.
6. At the end, each child should have just one cookie.

✚ *Shelley F. Hoster, Norcross, GA*

Dress the Doll

patterns

Materials

large doll
10 or more items of patterned doll clothes
real clothing items with a distinct pattern

What to do

1. Place the doll and the clothing items at a table or learning center.
2. Invite the children to practice dressing the doll.
3. As the child works, encourage him to identify the pattern on each item of clothing. Invite the child to make a pattern with the clothes, such as sock, shirt, sock, shirt, and so on.
4. Gather a collection of real clothing items that have a distinct pattern. Place them in the dramatic play center. Invite the children to try on the dress-up clothes and verbalize the pattern on each clothing item.
5. Have the children make patterns out of the clothing, for example, striped sock, black sock, striped sock, black sock.

More to do

Art: Cut out an assortment of clothing items from colored construction paper (socks, hats, dresses, shirts, and pants). Place the paper clothing and a variety of art supplies at the art table and invite the children to create a pattern on one or more items of clothing. Display the patterned clothing items on a bulletin board.

✚ *Mary J. Murray, Mazomanie, WI*

Driving the Car

matching, numeral recognition

Materials

blank stickers
marker
basket or box containing 10 small toy cars
12" x 18" piece of black construction paper
large sheet of colored paper
large and small books
5" x 7" note card
wooden block
tape
scissors

Preparation

1. Print the numerals 1–10 on blank stickers. Attach one to each car.
2. Cut a 4" wide curvy road shape from the black paper.
3. Draw a 10-part grid on the colored paper. Number the spaces 1–10 to create a "parking lot."
4. Make a ramp for the cars by stacking several small books in a pile, then leaning one end of the largest book on the stack.
5. Place the road near the end of the ramp and the parking lot near the other end of the road.
6. Write "Parking Lot" on the note card and tape it to the wooden block so it will stand up. Display the sign near the parking lot.
7. Place the basket of cars near the top of the ramp. (See illustration on the following page.)

What to do

1. Demonstrate the activity so that children can do it on their own or with a partner. Remove one car from the basket and place it at the top of the ramp.
2. Identify the numeral on the car and hold it at the top of the ramp.
3. Let the car go down the ramp. Drive the car onto the road and into the parking lot.
4. Park the car in the space with the matching numeral.
5. The game continues until all the cars are parked in the correct spaces.

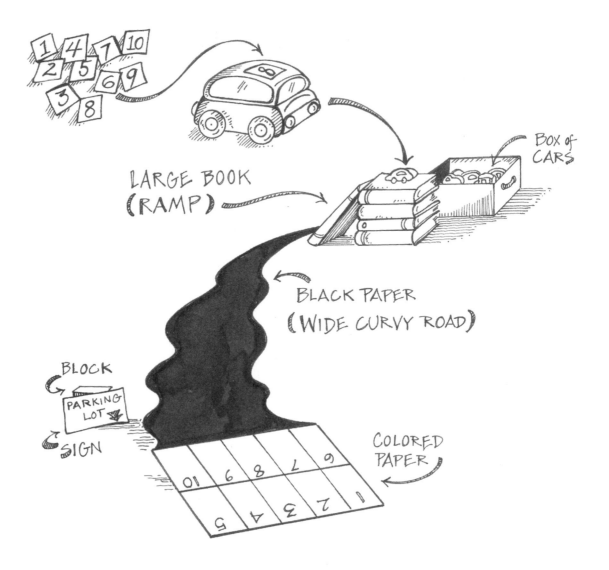

More to do Create a parking lot without numerals. Have the children park the cars in order from 1 to 10.

Fine Motor: Have children take turns rolling a number cube and manipulating the designated number of cars down the ramp and into the parking lot.

✚ *Mary J. Murray, Mazomanie, WI*

The Elves and the Shoemaker

odd and even, pairs

Materials

The Elves and the Shoemaker by Jacob Grimm and Jim Lamarche
pairs of shoes, boots, and other footwear

What to do

1. Read *The Elves and the Shoemaker* to the children.
2. Invite the children to take turns acting out the different parts of the book as you read it.
3. Talk with the children about *pairs* of shoes, and doubling the number of shoes the elves can make.
4. Play matching games with the children's own shoes, and introduce the children to odd and even numbers using their shoes (one shoe is an odd number, two shoes are an even number).

✚ *Ellen Javernik, Loveland, CO*

Fruit Market Fun!

addition, counting, money value, problem solving

Materials

assorted plastic fruit
money: pennies, nickels, dimes, and quarters (each pair of children will need a minimum of $1 in various coins)

What to do

This is an activity for older children. If doing this activity with younger children, you will need to revise it somewhat and help a lot.

1. Explain to the children that you are the "farmer" who owns the market. You will be giving them money to shop, and they will need to count out the correct amount of money to buy a piece of fruit.

2. Pass out money, giving each pair of children approximately one dollar in coins (adjust according to age and ability). You may want to distribute the change prior to the activity and place in small containers, such as clean yogurt containers, for easier transition and cleanup.

3. Hold up a piece of fruit and name a price. Instruct each pair of children to count their money, working together, until they have the correct sum of change.

4. As each pair finds the correct amount, ask them to raise their hands quietly. When everyone is finished, choose groups to share their money combinations with the class. (For example, if the price was 15 cents for a banana, one pair of children may have three nickels, another may have 15 pennies, and so on.)

5. Play until every pair has at least one chance to share their money combinations.

6. Let the children take turns with each other in groups of two or three being the farmer and the shoppers.

✚ *Dawnelle Breum, London, ON, Canada*

The Garden Party

addition, counting

Materials   different colors of construction paper (1 sheet per child)
scissors

adhesive circles
safety pins
3 large grocery bags
scissors
red paint

What to do   1. Make butterfly wings for each child. Cut out large bowtie shapes and let the children decorate them with adhesive circles. Safety pin the butterfly wings to the children's backs. For this activity, you will only need to make two pairs of wings, but it's fun for each child to make his own wings to keep.

2. Make three ladybug vests. Cut off the bottoms of three grocery bags, cut openings on each side of the bags for arm holes, and cut the front of the bag through the middle. Paint the bag red and let it dry. Attach adhesive black circles when dry.

3. Choose 10 children to be the "bugs." One child should wear a yellow and black smock or shirt, if available. Two children should wear butterfly wings, three children should wear the ladybug vests, and the remaining four children should be wearing sneakers.

4. Invite the children to recite the following rhyme as the 10 bugs stand in front of the class and act out their insect characters when mentioned. Let the children take turns acting out different bugs.

A LADYBUG

In my garden, 'round the tree
Danced one bumblebee.

And two large butterflies
Wearing polka-dotted ties.

The three ladybugs looked their best
Each in a red velvet vest.

While the four caterpillars were real neat
Wearing sneakers on their feet.

How many bugs are there then?
You're right, if you count ten!

Ingelore Mix, Gainesville, VA

Grocery Shopping

counting, matching, one-to-one correspondence

Materials
grocery items (empty boxes, cans, and containers; plastic fruit and vegetables; real food items such as potatoes, oranges, onions, and cans of soup)
brown paper bags
apron
purse
pennies
small toy shopping cart
cash register or shoebox
sheet of black paper

What to do
1. Set up a grocery store in the dramatic play area. Stock the area with the food boxes and containers. Place the pennies in the purse.
2. One child is the grocer and one or more other children go "shopping." The grocer wears the apron.
3. When the shoppers arrive, they greet the grocer. They choose sets of objects to purchase, and place them in their cart (two apples, five yogurt, three potatoes, and so on).
4. Encourage the grocer to count the items as he "scans" them (over the black sheet of paper) and then tells the shoppers how many pennies they owe. To teach the concept of one-to-one correspondence, have each item worth one penny.
5. The shoppers count out the pennies they need and pay the grocer. For example, if a child has five items, she would give the grocer five pennies.
6. The grocer places the items in a bag, then collects and counts the money.
7. Encourage the shoppers to take their items "home," to sort, classify, and count them again.
8. Make sure all the children have turns as the grocer.
9. For older children, label each item with a picture of a coin (penny, nickel, dime, or quarter). Provide real coins for them to pay for their purchases.

More to do
Dramatic Play: Change the grocery store into a clothing store. Stock the store with various shoes, socks, and other fun clothing items. Change the type of store each week.

✚ *Mary J. Murray, Mazomanie, WI*

Home from the Grocery Store

sorting

Materials   play kitchen equipment
empty food containers and boxes
plastic food
paper shopping bags

What to do   1. Provide a variety of empty food containers and plastic food in shopping bags.
2. Encourage the children to remove the items from the bags and sort them items by what goes in a refrigerator, freezer, or on the shelves.
3. Children can also sort the items by what needs to be cooked before eating and what can be eaten without cooking.

✚ *Sandy L. Scott, Meridian, ID*

Let's Make Cupcakes!

counting, one-to-one correspondence

Materials   muffin tin
cupcake liners
playdough
large bowl
birthday candles

What to do   1. Invite the children to make pretend cupcakes for a party. Have one child count the number of cupcakes that can be made using the muffin tin (six or 12).
2. Put the muffin tin in the middle of the table. One child places a cupcake liner in each compartment.
3. Put playdough into a large bowl. Invite the children to make six (or 12, depending on the muffin tin) playdough balls. Have them put one ball in each liner.

4. One child places a candle into each "cupcake." Another child counts the number of cupcakes and then asks that many children to sit at the table.

5. The children pretend to have a party!

✚ *Shelley F. Hoster, Norcross, GA*

Mail Box

matching numbers

Materials

large number of 3" x 5" pieces of colored paper
marker
10 small shoeboxes
scissors or craft knife (adult only)
rubber stamp and stamp pad or stickers

What to do

1. In advance, print a numeral between 1–10 on each piece of colored paper. Attach one number card to each shoebox. Cut a slit in the lid of each box and display the boxes randomly around the room.

2. Tell the children that they are going to practice being mail carriers.

3. Let the children help write numerals (1–10) on many pieces of colored paper to make "postcards" (one number per card). You may want to do this step ahead of time, without children's help.

4. Demonstrate how to pick up a numbered postcard, identify the numeral, and then use the rubber stamp and pad to make a "stamp."

5. The mail carriers "mail" the postcards by placing them in the "mailboxes" with the matching numeral.

6. Empty the mailboxes and invite the children to practice numeral sequencing or recognition.

7. A similar activity is to use paper shapes in place of numbered postcards. Attach one shape to each of six shoeboxes and have children match shapes.

✚ *Mary J. Murray, Mazomanie, WI*

Mail Call

matching, numeral recognition

Materials
large box
craft knife (adult only)
shoeboxes with lids (one for each child)
list of the children's addresses
self-stick folder labels
permanent marker
envelopes
ride-on toy or toy cart

What to do

1. Work as a group to make the mailbox. Cut a mail slot (adult only) in the front of a large box that will fold up and down so the mail can be deposited.
2. Give each child a single shoebox. Help them write their house numbers on two self-stick labels. Ask them to attach one to their boxes and keep the others to attach to a letter.
3. Cut a slit in the top of each shoebox (adult only), large enough for a letter to fit through. Children can remove the lid to get mail.
4. Set up the mailboxes on the opposite sides of the room from each other, so that the mail carriers can "deliver" the mail to the boxes on their cart.
5. Encourage the children to draw pictures and dictate or write messages to each other and put them in an envelope. You might want to assign pairs of children to write letters to each other. This ensures that every child will receive mail.

6. Children can attach the second address labels to their envelopes and put them in the mailboxes.
7. Give each child a chance to deliver the mail.

✚ *Ellen Javernik, Loveland, CO*

Matchbox™ Car Parking

matching, numeral recognition

Materials

corrugated box (a lid to box of copy paper is ideal)
Matchbox™ cars
number stickers or tape
ruler
markers
cutting tool (adult only)

What to do

1. Use a corrugated box or lid to a copy paper box to create a parking lot for Matchbox™ cars. Using a ruler and a marker, draw parking spaces on the box lid.
2. Write a numeral in each parking space. Vary this activity depending on the age and skill level of the children. For very young children, you might make parking spaces using the numerals 1–5. For older children, you might use numeric words to match to the numerals.
3. Apply number stickers or tape with numerals written on them to the cars. Number them to match the parking spaces.
4. As the children return vehicles to the parking area, they will have the challenge of finding the correct spot.
5. This is a great addition to the road play mats or block construction zones.

✚ *Bev Schumacher, Racine, WI*

Number City

counting, numeral recognition, sequencing

Materials

large paper or cardboard
empty egg cartons, cereal boxes, and so on
markers and/or paints
glue and tape
wooden clothespins, pipe cleaners, scraps of material, cotton balls, or other interesting objects
blank stickers
toy cars, plastic trees (for more fun, use grass, sand, shells, and so on)

What to do

1. Place the large paper or cardboard on the floor.
2. Mark roads, parks, beaches, and other landmarks on the paper.
3. Help the children make items such as buses, houses, buildings, trees, playground equipment, and so on using egg cartons or cereal boxes and paint.

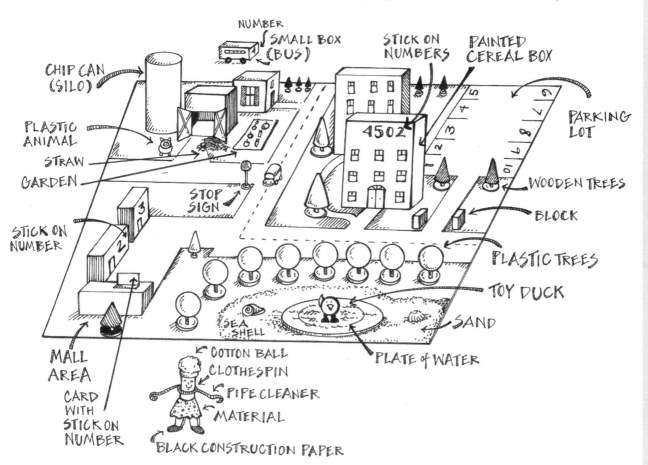

CHIP CAN (SILO)
PLASTIC ANIMAL
STRAW
GARDEN
STICK ON NUMBER
MALL AREA
CARD WITH STICK ON NUMBER

NUMBER
SMALL BOX (BUS)
STICK ON NUMBERS
PAINTED CEREAL BOX
PARKING LOT
WOODEN TREES
BLOCK
PLASTIC TREES
TOY DUCK
SAND

STOP SIGN
4502
SEA SHELL
PLATE of WATER

COTTON BALL
CLOTHESPIN
PIPE CLEANER
MATERIAL
BLACK CONSTRUCTION PAPER

4. After the children paint the items, allow them to dry.
5. Help the children glue or tape each item in place on the cardboard.
6. Invite them to make people using clothespins, with pipe cleaners for arms and legs, and material for clothes.
7. Provide blank stickers for children to mark numerals on houses, buses, stores, and so on.
8. As you and the children make the Number City, ask some of the following questions:
   - How should street addresses be arranged?
   - How many floors are in the high-rise building?
   - How many people live in each house?
   - How many wheels are on the bus?
   - How far is the bus from the beach?
   - How many swings are on the playground?

➕ *Sandra Saunders, Carrum Downs, Victoria, Australia*

Pet Store

classification

Materials   stuffed pet animals (dogs, cats, snakes, mice, rabbits, and birds)
variety of boxes

What to do   1. Set up an area in the classroom for the children to have a pet store. Provide stuffed animals and a variety of containers.
2. Have the children sort the animals by type, color, or size, and place them in the correct box.
3. Invite the children to create a pet store with the animals. They can make signs, prices, and so on.

Related books   *Millions of Cats* by Wanda Gag
The Poky Little Puppy by Janette Sebring Lowrey

➕ *Sandy L. Scott, Meridian, ID*

Post Office

matching, sorting

Materials

envelopes of various sizes
card stock cut to fit the various envelopes
stickers

What to do

1. Set up a table, chairs, cash register, and box ("mailbox"). Provide envelopes, card stock, and stickers, and invite the children to pretend they are in a post office.
2. Spread the cards and envelopes on the table, with the stickers nearby for use as stamps.
3. Encourage the children to match the different sizes of card stock to the different sizes of envelopes, then add stamps and deliver their letters.

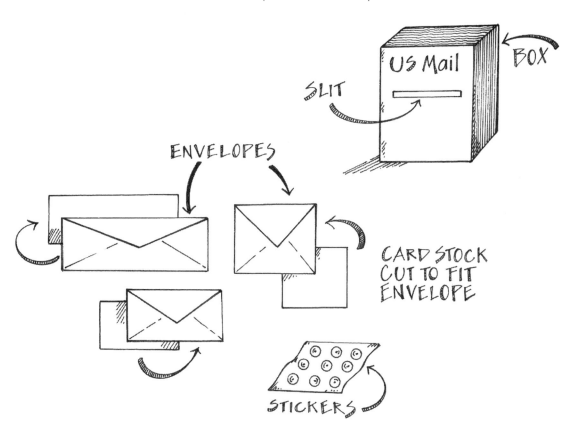

✚ *Maxine Della Fave, Raleigh, NC*

Puppet Story

counting, representing numbers

Materials

paper
scissors
paint or crayons
cardboard
glue
craft sticks
tape
stories or songs with numbers, such as "The Three Little Pigs," "The Three Bears,"
   or "Ten in the Bed"

What to do

1. Familiarize children with several stories and rhymes that include numbers.
2. Cut out oval shapes from paper.
3. Encourage the children to paint or color pictures on the oval paper shapes. For example, if you are doing "The Three Pigs," they might draw three pigs (on three ovals), a wolf, and three houses (on three different ovals).
4. Glue the ovals to a piece of cardboard.
5. Tape a craft stick to the figure.
6. Encourage the children to act out the stories using the puppets.

✚ *Sandy L. Scott, Meridian, ID*

Roll Over

subtraction, counting backwards

Materials

large quilts or blankets
3 or 4 pillows

What to do

1. Put the quilts and pillows on the floor (for safety) to make a "bed" big enough for 10 children.
2. Choose 10 children to lie down on the bed, with the smallest child on the left.
3. Explain to the children that everyone must roll over *once* when they hear "all rolled over" and when they hear "one fell out" the child nearest to you standing at the right side of the bed must roll right off the quilt and get up.

4. Sing the first verse of "There Were Ten in the Bed."

   There were ten in a bed and the little one said,
   "Roll over, roll over."
   So they all rolled over (everyone rolls once) and one fell out. (child on right end
   rolls off the blanket)

5. Continue singing, counting down to one in the bed. End with the following lyric:

   There was one in the bed and the little one said, "Good night."

6. For very young children, count the number of children left each time before singing the next verse.

✚ *Anne Adeney, Plymouth, United Kingdom*

Set the Table

one-to-one correspondence

Materials

dishes
silverware
cups
napkins
placemats
table

What to do

1. Gather the children into groups of four to six.
2. Give each child a different item to set the table for "dinner." One child gets plates, one gets the cups, and so on.
3. Ask them to figure out which item goes on the table first (placemats). Then, ask how many placemats need to be placed on the table and invite the child to put one at each seat.
4. Continue letting each child take turns setting the table with his item—one at each place at the table.
5. When the table is set, sit down together and enjoy dinner. Talk about what each child might be eating at dinner.

✚ *Shelley F. Hoster, Norcross, GA*

Space Explorers

counting backwards, position order

Materials   none

What to do

1. Choose five children to be space explorers. Have them stand in a row.
2. Tell each child which space explorer he is. For example, "Ryan, you're the first space explorer; Adam, you're the second explorer…"
3. If you have a large group of children, have them join hands to make a circle around the space explorers and become the "flying saucer."
4. Sing the song below with the actions mentioned, and try to get everyone looking left and right at the same time.
5. When each space explorer "zooms away," he spreads out his arms and "flies" out of the flying saucer, under the joined hands of the other children.
6. In the last verse, all the children who make up the flying saucer spread their arms and zoom away too.

Spacemen by Anne Adeney
*Five spacemen in a flying saucer
Zoomed 'round the earth one day.
They looked left and right,
But they didn't like the sight
So the first man zoomed away.*

*Four spacemen in a flying saucer
Zoomed 'round the earth one day.
They looked left and right,
But they didn't like the sight
So the second man zoomed away.*

*Three spacemen in a flying saucer
Zoomed 'round the earth one day.
They looked left and right,
But they didn't like the sight
So the third man zoomed away.*

*Two spacemen in a flying saucer
Zoomed 'round the earth one day.
They looked left and right,
But they didn't like the sight
So the fourth man zoomed away.*

One spaceman in a flying saucer
Zoomed 'round the earth one day.
He looked left and right,
But he didn't like the sight
So the fifth man zoomed away.

NO spacemen in a flying saucer
Zoomed 'round the earth one day.
It looked left and right,
But it didn't like the sight
So it just zoomed away.

✚ *Anne Adeney, Plymouth, United Kingdom*

Sort It Out

sorting

Materials   pairs of socks of different colors and sizes
various laundry items (shirt, shorts, towels, washcloths, and so on)
small laundry basket

What to do
1. Place the socks in the laundry basket.
2. Hold up a pair of matching socks and say, for example, "These socks go together because each sock is red and each one fits the same size foot."
3. Pick up another sock and ask the children to look through the pile for the sock that matches it.
4. When a child has chosen a sock, encourage him to use descriptive words to tell you how he knows it is the right one.
5. Continue holding up socks until the children have paired them all. If they mismatch any socks, provide clues such as "What is the color of each sock?"
6. Remove the socks from the laundry basket and put the laundry items in.
7. Encourage the children to help sort the laundry. Ask one child to find all the blue items in the basket.
8. Have the children count the items as the child finds them.
9. Ask another child to count all the towels in the basket.

10. Continue by having the children take turns sorting items by type (all shirt, all towels.) or color until the basket is empty and all items have been sorted.
11. Leave the basket in the dramatic play center. String a laundry line along one wall and attach clothespins. Encourage the children to sort the laundry items and hang them out to dry.

Related song   **Sort the Laundry** (Tune: "Row, Row, Row Your Boat")

Sort, sort, sort the laundry
Into different piles.
Red or blue or shirts or pants
Sorting all the while.

Sort, sort, sort the laundry.
Put the shirts right here.
Sorting can be lots of fun.
Sort the things you wear.

Match, match, match the socks.
See what you can find:
Red with red and blue with blue.
They match all the time.

✚ *Virginia Jean Herrod, Columbia, SC*

The Three Bears

* *

matching, one-to-one correspondence

Materials   any version of "Goldilocks and the Three Bears"
girl doll
3 stuffed bears (small, medium, and large)
3 bowls (small, medium, and large)
3 chairs (small, medium, and large)
3 beds (small, medium, and large)

What to do

1. Put out the story props.
2. Pick four children to play the parts of Goldilocks and the three bears.
3. Tell the four children they will be helping Goldilocks and the bears do their parts in the story.
4. Read "Goldilocks and the Three Bears" to the children.
5. During the story, the children will pair the small, medium, and large bears with the similarly sized bowls, chairs, and beds.
6. Select other children to help act out the story and do it all over again.

Related books   *The Three Little Javelinas* by Susan Lowell
The Three Little Pigs by Steven Kellogg
The Three Pigs by David Wiesner

✚ *Monica Hay Cook, Tucson, AZ*

The Toy Store

addition, counting, writing numerals

Materials
toys
tagboard
markers
play money
cash register
sales receipt pad

What to do

1. Create a simple price list for the toys using tagboard. Draw a picture of each toy and write the price next to it. Children can help with this step.
2. Invite the children to take turns as cashier and customer.
3. The customer chooses a toy or toys he wants to purchase and gives the cashier the appropriate number of dollars.

Related books   *Corduroy* by Don Freeman
Curious George Visits a Toy Store by H.A. Rey
I Use Math at the Store by Joanne Mattern

✚ *Kristi Larson, Spirit Lake, IA*

What's in My Tackle Box?

counting, sorting

Materials
fishing props (fishing hats, vest, fishing poles, and string)
chairs
child's wading pool filled with blue cellophane
die-cut fish from assorted colored foam sheets
small plastic containers with a lid and handle (at least 4–6)
assortment of plastic insects, worms, frogs, and snakes
labels
crayons
copy of tackle box chart (see illustration)

What to do
1. Place the fishing props, chair, wading pool (filled with cellophane and die-cut fish) in the dramatic play area.
2. Provide plastic containers ("tackle boxes") filled with an assortment of plastic bugs, worms, frogs, snakes, and so on.
3. Let the children help label each box.
4. Encourage the children to visit the dramatic play area and pretend to fish. Have them open their tackle box and take out all the things in their box.
5. Ask them to sort and count the items in their tackle box and draw their findings on the chart.

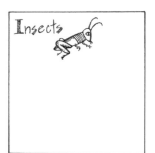   

Draw the number of animals (insects, frogs, snakes, worms) in your Tackle Box.

✚ *Quazonia J. Quarles, Newark, DE*

Bracelet Patterns

patterns

Materials

pipe cleaners
beads
small bowls or cups for the beads

What to do

1. The children pick two or three bead colors to string on a pipe cleaner in an ABABAB or ABCABC pattern.
2. When the bracelet is long enough to go around the child's wrist, the child stops and twists the ends together. It should be loose enough to slide on and off without having to untwist the ends.
3. Make sure the ends of the pipe cleaner are turned inward so the child is not scraped by the wire on the ends.
4. More complex patterns can be created for older children who are ready to expand pattern making.

More to do

Holidays and Special Days: Children can exchange bracelets as part of a Valentine's Day or Friendship Day activity. Use holiday colors to create holiday bracelets (red, pink, and white for Valentine's Day, orange and black for Halloween, and so on).

✚ *Sandra Nagel, White Lake, MI*

Button Button

sorting

Materials

old buttons
egg cartons

What to do

1. Let the children sort buttons into egg cartons according to attributes they choose.
2. Then ask them to sort according to a specific attribute, such as by color, number of holes, size, and so on.

✚ *Jean Potter, Charleston, WV*

Clay Numerals

number formation

Materials
modeling clay
sentence strips with numerals 1–10

What to do
1. Give each child a sentence strip.
2. Show the children how to roll the clay into a long, thin rope.
3. Encourage them to use the ropes of clay to form numerals using their sentence strip as a model.

Related book
One Fish, Two Fish, Red Fish, Blue Fish by Dr. Seuss

✚ *Barbara Saul, Eureka, CA*

Colored Straw Necklace

patterns

Materials
string or yarn
masking tape
index cards
colored straws which reflect the season or holiday (red and green for Christmas; red, pink, and white for Valentine's Day; orange, yellow, red for fall)
markers in the same colors as the straws
scissors

What to do
1. In advance, cut pieces of string or yarn for children to use as necklaces or bracelets. Wrap masking tape around the ends of each piece to help with lacing.
2. Make index cards with pattern colors for the children to follow while creating their necklace or bracelet.
3. For younger children, use colored lines to create the pattern on the card, and for older children use letters (for example: RGRGR). Make sure to write the letter in the same color marker (R should be red, G should be green).

4. Cut straws into ½" pieces.
5. Give each child a string, some straws, and an index card.
6. Help them follow the index card to create a pattern or help them make their own pattern.

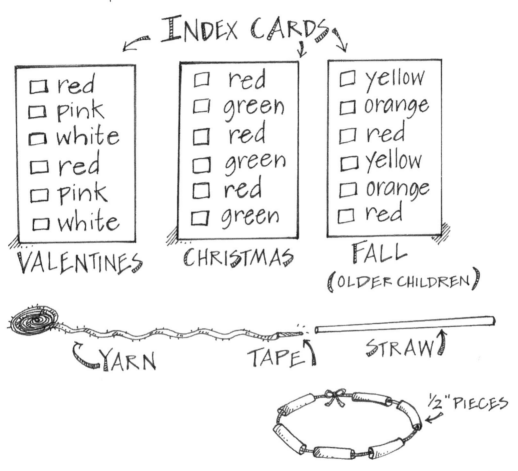

← INDEX CARDS →

VALENTINES	CHRISTMAS	FALL
☐ red	☐ red	☐ yellow
☐ pink	☐ green	☐ orange
☐ white	☐ red	☐ red
☐ red	☐ green	☐ yellow
☐ pink	☐ red	☐ orange
☐ white	☐ green	☐ red

FALL (OLDER CHILDREN)

YARN — TAPE — STRAW

½" PIECES

✚ *Sandy L. Scott, Meridian, ID*

Cotton Ball Math

one-to-one correspondence

Materials   paper
scissors
tape
clean, plastic fruit or vegetable tray (from grocery store)
cotton balls
spring-type clothespins

What to do
1. Cut out the numerals 1–10 from paper. Tape one numeral in each divided section of the plastic tray. You may want to use two trays and tape 1–5 in one tray and 6–10 in the other tray (depending on the number of sections).
2. Put the tray on a table with a bunch of cotton balls and a few clothespins.
3. Ask the children to place the correct number of cotton balls in each section of the tray by picking them up with the clothespins.
4. If desired, label the cotton balls depending on your theme. For example, they can be "clouds" for a weather theme, "snowballs" for a winter theme, or "marshmallows" for a food theme. This provides a great opportunity to bring this activity out many times during the year for children to practice counting and using fine motor skills.

✚ *Gail Morris, Kemah, TX*

Magic Puzzles

numeral identification, spatial relationships

Materials   tagboard
scissors
markers
clear contact paper or laminator

What to do
1. Cut the tagboard in 8" x 8" squares.
2. With markers, write a large numeral on each card.
3. Have the children color the numerals.
4. Cover the numerals with contact paper or laminate them.

5. Cut the squares into four to six pieces to make a puzzle.
6. The children assemble the puzzles together to figure out the numeral.

✚ *Monica Hay Cook, Tucson, AZ*

Magnetic Puzzles

matching

Materials
advertisement refrigerator magnets (free from restaurants, realtors, dental and
  doctor offices, lawn services, and so on)
scissors
magnet board

What to do
1. Collect free advertisement magnets. Ask parents for donations.
2. Cut each one into two pieces. Use straight, zigzag, and curved lines.
3. Place these magnet puzzles at your magnet board and challenge the children
   to put them together. These provide great environmental print for the
   children too.

✚ *Gail Morris, Kemah, TX*

Math Muffins

counting, sorting

Materials
cupcake liners
marker
buttons

What to do
1. Write a numeral on each of the cupcake liners.
2. Children count and sort that many buttons into each liner.

✚ *Jean Potter, Charleston, WV*

Mix and Match

matching sizes

Materials
different sizes of plastic bottles with lids
bucket (for storing the jars and lids)

What to do
1. Collect and wash a variety of plastic bottles. Make sure they are different sizes.
2. Begin the activity with all the tops on the bottles. Invite a small group of children to remove the lids, then mix them up, and replace them on other bottles.
3. Encourage the children to discuss why they thought the lids would fit on the bottles on they chose.
4. Store the bottles and lids in a bucket.

✚ *Ellen Javernik, Loveland, CO*

Nature Garland

patterns

Materials

blunt needle
thick thread
large bowls
popcorn
raisins

What to do

1. Give each child a pre-threaded blunt needle. Place a knot at the end of the thread.
2. Put a large bowl of popcorn and a large bowl of raisins on the table.
3. Show the children how to string the popcorn and raisins on the thread.
4. Make a pattern for the children to follow, or have them make their own patterns (for example, three pieces of popcorn, one raisin, three pieces of popcorn, and so on).
5. You may want to make several different patterns by gluing the items to a piece of paper before starting the project.
6. Go outdoors to hang the completed garland for the birds to eat. You may find that squirrels also enjoy the garland!

✚ *Sandy L. Scott, Meridian, ID*

Number Writing Center

printing numerals

Materials

assortment of writing utensils and art supplies
modeling clay
dry-erase boards and markers
chalkboards and erasers
cups of water, colored paper, and paintbrushes
newspapers and magazines
4 solid-colored art shirts or aprons
permanent marker or fabric paints

Fine Motor

What to do

1. Prepare a writing center for children to practice forming numerals. Make a large sign that reads "Writing Center" and place it on the table. Hang a large numeral poster in the center. Stock the center with the materials listed on the previous page so the children can practice writing and forming numerals using a variety of materials and mediums.

2. Use a permanent marker or fabric paint to print numerals randomly on the art shirts. Let the shirts dry, and put them in the writing center.

3. Read one of your favorite number or counting books to the children.

4. Demonstrate how to form each numeral on a chalkboard or dry-erase board.

5. Explain that you've set up a new writing center so that the children can practice writing or forming numerals in many fun ways. Explain that they can mold numerals out of clay, paint numerals with water, look for and circle numerals in newspapers, and so on.

6. Explain that four children can work at the center at one time and that each person working must wear an art shirt or apron.

7. Model how to use each of the supplies at the center to form numerals. Instruct children about special rules or guidelines for using materials.

8. Invite the children to work at the center to create numerals during learning center time or free play.

9. Have a designated place at the center for children to display their work.

✦ *Mary J. Murray, Mazomanie, WI*

Pattern Match

* *

patterns

Materials

decorative pencil erasers (found in dollar stores and discount stores)

What to do

1. Give the child enough erasers to make patterns (for example, one witch, one bat, one witch, one bat, and so on).

2. Encourage the child to make AB; ABB; or ABC patterns.

✦ *Jean Potter, Charleston, WV*

Ping Pong Math

numeral recognition, one-to-one correspondence

Materials
water table
egg carton (numbered 1–12)
Ping Pong balls (numbered 1–12)
tongs

What to do
1. Place the Ping Pong balls in the water table.
2. Have the children use the tongs to grab the balls, then place the correct numbered ball into the correct numbered section of the egg carton.

✚ *Wanda Guidroz, Santa Fe, TX*

Rectangle Puzzle

matching, spatial awareness

Materials
any picture, approximately 6" × 8"
smaller copy of the above picture
scissors
glue stick
9" × 12" colored envelope with a clasp closure
tagboard
marker
laminator
X-acto knife (adult only)
self-adhesive Velcro

What to do
1. Locate a picture approximately 6" × 8" turned horizontally. It could be a picture of anything relating to your current theme.
2. Cut out 16 rectangles from the picture (like windows), leaving part of the picture intact surrounding each rectangle to make a puzzle frame.
3. Glue the remaining picture (the frame), with the rectangles removed, to the bottom of the front of a 9" × 12" envelope.

4. Glue the smaller identical picture above it along with the directions: "Put the puzzle together." Laminate the envelope with the flap open.

5. Glue the 16 rectangles on tagboard and laminate. Cut out each rectangle. These will be the puzzle pieces.

6. Use an X-acto knife to slit the top opening of the envelope.

7. Attach self-adhesive Velcro pieces to the back of each puzzle piece and to each rectangle on the picture on the envelope.

8. To do this activity, a child looks at the smaller picture as a model and places the puzzle pieces, stored inside the envelope, on the envelope to complete the puzzle.

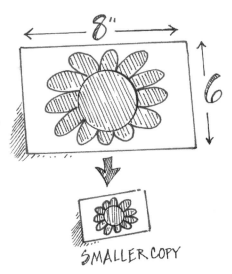

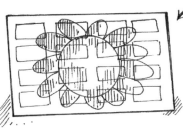

SMALLER COPY

CUT OUT 16 RECTANGLES FROM the LARGER PICTURE

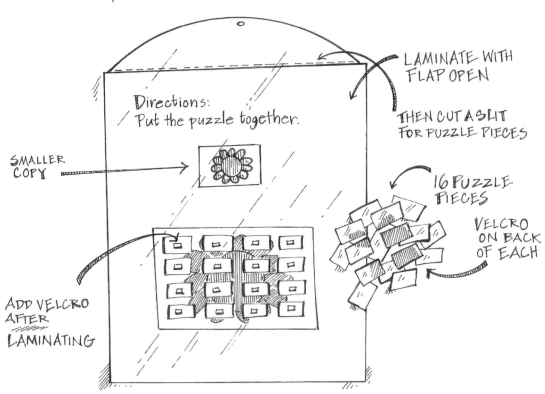

Directions: / Put the puzzle together.

SMALLER COPY

ADD VELCRO AFTER LAMINATING

LAMINATE WITH FLAP OPEN

THEN CUT A SLIT FOR PUZZLE PIECES

16 PUZZLE PIECES

VELCRO ON BACK OF EACH

✚ *Jackie Wright, Enid, OK*

Salt Boxes

printing numerals

Materials   shallow boxes
2 containers of salt

What to do
1. Pour the salt into boxes, about ½" deep.
2. Using one box per child, show the children the numerals, and encourage them to use their fingers to write the numerals in the salt.
3. When one number is done, shake the box to erase it, and let the children continue making different numerals.

Related book   *Splash!* by Ann Jonas

✚ *Barbara Saul, Eureka, CA*

Shape Puzzle

matching, shape recognition

Materials   large rectangular piece of cardboard or tagboard (11" x 17" or larger)
marker
shape stencils
craft knife
paint
re-sealable bag

What to do
1. Using a marker, divide the piece of cardboard into six equal sections.
2. In each of the sections, trace a shape using a stencil. Choose six different shapes (circle, square, triangle diamond, heart, star, rectangle, and so on).
3. Using a craft knife, cut them out so that they leave a hole where they should go. Set the pieces aside. These will be the puzzle pieces and the cardboard will serve as the frame.
4. Paint each section and its corresponding shape the same color, using a different color for each shape pair. Let dry.

5. Write the name of the shape on each of the pieces and under or above the cut holes in the frame.

6. When it is ready, let the children come over and see if they can match up each shape with the correct hole.

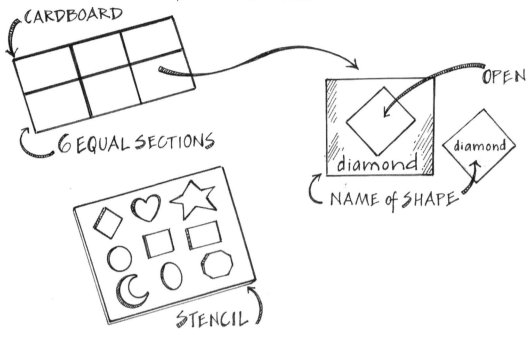

More to do For older children, you can use different colors to make it more challenging. You can even paint the entire puzzle the same color so that children pay attention to matching the shape, not the color.

✚ *Shelley F. Hoster, Norcross, GA*

Sorting Items

* *

counting, numeral recognition, sorting

Materials small plastic baggies
small items that will fit in the baggies (pennies, paper clips, pennies, marbles, crayons, and so on)
marker

What to do
1. Mark each bag with a numeral.
2. Put out several items for the children to sort into the bags.
3. Demonstrate how to sort the items.
4. Explain that they should carefully look at their items so that they can sort correctly; for example, if they only have one crayon then they should use that in the first bag and not save it for the bag that needs five items.

✛ *Sandy L. Scott, Meridian, ID*

Sorting Keys

sorting

Materials   several keys

What to do
1. Give each child an assortment of keys to sort. Since keys often look very similar to each other, make sure they are very different from each other (different shapes, colors, and sizes).
2. Ask the children to describe the methods they used to sort the keys, such as color, shape, size, and so on.
3. Mix up the keys and have the children regroup them using different categories from the previous sorting.
4. When the children have sorted the keys a second time, ask them to count how many keys they have.

Related book   *One Gorilla: A Counting Book* by Atsuko Morozumi

✛ *Barbara Saul, Eureka, CA*

Spooning Numbers

counting, numeral recognition

Materials   1 ice cube tray for each child
black marker
5 spoons and 5 colorful cereal bowls
spooning items (cotton balls, colored beads, marbles, buttons)

What to do

1. Label five compartments on the inside (not the bottom) of ice cube trays (1–5) with a black marker. Start at the left hand side of the tray and continue in numerical order from left to right.
2. Set up five spooning stations. At each station, place a spoon and a cereal bowl.
3. Fill each bowl with a spooning item. For example, fill the bowl at station one with cotton balls, colored beads at station two, and so on.
4. Ask the children to rotate through the stations and use the spoons to fill their ice cube trays with the appropriate number of items that corresponds to the numeral written on the ice cube tray.
5. As the children learn more numbers, label the ice cube tray compartments with the numerals 6–10. Add five more stations and spooning items such as paper clips, pencil erasers, and small seashells.

✚ *Randi Lynn Mrvos, Lexington, KY*

Sticker Beads

sequencing

Materials

small numeral stickers
blocks or beads
yarn or thread
large needles

What to do

1. Stick a different numeral on each of the beads or blocks.
2. Provide children with a pre-threaded piece of yarn that is knotted at one end. Have them place the beads on the yarn according to the numerals on the beads.
3. If using blocks, they can stack them starting with 1 or put them in a line from 1 to 10.

✚ *Jean Potter, Charleston, WV*

Bakery Shop

counting backward, subtraction

Materials

tagboard in a variety of colors
laminator
craft sticks
tape

What to do

1. Cut out "cupcakes" from tagboard in a variety of colors (colors can be repeated). Make one cupcake for each child.
2. Laminate each cupcake.
3. Attach a craft stick to the back of each cupcake using tape.
4. Put the cupcakes in the center of the circle on the floor.
5. Hold hands and walk around the circle while singing the following verse.

   Down around the corner at the bakery shop,
   There were 15 little cupcakes with frosting on top.
   Along came (child's name) all alone,
   And she took the red one home.

6. The child picks up the cupcake and rejoins the group.
7. Continue until all the children have picked up a cupcake.

✚ *Sandy L. Scott, Meridian, ID*

Beehive

counting, printing numerals

Materials

8" x 9" card stock, 1 for each child
5" x 5" card stock, 1 for each child
5 pieces of scrap card stock (about 2" x 2 ½") for each child
crayons or paint
glue or tape
5" – 6" lengths of transparent fishing line, 5 for each child

What to do

1. Help older children make their own beehives. You may need to cut out all the pieces and prepare beehives for younger children.

2. Round off the top of the 5" × 5" card stock to make an arched entrance to a "beehive."

3. Fold up about 1" on the bottom of the 8" × 9" card stock (beehive).

4. Place the entrance of the beehive centrally at the bottom of the beehive and mark its edges on the folded-over piece.

5. Cut off the bits of the fold on either side of the entrance, so there is a small flap under the entrance (this will keep the bees from falling out).

6. Cut the larger piece of card stock into a beehive shape (basically a dome with slightly curvy sides).

7. Glue or tape the top of the entrance in place, with a fold at the top so it can be lifted easily.

8. Make five simple bees from the small pieces of card stock. Stripe their bodies with yellow and black crayons or paint.

9. Write the numerals 1–5 on the bees' heads.

10. Tape one end of each piece of fishing line to the back of each bee.

11. Tape the other ends in different places on the bee hive, under the entrance, so when the bees are "flying" they will all be at different levels. Keep the bees in numerical order.

12. Paint or color the beehive.

13. Tuck all the bees inside the little flap.

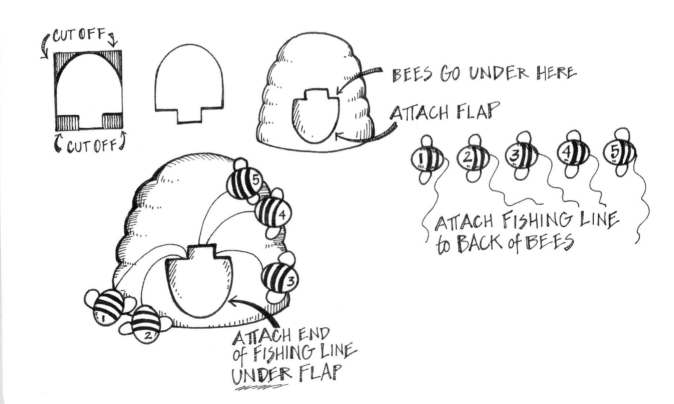

14. Sing "Here Is the Beehive" as the children release their bees, one by one.

Here Is the Beehive
Here is the beehive,
Where are the bees?
Hidden away where nobody sees.
Soon they come buzzing,
Out of the hive,
One!
Two!
Three!
Four!
Five!

✚ *Anne Adeney, Plymouth, United Kingdom*

Busy Bees

counting

Materials none

What to do Teach the children the following rhymes, making the appropriate gestures when indicated.

Counting Bees
One, two, three, four, five, (hold up appropriate fingers on one hand)
Bees flew out of a hive. (wiggle fingers in the air)
Six, seven, eight, nine, ten, (hold up appropriate fingers on other hand)
They flew back in again! ("fly" the five original fingers under your other arm)

One Bee on Your Nose
One bee on your nose. (one finger touches your nose)
Two bees on a rose. (two fingers on your other little finger)
Three bees on a daisy. (three fingers on your other thumb)
Four bees are not lazy. (wiggle four fingers while shaking head "no")
Five bees in a dive, (five fingers swoop from high to low)
Fly to the bee hive. (place five fingers under your other arm)

✚ *Christina R. Chilcote, New Freedom, PA*

Busy Squirrels

addition

Materials
grey and brown felt
scissors
marker
flannel board

What to do
1. Trace and cut out the outlines of three squirrels from grey felt. Trace and cut out the outlines of nine acorns from the brown felt.
2. Recite the following rhyme with the children, placing the squirrels and acorns on the flannel board as the rhyme mentions them.
3. Let the children take turns manipulating the squirrels and acorns as they are mentioned in the rhyme.

Busy Squirrels
Running up and down the tree,
Busy squirrels I do see.
One scurries here, one scurries there,
One hurry-scurries everywhere.

Giant acorns they
*   have found,*
And bury them in
*   the ground.*
Three acorns here,
*   three acorns there,*
Three acorns in the
*   city square.*

How many squirrels have you found?
How many acorns have you found?
There are three squirrels all around,
And nine acorns in the ground!

 Ingelore Mix, Gainesville, VA

Change in My Pocket

addition, money values

Materials   none

What to do   Invite the children to recite the following rhyme.

Change in My Pocket
One brown penny,
It's worth just a cent.
The lowest amount I know,
And very easily spent.

A shiny new nickel,
It's a little fat.
It's worth five cents,
Now you know that.

A little dime,
That is so thin and trim.
It's worth ten cents,
And can be spent on a whim.

Finally, an old quarter
That is big and bold.
It's worth 25 cents,
So I'm told.

Now how much money
Do I have? Do you know?
I can hear the ice cream truck,
And I want to hurry up and go!

✚ *Geary Smith, Mexia, TX*

Cold Countdown

counting backwards

Materials 10 silly dress-up hats

What to do

1. Give a different hat to 10 children.
2. Invite all the children to recite the following story. Repeat it 10 times, reducing the number with each verse by choosing a "snowman" to "melt" (child takes off his hat and sinks to the floor).

Cold Countdown

Ten little snowmen,
Each in a funny hat.
Out came the sun
And melted one.
What a sad, sad sight was that.

Nine little snowmen…
Eight little snowmen…

No snowmen were left
On that snowy day.
But I found ten hats
When I went out to play.

✚ *Ellen Javernik, Loveland, CO*

David Plays with One Hammer

counting

Materials   none

What to do   Invite the children to recite the following chant, making the appropriate gestures when prompted:

David Plays with One Hammer
David plays with one hammer, one hammer, one hammer.
David plays with one hammer all day long. (move one arm up and down)

David plays with two hammers, two hammers, two hammers.
David plays with two hammers all day long. (move both arms up and down)

David plays with three hammers, three hammers, three hammers.
David plays with three hammers all day long. (Move both arms and one foot)

David plays with four hammers, four hammers, four hammers.
David plays with four hammers all day long. (move both arms and both feet)

David plays with five hammers, five hammers, five hammers.
David plays with five hammers all day long. (move both arms, both legs, and head)

David goes to sleep, sleep, sleep.
David goes to sleep, all night long. (use hands as pillows and close eyes)

✚ *Barbara Saul, Eureka, CA*

Dimes and Dollars

coin identification, money values

Materials
pennies, nickels, and dimes
plastic bowl
big handkerchief

What to do

1. Teach the children the following rhyme.

   How Many Cents Make a Dime by Shyamala Shanmugasundaram
   How many cents make a dime?
   I need to buy a swaying wind chime.
   Ten cents make a dime.
   It's not enough money to buy a swaying wind chime.
   How many dimes make a dollar?
   I need to buy a dog collar.
   Ten dimes make a dollar.
   It's not enough money to buy a dog collar.
   I'll break my piggy bank to buy a dog collar.
   It has a few dimes, cents, and dollars.
   As I sleep I will watch the stars twinkle
   And my wind chime will go tinkle, tinkle, tinkle.

2. Show the children a penny, a nickel, and a dime. Explain that 10 pennies equal 10 cents, 2 nickels equal 10 cents, and 1 dime equals 10 cents. For older children, you can show them the coins that make up a dollar (100 pennies, 20 nickels, 10 dimes, and four quarters).

3. Place 10 pennies, 10 nickels, and 10 dimes in a plastic bowl.

4. Blindfold a child and ask her to take 10 dimes from the bowl to make a dollar using her sense of touch. Depending on the age of the child, you may want to use dimes and quarters, and have the child remove only three or four dimes.

5. When the child is finished, remove the blindfold and ask her if she has a dollar. If not, ask her how many more dimes she needs to make a dollar.

✚ *Shyamala Shanmugasundaram, Nerul, Navi Mumbai, India*

Elizabeth's Eggs

subtraction

Materials   nest (real or pretend)
5 plastic eggs

What to do
1. Ask the children to count the eggs in the nest.
2. Practice subtraction by removing some eggs from the nest each time and asking how many are left.
3. Invite the children to take turns making up a subtraction equation of their choice. For example, "I'm taking three eggs out of the nest. Three eggs taken away from five eggs is two eggs. There are two eggs left in the nest."
4. Explain to the children what a riddle is. Recite the following riddle, "Elizabeth."

   Elizabeth, Elspeth, Betsy, and Bess,
   They all went together to seek a bird's nest;
   They found a bird's nest with five eggs in,
   They all took one, and left four in.

5. See if the children can figure out the riddle. Give them clues, if needed. If there are any children who use both their real name and a shortened form or nickname, use their names saying, for example, "Are John Smith, and Johnny Smith two people or one? Are Robert Jones, Bob Jones, and Bobby Jones three people, two people, or one person?"
6. Talk about words, other than names, that are all different ways of describing the same thing such as *dog, pup, mutt, man's best friend,* and *doggy.*

✚ *Anne Adeney, Plymouth, United Kingdom*

Elmore Donkey

counting

Materials

sheets of different colored paper
scissors

What to do

1. Trace and cut out outlines of a unicycle, a bicycle, a tricycle, and a tractor.
2. Give a cutout to four different children.
3. Recite the following poem with the children. The children with the cutouts hold up their cutout at the appropriate time.
4. Repeat to let other children have a turn holding the cutouts.

Elmore Donkey

*Elmore Donkey lives in the country
And rides a unicycle, which is fun.
How many wheels does it have?
It has only one.*

*Elmore Donkey lives in the country
And rides a bicycle, which is blue.
How many wheels does it have?
It has but two.*

*Elmore Donkey lives in the country
And rides a tricycle around a tree.
How many wheels does it have?
It has exactly three.*

*Elmore Donkey lives in the country
And rides a tractor with farmer Moore.
How many wheels does it have?
It has precisely four.*

 Ingelore Mix, Gainesville, VA

Finger Math

addition, subtraction

Materials none

What to do 1. Recite the following number problems, inviting the children to hold up the appropriate number of fingers for each line:

There are five monkeys, and they each want a banana (hold up five fingers).
The zookeeper has four bananas to give (hold up four fingers of your other hand). Does the zookeeper need more or fewer bananas to feed each monkey one?
How many?

I have six goldfish, but I want ten. How many more do I need?

2. Think up different problems of your own, with the children adding and subtracting numbers together on their fingers.

✚ *Ingelore Mix, Gainesville, VA*

Five Apples

subtraction

Materials red tagboard or construction paper
scissors
glue
craft sticks
marker

What to do 1. Cut out apples from red tagboard, one for each child.
2. Glue each apple to a craft stick and write a numeral from 1 to 5 on each apple. For example, if there are 20 children in the class, make four apples with each numeral.
3. Give each child an apple.

4. Have all the children with the numeral 1 apples stand together in a small group, the children with the numeral 2 apples stand together, and so on.

5. Invite the children recite the following poem.

Five Little Apples

Five little apples hanging on a tree,
The juiciest apples you ever did see.
The wind came past and gave an angry frown.
And one little apple came tumbling down.

6. At the end of the poem, ask the group of children holding the numeral 5 apple cutouts to sit down.

7. Repeat the poem, inserting the numbers four, three, two, and one until all the children are sitting down.

Related book   *The Apple Pie Tree* by Zoe Hall

✚ *Sandy L. Scott, Meridian, ID*

Five Busy Farmers

counting, number sequence

Materials none

What to do Invite the children to act out the following poem, performing the movements as noted.

Five Busy Farmers

Five busy farmers (yawn)
Woke up with the sun, (stretch)
For it was early morning (pretend to get dressed)
And chores must be done. (put hat on)

The first busy farmer (hold up one finger)
Went to milk the cow. (make milking motions with both hands)
The second busy farmer (hold up two fingers)
Thought he'd better plow. (rotate hands as if on a steering wheel)

The third busy farmer (hold up three fingers)
Fed the hungry hens. (pretend to scatter grain)
The fourth busy farmer (hold up four fingers)
Mended broken pens. (pretend to use a hammer)

The fifth busy farmer (hold up five fingers)
Took his vegetables to town. (pretend to dig up vegetables)
Baskets filled with cabbages (pretend to cut and box cabbages)
And sweet potatoes, brown. (pretend to dig and shake dirt off)

When the work was finished (mop brows and take hats off)
And the western sky was red, (look into distance with hand above eyes)
Five busy farmers (hold up five fingers)
Tumbled into bed. (fold hands beneath cheek and close eyes)

✚ *Anne Adeney, Plymouth, United Kingdom*

Five Little Candles

ordinal words

Materials   none

What to do   Teach the children the following fingerplay (similar to "Five Little Pumpkins").

Five Little Candles
Five little candles on a birthday cake. (hold up five fingers)
The first one said, "We'd better stay awake!" (point to each finger)
The second one said, "Let's give off some light."
The third one said," My, we sure are bright."
The fourth one said, "Your birthday's here!"
The fifth one said, "Let's give a big cheer!"
"Oooh" went the wind that blew the candles out, (bend fingers down)
And everybody gave a great big shout:
"Happy Birthday!"

More to do   **Art:** If desired, decorate a white, pink, or brown glove or mitt to look like a birthday cake. Cut out yellow flames from felt and attach to each finger of the glove (the fingers are the candles).

✚ *Shelley F. Hoster, Norcross, GA*

Five Little Ducks

counting

Materials   none

What to do   Invite the children to recite the following rhyme.

Five Little Ducks

Five little ducks went out to play, (hold up five fingers)
Over the hills and far away, (make hills in air with hand)
Mama duck said, "Quack, quack, quack." (use hands for quacking motion)
Four little ducks came waddling back. (flap arms like wings)

(repeat until the last duck waddles away)

No little ducks came waddling back.
So papa duck said, "Quack, quack, quack." (say in low, slow voice, use arms for
   the quacking motion)
And five little ducks came waddling back!

✚ *Sandy L. Scott, Meridian, ID*

Five Little Fingerprints

counting

Materials   magnifying glasses

What to do
1. Discuss fingerprints and their unique designs for each person. Explain what the word *whorl* means.
2. Provide magnifying glasses for the children to examine their own fingerprints, and the fingerprints of friends.
3. Introduce the children to the following rhyme and practice counting to five.

Five Little Fingerprints

Five little fingerprints on each hand,
Like no other in the land.
Lines and whorls: they're all my own,
They belong to me alone.

More to do   **Art**: Press the fingertips in ink pads to make fingerprints. Use the magnifying glasses to examine them more closely.

✚ *Susan Oldham Hill, Lakeland, FL*

Five Little Monkeys

counting backwards

Materials   none

What to do   Invite the children to recite the following rhyme.

Five Little Monkeys
Five little monkeys swinging in a tree, (hold up number of fingers)
Teasing Mr. Alligator, (use finger to point and tease)
"Can't catch me, (wave finger back and forth)
Can't catch me."
Along comes Mr. Alligator (make quiet swimming motion with arms as if in water)
Quiet as can be (say very quietly)
And he snatched that monkey right out of the tree. (make an opening and closing
   motion with hands)

Four little monkeys swinging in the tree…
Three little monkeys swinging in the tree…
(continue until Mr. Alligator snatches the last of the monkeys from the tree)

No little monkeys swinging in the tree,
Teasing Mr. Alligator:
"Can't catch me."
So Mr. Alligator says, "Yum, yum, yum."

✚ *Sandy L. Scott, Meridian, ID*

Five Little Owls Counting Poem

counting, subtraction

Materials   none

What to do Invite the children to recite the following original poem, making gestures to dramatize the action of the owls in each stanza.

Five Little Owls

Five little owls sitting in a tree.
One fell off and bumped his knee.
The mother called the doctor and the doctor said,
"No more owls sitting in the tree!"

Four little owls sitting in a tree.
One saw a mole and then there were three.
The mother called the doctor and the doctor said,
"No more owls sitting in the tree!"

Three little owls sitting in a tree.
One flew away and then there were two.
The mother called the doctor and the doctor said,
"Only two more owls to hoot 'WHOOOOO!'"

Two little owls sitting in a tree.
One went "Achoo!" and flew away for some tea.
The mother called the doctor and the doctor said,
"No more owls sitting in the tree!"

One little owl sitting in a tree.
He flew up in the sky to see what he could see.
The mother called the doctor and the doctor said,
"No more owls sitting in the tree!"

Now there are no little owls sitting in the tree.
"No little owls!" the mother did sigh.
The mother called the doctor and the doctor said,
"Let those owls soar way up high."

Related books *Owl Moon* by Jane Yolen
The Sleepy Owl by Marcus Pfister

✚ *Cookie Zingarelli, Columbus, OH*

Five Little Snowmen

ordinal words, representing numbers

Materials none

What to do Invite the children to recite the following rhyme, making the necessary gestures as the rhyme indicates.

Five Little Snowmen
Five little snowmen
Were standing in a row. (hold up five fingers on one hand)

The first little snowman said,
"I wish I could grow!" (point to thumb)

The second little snowman said,
"My button nose is flat." (point to pointer finger)

The third little snowman said,
"Look at my tall hat." (point to the middle finger)

The fourth little snowman said,
"My scarf is very warm." (point to ring finger)

The fifth little snowman said,
"My broom will sweep the barn." (point to pinky)

Then all five snowmen
Put on a happy smile, (hold up all five fingers)

"We're glad it is so cold,
So we can stay awhile!"

✚ *Mary Brehm, Aurora, OH*

Five Little Stars

counting

Materials numeral cards (1–5)

What to do
1. Teach the children the following fingerplay.
2. Choose five children to hold up numeral cards as the others recite the words and do the motions.

Five Little Stars

One little star up in the sky. (open and close fingers with hand held up)
Two little stars just shooting by. (point index fingers in different directions)
Three little stars shining, oh, so bright. (cross straightened arms, then sweep out)
Four little stars twinkling in the night. (both hands held high, opening and closing fingers)
Five little stars just fading away. (wiggle fingers, slowly lowering hands)
Sleep, little stars, here comes the day.

✚ *Susan Oldham Hill, Lakeland, FL*

Five Snow Bunnies

counting backwards

Materials none

What to do
1. Teach the children the motions that go with the following rhyme.
2. Repeat the rhyme and motions with the class.

Five Snow Bunnies

Five snow bunnies (show five fingers)
Sliding on a sled, (glide hand from high to low)
One fell off (roll both hands)
And hurt his head. (hold head and shake it side to side)

Papa called the doctor, (using little finger and thumb, pretend to be on the telephone)
The doctor said,
"No more bunnies (wag finger vigorously)
Sliding on the sled." (glide hand from high to low)

Four snow bunnies…
Three snow bunnies…
Two snow bunnies…
One snow bunny…
No more bunnies sliding on the sled!

✚ *Christina Chilcote, New Freedom, PA*

Flashlight, Flashlight

numeral recognition

Materials large number cards from 1–10
flashlight

What to do
1. Ahead of time, place the number cards on a chalk rail or other visible place in the room. Choose one child to hold the flashlight.
2. Teach the children the following rhyme.

   Flashlight, Flashlight
   Flashlight, flashlight, shine so bright.
   Like a glowing star at night.
   Shine on the numerals one to ten.
   Turn the lights out! Let's begin.

3. Turn out the lights and call out a number from 1–10.
4. Ask the child to shine the flashlight on the number card that matches the number called out.
5. Then ask the rest of the group to clap the matching number of claps.
6. Repeat so that others have a turn with the flashlight.

✚ *Susan Oldham Hill, Lakeland, FL*

Four Little Chickens

ordinal numbers

Materials none

What to do
1. Talk about chickens and what they eat.
2. Teach the following rhyme to the children.
3. Have the children practice the actions mentioned in the rhyme. Encourage them to put a lot of facial, body, and vocal expression into the reaction of the little chicks.
4. Choose four children to be the chicks and one to be the mother hen. These five children act out the rhyme as the other children sing it.
5. Choose a different group of children to do the actions or, alternately, all the children can do all the actions each time.

Four Little Chickens
Said the first little chicken,
With an odd little squirm,
"I wish I could find a fat little worm."

Said the second little chicken,
With an odd little shrug,
"I wish I could find a fat little bug."

Said the third little chicken,
With a small sigh of grief,
"I wish I could find a green little leaf."

Said the fourth little chicken,
With a faint little moan,
"I wish I could find a little gravel stone."

"Now, see here!" said their mother,
From the green garden patch.
"If you want any breakfast,
You must scratch, scratch, scratch!"

✚ *Anne Adeney, Plymouth, United Kingdom*

Four Little Ducks

number sequence

Materials

large yellow feather

What to do

1. Teach the children the following counting rhyme.

   Four Little Ducks
   Four little ducks that I once knew
   Fat ducks, skinny ducks, they were, too.
   But the one little duck with a feather on her back,
   She ruled the others with a "Quack! Quack! Quack!"

   Down the river they all would go,
   One, two, three, four, all in a row.
   But the one little duck with a feather on her back,
   She ruled the others with a "Quack! Quack! Quack!"

   Quack! Quack! Quack! Quack!

2. Say the rhyme several times with the children. When they can say the rhyme all the way through, give one child a feather and have her lead three other children around the room as everyone sings.
3. Sing the song several times in a week, giving each child a chance to lead the group in a merry march around the room.

More to do

Sensory: Create a feather chart. Divide a standard piece of paper down the middle, then lengthwise in four equal sections. On the left side of the paper, print the numerals 1–4, with one numeral in each square. Have the children glue the appropriate number of feathers in the square on the right side of the paper.

✚ *Virginia Jean Herrod, Columbia, SC*

Friendship Walk

counting

Materials   none

What to do   1. Teach the children the following song to the tune of "One Elephant Went Out to Play."

Frienship Walk

One little friend walks all alone.
He finds a good friend he has known.
Two walk along and then they see
Another friend coming to make it three.

Three friends wishing for just one more.
Here comes another; now they're four.
It's just so good to be alive!
Let's ask another so we'll have five.

2. Have the children sit in a circle. Choose one child to start the game by walking in a circle around the children.
3. Ask the rest of the children to sing along. The child chooses new friends whenever the lyrics mention adding one more friend. The chosen children walk with the child around the circle.
4. Repeat the song, letting the fifth child be the leader, until everyone has had a turn.

Related books   *A Bargain for Frances* by Russell Hoban
Frog and Toad Are Friends by Arnold Lobel
Swimmy by Leo Lionni
The Velveteen Rabbit by Margery Williams

✚ *Susan Oldham Hill, Lakeland, FL*

Geometry Jingles

shape identification

Materials   large shapes (circles, squares, rectangles, ovals, and triangles)

What to do
1. Introduce the children to the names of the different shapes.
2. Invite the children to recite the following original poem. Be sure to point out that squares are rectangles, but not all rectangles are squares. This is a tricky concept, especially for younger children.

   I like to look for circles,
   It's so much fun to do.
   They're round, and have no corners.
   Can you find circles, too?

   An oval looks just like an egg.
   Its shape is almost round.
   And if you're looking carefully,
   Lots of ovals can be found.

   The triangle is a special shape.
   Look and you will see
   That its sides and corners
   Always equal three.

   There's another shape to look for.
   Square is its special name.
   It has four corners and four sides
   That measure just the same.

   The world is full of rectangles.
   You see them everywhere.
   They have four sides and corners,
   And some of them are squares.

3. Encourage the children to look around the room and locate different examples of the shapes. Invite them to use the large cutouts of the shapes to remind them what each shape looks like.

✚ *Ellen Javernik, Loveland, CO*

Going on a Shape Hunt

shape identification

Materials
chart paper
digital or Polaroid camera

What to do
1. Copy the poem below onto chart paper, giving each stanza its own section, and recite it with the children

2. Invite the children to make the shapes and movements, using their hands or bodies. Practice making a variety of shapes with the children before doing the rhyme.

A circle, a circle,
Let's all form a circle.
A shape so round
It rolls on the ground
And can form a ring
Around anything!

A triangle, a triangle,
Let's all form a triangle.
A space with peaks
Like birds and their beaks,
Or let's be fins
On fish that swim.

A heart, a heart,
Let's all make a heart.
A shape so fine,
Like a Valentine,
Or what grows on trees,
Pretty little leaves.

A square, a square,
Let's all form a square.
A shape that's tame
Each side is the same,
They make a great box,
And lots of fun blocks.

3. Take photos of the children as they create the shapes. Hang the photos around the room.

✚ *Kaethe Lewandowski, Centreville, VA*

Halloween Counting

counting

Materials   5 real or paper cutout pumpkins

What to do   1. Show the children five pumpkins.
2. Invite the children to recite the following rhyme, making the appropriate gestures when prompted. Point to a pumpkin on each line.

> *Five little pumpkins sitting on a gate.* (hold up one arm as the gate and five
>   fingers as the pumpkins)
> *The first one says, "Oh my, it's getting late!"*
> *The second one says, "There are witches in the air."* (use hands to fly like a witch)
> *The third one says, "But we don't care."* (shake head back and forth)
> *The fourth one says, "Let's have a little fun!"*
> *The fifth one says, "Let's run and run and run!"* (use fingers to make running
>   motion)
> *"Oooh," went the wind, and out went the light,*
> *And the five little pumpkins rolled out of sight!* (make a rolling motion
>   with arms)

✚ *Barbara Saul, Eureka, CA*

Hanging Up Clothes

matching, patterns

Materials
colored paper
scissors
glue or glue stick
tagboard
string
2 chairs
clothespins

What to do

1. Cut out four T-shirt shapes from each color of paper and glue each shape to a piece of tagboard. If there are 20 children in the class, for example, you would have five different colors of T-shirt (four red, four blue, and so on).
2. Place two of each color of T-shirt in a laundry basket and stack the remaining T-shirts in a in a pile.
3. Make a clothesline within the children's reach by tying a string between two chairs.
4. Give each child a T-shirt (from the pile).
5. Have them look at their T-shirt and then lay it face down in front of them.
6. Explain that you are going to hang the laundry. As you pin each shirt (from the laundry basket) to the clothesline, the children sing the following song.

This is the way we wash our clothes,
Wash our clothes, wash our clothes.
This is the way we wash our clothes so early in the morning.

Additional verses:
This is the way we hang our clothes...
This is the way we dry our clothes...

7. As the children sing, the two children with the matching color T-shirt should turn over their cards and show the class. Ask one of the two children to hang her matching T-shirt next to yours on the clothesline.
8. Continue singing and playing the game. Select a different color T-shirt and repeat the above step. Do this until all five colors are represented.
9. Start over again so that the remaining children hang their T-shirts the same way. You should have a pattern like this: red, red, blue, blue, black, black, brown, brown, pink, pink; red, red, and so on.

CUT TWO

✚ *Mary J. Murray, Mazomanie, WI*

Hide and Seek

counting

Materials   none

What to do
1. Ask the children if they have ever played hide and seek. Invite them to describe some of their experiences with the game.
2. Do the following activity, modeling the gestures for the children.

   One: Close your eyes and turn around. (turn around)
   Two: Don't look up, and don't look down. (shake head "no" and point up and down)
   Three: Listen well to where I go. (hand cups ear)
   Four: There's no noise; I'm on tiptoes. (rise up on toes)
   Five: Feel a breeze? Am I nearby? (wave hand to create breeze)
   Six: Careful not to blink your eye! (blink)
   Seven: Am I on your left or right? (point each way)
   Eight: When you find me, hold me tight. (put arms around self in a hug)
   Nine: My only noise is a squeak. (make a squeaking noise)
   Ten: I'm all hidden; time to seek! (arms bent over heads as a "cover" to hide, or children run to an area designated as "home" or back to their seats on "seek")

More to do
Games: Play traditional hide and seek. Make sure to count as children hide.

Related book
Hide and Seek by Janet S. Wong

✚ *Theresa Callahan, Easton, MD*

House of the Bears

* *

comparison

Materials
large, medium, and small bowls
large, medium, and small chairs
large, medium, and small doll beds
large, medium, and small bears (cutouts or stuffed animals)

What to do
1. Tell the children the story of "Goldilocks and the Three Bears."
2. After talking about the story, read them the following poem, "House of the Bears."
3. Show the actions to accompany the poem: searching with hand above eyes; indicating size with hands, from big to tiny; and the first two fingers making "running away legs" at the end.

4. Pause after each verse and ask what Goldilocks saw next.

House of the Bears

When Goldilocks went to the house of the bears,
What did her blue eyes see?
A bowl that was big, a bowl that was small,
A bowl that was hardly there at all.
Too hot! Too salty!
Just right: yummy!

When Goldilocks went to the house of the bears,
What did her blue eyes see?
A chair that was big, a chair that was small,
A chair that was hardly there at all.
Too high! Too low!
Just right: crash!

When Goldilocks went to the house of the bears,
What did her blue eyes see?
A bed that was big, a bed that was small,
A bed that was hardly there at all.
Too hard! Too soft!
Just right: sleepy!

When Goldilocks went to the house of the bears,
What did her blue eyes see?
A bear that was big, a bear that was small,
A bear that was hardly there at all.
Ferocious! Scary! Angry!
HELP!

5. As you read the poem point to the different sizes of objects as they are mentioned. Talk about *big*, *smaller*, and *smallest*. Ask the children to point out similar items in the room that have different sizes (pencils, tables, paper, and so on).

✚ *Anne Adeney, Plymouth, United Kingdom*

How Many Things Will You Clean Up?

addition, counting

Materials   none

What to do: 1. During cleanup time, sing the following song to the tune of "London Bridge."

How Many Things Will You Clean Up?
How many things will you clean up?
You clean up?
You clean up?
How many things will you clean up?
Tell us, (child's name).

(The child, Michael, for example, calls out a realistic number, such as "five.")

(Michael) *says find* (five) *things.*
Find (five) *things.*
Find (five) *things.*
(Michael) *says find* (five) *things.*
Thank you, (Michael).

2. Give the children a chance to clean up, then repeat, if necessary, using a different child.

Related books   *Messy Bessey and the Birthday Overnight* by Pat McKissack
Skip to My Lou by Mary Ann Hoberman

✚ *Cassandra Reigel Whetstone, Folsom, CA*

It Must Be Spring

addition

Materials   none

What to do   Recite the following fingerplay with the children, using fingers as the flowers popping up out of the ground.

It Must Be Spring

Two flowers pop up from the ground
And listen to the sound...
Wake up, wake up,
It's spring, it's spring.
They hear the robin sing.

Two more pop up from the ground
And listen to the sound...
Wake up, wake up,
It's spring, it's spring.
They hear the robin sing.

Two more pop up from the ground
And listen to the sound...
Wake up, wake up,
It's spring, it's spring.
They hear the robin sing.

Four more pop up from the ground
And listen to the sound...
Wake up, wake up,
It's spring, it's spring.
They hear the robin sing.

I have a pretty bunch of flowers now,
As pretty as can be.
I keep these pretty flowers,
Because they are for me!

✚ *Ingelore Mix, Gainesville, VA*

Little Mice

counting backwards

Materials

Seven Blind Mice by Ed Young
7 felt mouse shapes corresponding to the colors of the mice in the story
flannel board

What to do

1. Do the following fingerplay with the children. Repeat it two or three times, so children are comfortable with it.

Seven Little Mice

Seven little mouse tails (show seven fingers)
Sticking up so high, (seven fingers raised high)
One mouse sits (lower one finger)
And six go by. (wave six fingers)
Six sets of whiskers (run a finger horizontally under your nose)
Wiggling to and fro, (wiggle six fingers)
One mouse stops, (lower one finger)
Leaving five to go. (show five fingers)
Five little bodies
Creeping on the ice, (creep fingers of right hand over horizontal left arm)
One mouse slips away (slide one finger down the arm)
From four other mice. (show four fingers)
Four pairs of big ears (place spread out hands on either side of head)
Listening for a sound, (cup hand to one ear)
Three mice go ahead, (show three fingers)
One turns around. (show one finger, hide it behind your back)
Three sets of tiny paws, (show three fingers)
Dancing in the dew, (lightly bounce fingers of right hand on horizontal left arm)
One mouse gets tired (show one finger and yawn)
And then there are two. (show two fingers)
Two sleepy little mice,
Now their day is done. (yawn)
One went to bed, (put one finger down)
Leaving only one. (show one finger)
One pair of shiny eyes (point to eyes)
In the bright moon light,
One mouse goes to bed (show one finger)
And says, "Good night!" (hands together, head on hands, pretend to sleep)

2. After the children have learned the fingerplay, give seven children each a felt mouse.

3. Read the book *Seven Blind Mice* to the children. As you read the story, the children place the colored felt mouse that corresponds to the one you are reading about on the flannel board.

4. Before you reveal what the mice have been climbing on, let the children guess.

5. Finish the story, revealing that the mice have been climbing on an elephant.

✚ *Christina Chilcote, New Freedom, PA*

The Me Counting Song

counting, identifying symmetry

Materials   none

What to do   With the children, sing the following song to the tune of "Mary Had a Little Lamb."

The Me Counting Song
I've got two eyes on my face, on my face, on my face,
I've got two eyes on my face, count them—one, two.

I've got one nose on my face, on my face, on my face,
I've got one nose on my face, count it—only one.

I've got two arms on my body, on my body, on my body,
I've got two arms on my body, count them—one, two.

I've got five fingers on each hand, on each hand, on each hand,
I've got five fingers on each hand—one, two, three, four, five.

Related book   *My Five Senses* by Aliki

✚ *Kristi Larson, Spirit Lake, IA*

My Leopard Has 10 Spots

subtraction

Materials   none

What to do   1. Gather the children together, and ask them to hold out all 10 of their fingers.
2. Recite the following poem, encouraging them to use their fingers to keep track of the diminishing number of spots.

My Leopard Has 10 Spots

My leopard has ten spots.
I don't know how,
I don't know where,
But my leopard lost two spots somewhere.
It's getting dark, it's getting late,
To sleep he goes, with only eight.

(Continue making up verses that diminish the number of spots on the leopard until he has none.)

✚ *Ingelore Mix, Gainesville, VA*

A Name for Nothing

recognizing zero

Materials   none

What to do   Recite the following original poem with the children:

Zero the Hero

I'm Zero the Hero, oh, marvelous me.
When you look at numbers,
I know that you'll see
How very important zero can be.

Before you count anything, even one,
You have zero, nothing, none.
If you count backwards, three, two, one,
You can say zero to show that you're done.

When you add zero, it's very strange,
The number you started with doesn't change.
In subtraction it's also true,
Take away zero and you get nothing new.

I'm Zero the Hero, oh, marvelous me.
When you look at numbers,
I know that you'll see
How very important I can be.

✛ *Ellen Javernik, Loveland, CO*

The Number in My Hand

numeral recognition

Materials construction paper
scissors
tape
craft sticks or straws

What to do 1. Cut out large numerals and tape them to craft sticks or straws.
2. Invite the children to sing the following song to the tune of "He's Got the Whole World in His Hands." Begin the first verse by holding up the numeral 1:

I've got the number one in my hand.
I've got the number one in my hand.
I've got the number one in my hand.
I've got the number one in my hand.

3. Hold up signs with different numerals on them and invite the children to sing the song using those numerals instead of the numeral 1.

4. Let different children hold the numerals and vary the song as follows.

Who's got the number one in her hand?
Who's got the number one in her hand?
Who's got the number one in her hand?
(Child's name)*'s got number one!*

5. Sing it through and have the child who has the numeral stand up and hold the numeral up.

✚ *Shelley F. Hoster, Norcross, GA*

Numbers in the Circle

counting, numeral recognition

Materials   several sets of laminated numeral cards on strings from 1–10

What to do

1. Make several sets of number cards (1–10) and laminate them. Punch a hole in the upper right corner and the upper left corner of the cards and tie a string through the holes.

2. In this variation of "Farmer in the Dell," the children wear the number cards as necklaces and make a circle.

3. Choose a child wearing a "1" card to stand inside the circle.

4. As the children sing the song below, ask the child in the circle to choose a child wearing the "2" card to join her in the circle.

The one will choose a two,
The one will choose a two,
Here comes another one!
The one will choose a two.

5. With the two children inside the circle, sing the next verse. The second child picks a child wearing a "3" card to join her inside the circle.

The two will choose a three,
The two will choose a three,
Here comes another one!
The two will choose a three.

6. Continue until the tenth child is chosen and repeat until all the children are inside the circle.

✛ *Susan Oldham Hill, Lakeland, FL*

One Man Went to Mow

counting forward and backwards

Materials none

What to do
1. Explain to the children that a meadow is a field of grass.
2. Show them a picture of a person mowing grass with a scythe, and explain that was how it was done a long time ago.
3. Sing the song "One Man Went to Mow."

One Man Went to Mow
One man went to mow,
Went to mow a meadow.
One man and his dog,
Went to mow a meadow.

Two men went to mow,
Went to mow a meadow.
Two men, one man and his dog,
Went to mow a meadow.

Three men went to mow,
Went to mow a meadow.
Three men, two men,
One man and his dog,
Went to mow a meadow.

Four men went to mow,
Went to mow a meadow.
Four men, three men, two men,
One man and his dog,
Went to mow a meadow.

4. Continue singing up to whatever number you want.

✚ *Anne Adeney, Plymouth, United Kingdom*

One Happy, Two Happy, Three Happy Children

counting forward and backwards

Materials none

What to do 1. Invite the children to stand in a line and march forward one at a time while singing the following song to the tune of "Little Red Wagon."

One happy, two happy, three happy children,
Four happy, five happy, six happy children,
Seven happy, eight happy, nine happy children,
Ten happy children who know math!

2. Then have the children march backward (or back to the original spot) while singing the following.

Ten happy, nine happy, eight happy children,
Seven happy, six happy, five happy children,
Four happy, three happy, two happy children,
One happy child who knows math!

✚ *Susan Grenfell, Cedar Park, TX*

One, Two, Three

counting

Materials none

What to do
1. Discuss the steps people follow in order to complete a task, such as washing dishes (scrape off food, wash in soapy water, rinse, and dry).
2. Talk about the steps the children take to get ready in the morning: wake up, get dressed, eat breakfast, brush teeth and hair, and so on.
3. Explain that the little mice in this rhyme have to follow steps to get their food safely. Ask what the mice will look for.
4. Invite the children to recite the following rhyme, making the appropriate gestures when prompted. Ask them to count using their fingers for the "one, two, three" lines.

Little mice in a hungry mood
Look around to find some food. (look left and right)

Tiptoe! One, two, three… where?
On the table! Cheese is there! (point to imaginary cheese)

Sniff! One, two, three… yum! (rub stomach)
It's good cheese, let's get some!

Jump! One, two, three… stop!
Is that the cat on the table top?

Yes! One, two, three… scat!
Hurry home! Here comes the cat! (run in place, or to designated "home" area)

More to do   **Art:** Create a paper plate mouse face puppet. Attach a white paper plate to a craft stick. Discuss geometric shapes. Have each child glue on two small squares (eyes), two large ovals (ears), one medium triangle (nose) and one small circle (mouth). To convert the puppet into a mask, cut out the square openings instead. Invite the children to use the puppets or masks for the fingerplay.

✚ *Theresa Callahan, Easton, MD*

Over in the Meadow

counting, matching

Materials
copy of the song *Over in the Meadow* by Olive A. Wadsworth
light green or light blue shower curtain
permanent markers
pictures of each mother animal and baby animals mentioned in the song
laminator
tape or CD of *Over in the Meadow*
tape recorder or CD player

What to do
1. In advance, draw a meadow scene on the shower curtain using permanent markers.

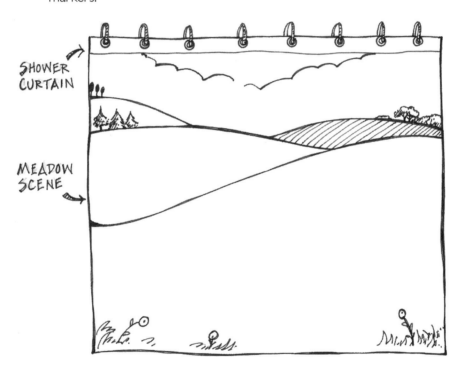

① TOADS ② FISH ③ BLUEBIRDS

④ MUSKRATS ⑤ BEES ⑥ CROWS

⑦ CRICKETS ⑧ LIZARDS ⑨ FROGS ⑩ SPIDERS

2. Prepare one picture of each mother animal as well as the number of baby animals mentioned in the song (one toad, two fish, three bluebirds, four muskrats, five bees, six crows, seven crickets, eight lizards, nine frogs, and ten spiders).

3. Laminate all of the pictures for longevity.

4. Show the children the animal pictures and talk about the different animals.

5. Sing the song with the children. Invite them to help place the mother animals on the shower curtain with the correct number of baby animals.

✚ *Quazonia J. Quarles, Newark, DE*

Phonic Counting Phrases

counting

Materials   none

What to do   1. Invite the children to listen carefully and see if they can hear which sounds are similar among the following words:

> *One wagon*
> *Two ties*
> *Three thrones*
> *Four feet*
> *Five fingers*
> *Six socks*
> *Seven snakes*
> *Eight eggs*
> *Nine nails*
> *Ten tents*

2. Repeat the words several times, so the children can hear their phonic similarities.

Related book   *Ten Little Rabbits* by Virginia Grossman

✚ *Barbara Saul, Eureka, CA*

A Pizza Is a Whole

fractions

Materials   whole pizza made out of construction paper
slice of pizza cut out of construction paper

What to do   Sing the following song to the tune of "London Bridge Is Falling Down" while showing the children the pizza shapes.

A pizza is a circle shape, circle shape, circle shape.
A pizza is a circle shape, it is a whole.
A slice of pizza is a triangle shape, triangle shape, triangle shape.
A slice of pizza is a triangle shape, it is a part.

Related books   *Apple Fractions* by Jerry Pallotta
Parts of a Whole by Janet Reed

✚ *Renee Kirchner, Carrollton, TX*

Shapes All Around

geometric shapes

Materials   square box
shoebox
orange
paper with a large V written on it
marker

What to do   1. Read the following poem to the children. Hold up the different objects as they are mentioned.

See that box sitting over there? (point to square box)
Its equal sides make it a square.
Here is a box that held a shoe. (hold up shoebox)
A box can be a rectangle too.
Here's an orange so round and fat, (hold up an orange)
A circle is a shape like that.
Take the letter V, add a line, (hold up the letter V, and draw a line)
That new triangle looks just fine.
Shapes are everywhere, it is true;
Just look and they'll appear to you.

2. Hold up the objects again and have the children call out the shape.

3. Invite the children to "draw" the shapes in the air.

4. Ask the children to look for these shapes in classroom objects and pictures.

Related books   *Color Farm* by Lois Ehlert

The Missing Piece Meets the Big O by Shel Silverstein

✚ *Theresa Callahan, Easton, MD*

Shapey Gapey

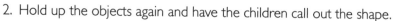

shape recognition

Materials   cutouts of triangles, circles, rectangles, squares, diamonds, and so on (1 per child)

What to do

1. Give each child a shape cutout.

2. Sing the following song with the children to the tune of "Hokey Pokey," inviting them to hold out their shape when it is mentioned.

   You put your (name of a shape) in,
   You take your (name of a shape) out,
   You put your (name of a shape) in,
   And you shake it all about.
   You do the shapey gapey
   And you turn yourself around.
   That's what it's all about.

3. Repeat the verse, naming a different cutout shape each time.

4. For the final verse, sing: *You put all your shapes in.*

✚ *Margery Kranyik Fermino, West Roxbury, MA*

Six Little Donkeys

counting

Materials   none

What to do   Invite the children to recite the following rhyme.

Six Little Donkeys
One little donkey went walking one day.
Another joined him, and the two did bray.

One...   Two did bray

Two little donkeys were looking for their lunch,
And they found some carrots to munch.

...carrots to munch

Three little donkeys wearily sat down.
They would not budge to go to town.

...wearily sat down.

Four little donkeys walking to and fro.
Slowly down the hill they did go.

...down the hill they did go.

Five little donkeys carried sticks on their backs.
They ate some thistles for noontime snacks.

Six little donkeys went to the barn at night.
They slept soundly until the morning light.

✚ *Mary Brehm, Aurora, OH*

Six Little Owls

counting, ordinal numbers

Materials   chart tablet

What to do

1. Discuss the changing of the seasons from summer to fall. Write the following original rhyme on chart paper, and teach it to the children.

   Six Little Owls
   The first little owl said, "Where can the squirrels be?"
   The second one said, "They're storing nuts in their tree."
   The third one said, "The geese just flew away!"
   The fourth one said, "It's colder out today."
   The fifth one said, "Where did summer go?"
   The sixth one said, "Fall is here, you know!"

2. After the children have memorized the words, choose six children to stand in a row. Each child says a line in the rhyme.

3. As a variation, give the children numeral cards to hold. Distribute them randomly for the children to put in the correct order.

More to do   **Art:** Put fall colors of paint on the easel and provide brown and yellow easel paper.

Related books   *Owl Moon* by Jane Yolen
Ten Black Dots by Donald Crews

✚ *Susan Oldham Hill, Lakeland, FL*

Sweet Potato Pie

counting

Materials   none

What to do   1. Invite the children to recite the following rhyme.

One potato, two potato, three potato, four.
Five potato, six potato, seven potato more.

2. Encourage the children to pound one fist on the top of the other fist, and back and forth, until the rhyme is over.
3. After they learn the original rhyme, say the rhyme in a new and different way:

One potato, two potato, three potato, four.
Five potato, six potato, seven potato more.
Eight potato, nine potato, ten potato high,
Now let's make a sweet potato pie.

4. Do the same hand motions with the new rhyme. This time, start pounding your fists low, and go higher as you count higher (like going up a ladder).

✚ *Judy Fujawa, The Villages, FL*

Ten Cartons of Milk

counting backwards and forwards

Materials   10 clean, empty ½ pint milk cartons
acrylic paint and brush, or foam or felt numerals (1–10) and glue (optional)

What to do   1. If desired, paint or glue the numerals 1–10 on the sides of 10 milk cartons.
2. Place the milk cartons on the edge of a desk, table, or shelf. If numerals are on the cartons, place the cartons in order from 1–10.

3. Ask the children to count from 1–10 with you while you point to each carton in ascending order. Then ask them to count from 10 – 1, while you point to each carton in descending order.

4. Sing the following song to the tune of "99 Bottles of Beer on the Wall."

Ten cartons of milk on the wall,
Ten cartons of milk,
If one of those cartons should happen to fall,
Nine cartons of milk on the wall. (remove one milk carton)

Nine cartons of milk on the wall…
Eight cartons of milk on the wall…

5. Continue counting down and removing milk cartons until you get to "No more cartons of milk on the wall."

6. Once everyone knows the song, let children take turns removing a carton. If it's the end of the day, and the children are getting antsy, pretend to knock down each carton "accidentally" in turn, always acting surprised or shocked that another carton has fallen.

✚ *Christina Chilcote, New Freedom, PA*

Ten Cows in the Dell

counting backwards

Materials   10 tagboard headbands with "cow ears" attached (optional)

What to do
1. Sing the song (below) with the children.
2. Have the children join hands and form a circle, walking clockwise while singing the first verse.
3. At the end of the first verse, choose a child to go inside the circle. If using cow ear headbands, the child puts one on.
4. Continue as the group sings about cow number 9, number 8, and so on going into the "barn" (inside the circle).
5. As fewer children are left in the "dell" it becomes harder (and sillier) to circle the cows in the "barn." If only 11 children play, the lone "farmer" has to try to circle the cows by himself!

Ten Cows in the Dell (tune: "The Farmer in the Dell")

The farmer in the dell
He had ten cows to sell.
One cow got hungry and went to the barn,
Nine cows left in the dell.

…He had nine cows to sell…
…He had eight cows to sell…

The farmer in the dell,
He had a cow to sell.
The cow got hungry and went to the barn,
No more cows to sell!

✚ *Christina Chilcote, New Freedom, PA*

Ten Little Ducklings

subtraction

Materials　　none

What to do　　1. Gather the children into one large group.
2. Choose 10 children to be "ducklings," and line them up in front of the other children.
3. Invite the children to recite the following rhyme, having the "ducklings" perform the actions described in the rhyme.

Ten Little Ducklings
10 little ducklings
Waddle down the path
Doing very fancy math.

If three of us could swim away,
And three of us slept all day,
And three hide behind a tree,
How many ducklings would we be?

✚ *Ingelore Mix, Gainesville, VA*

Ten Fingerplay

addition, counting backwards, subtraction

Materials none

What to do Invite the children to recite the following rhyme, making the appropriate gestures when prompted.

I have ten fingers as you can see. (hold up 10 fingers)
Put down seven, now I have three. (put down seven, so three are left)
Put up two for five on one hand. (hold up all fingers on one hand)
Wave all five to make a fan. (fan face with hand)

Put down three and hold up two. (make peace sign with two fingers up)
Hold a peace sign for all to view. (hold hand high above head)

Now show me ten for countdown fun, (hold up 10 fingers)
We'll count straight down from ten to one:
Ten, nine, eight, seven, six, five, four, three, two, one, (put down one finger
    at a time)
And now at last we've come to…none! (put down last finger)

More to do **Art:** Help the children trace around both of their hands (fingers spread) on a piece of paper. Ask them to dot the numbers 1–10 on the fingernails of the hand and write a numeral 1–10 on each finger. Color and decorate the hands.

✚ *Susan Grenfell, Cedar Park, TX*

Ten Little Bees

counting, representing numbers

Materials   none

What to do   Say the following rhyme with the children, holding up the correct number of fingers when mentioned.

Ten Little Bees

One little bee flew near a shoe,
Along came another, and that made two.

Two little bees flew into a tree,
Along came another, and that made three.

Three little bees flew near a door,
Along came another, and that made four.

Four little bees were buzzing around the hive,
Along came another, and that made five.

Five little bees landed on some sticks,
Along came another, and that made six.

Six little bees flew up toward heaven,
Along came another, and that made seven.

Seven little bees buzzed by the garden gate,
Along came another, and that made eight.

Eight little bees flew in a line,
Along came another, and that made nine.

Nine little bees flew to their hive again,
Along came another, and that made ten.

✚ *Mary Brehm, Aurora, OH*

Ten Little Instruments

counting

Materials   rhythm instruments (1 per child)

What to do   Invite the children to recite the following rhyme to the tune of "Little Red Wagon" while playing the instruments put out for them.

> **Ten Little Instruments**
> *One little, two little, three little instruments.*
> *Four little, five little, six little instruments.*
> *Seven little, eight little, nine little instruments,*
> *Ten instruments in the band!*

✚ *Margery Kranyik Fermino, West Roxbury, MA*

Ten Mosquitoes

counting, subtraction

Materials   10 felt mosquitoes and flannel board (optional)
fly swatter (optional)

What to do   1. Invite the children to sing the following song to the tune of "Little Red Wagon."

> **Ten Mosquitoes**
> *One little, two little, three mosquitoes,*
> *Four little, five little, six mosquitoes,*
> *Seven little, eight little, nine mosquitoes,*
> *Ten mosquitoes eating me!*

2. Add the mosquitoes to the flannel board as you sing them. If you don't want to use props, hold up fingers as you count.
3. Once the children are adept at the first verse, add the following verse to the song:

Squish one flat and that'll leave nine,
Squish one flat and that'll leave nine,
Squish one flat and that'll leave nine,
Nine mosquitoes eating me.

4. Hit the felt mosquito with a fly swatter and remove it from the flannel board at the end of the verse (or make a slapping gesture on your leg).
5. Repeat the verse, diminishing the number by one each time, and end with this verse:

Squish one flat and that'll leave none,
Squish one flat and that'll leave none,
Squish one flat and that'll leave none,
No mosquitoes eating me. But ooh, I'm itchy!

✚ *Kristi Larson, Spirit Lake, IA*

This Little Frog Has Two Eyes

multiplying by 2

Materials   none

What to do   1. Invite the children to squat down and hop around like frogs.
2. Ask them how many eyes, legs, mouths, and tails are on a frog.
3. Choose five children to act out the song as the others sing. One child acts out the first verse, another child joins him for the second verse, and so on. This will help the children visualize the numbers (four eyes, eight legs, and so on).
4. For beginning multipliers, you may need to stop and count between verses.

This Little Frog Has Two Eyes (Chinese nursery rhyme)
This little frog has two eyes,
Four legs,
One mouth, no tail,
Says "croak, croak" and
Plops into the water.
Two little frogs have four eyes,
Eight legs,

Two mouths, no tails,
Say "croak, croak" and
Plop into the water.

Three little frogs have six eyes,
Twelve legs,
Three mouths, no tails,
Say "croak, croak" and
Plop into the water.

Four little frogs have eight eyes…
Five little frogs have ten eyes…

✚ *Anne Adeney, Plymouth, United Kingdom*

Time to Rhyme

measuring time, numeral recognition

Materials

paper plates
scissors
construction paper
brad
markers

What to do

1. Make a clock using a paper plate. Cut out clock hands from construction paper and use a brad to attach them to the center of the plate.
2. Write the numerals 1–12 around the edge of the paper plate to mark the hours on the clock.

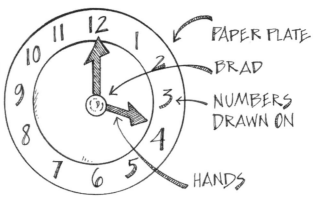

3. Read the poem "Hickory Dickory Dock" to the children.

Hickory, dickory, dock,
The mouse ran up the clock.
The clock struck one, (move the clock hands to 1 on your clock)
The mouse ran down,
Hickory, dickory, dock.

4. Continue on with the other verses, changing the clock hands as you go.

Related books *Bunny Day: Telling Time from Breakfast to Bedtime* by Rick Walton
Telling Time with Big Mama Cat by Dan Harper

✚ *Monica Hay Cook, Tucson, AZ*

Twice One Is Two

multiplying by 2

Materials large pictures of each flower or plant mentioned in the rhyme, with appropriate notation above it ($2 \times 4 = 8$ above picture of poppies)

What to do
1. Teach the children this garden rhyme with the help of the visual aids. (Memory experts say that associating anything with a picture will help children remember it.)
2. Add a rhyme and children will have several different clues to help them remember how to multiply by two. **Note:** The rhyme is a bit advanced, especially for younger children.

Twice One Is Two
Twice one is two,
Violets white and blue.
Twice two is four,
Sunflowers at the door.
Twice three is six,
Sweet peas on their sticks.
Twice four is eight,

Poppies at the gate.
Twice five is ten,
Pansies bloom again.
Twice six is twelve,
Pinks for those who delve.
Twice seven is fourteen,
Flowers of the runner bean.
Twice eight is sixteen,
Clinging ivy, evergreen.
Twice nine is eighteen,
Purple thistles to be seen.
Twice ten is twenty,
Hollyhocks in plenty.

✚ *Anne Adeney, Plymouth, United Kingdom*

Watch My Counting Shine

counting

Materials   sturdy number cards 1–10
                    large chart paper with the words to the song

What to do   1. Invite the children to sing the following song to the tune of "I've Been
                       Working on the Railroad."

                       I am always counting something,
                       Counting all day long.
                       One, two, three, four, five, I'm counting,
                       It's the reason for my song.

                       Next, I'm counting six and seven;
                       Then eight and nine belong...
                       You know what is coming next: it's ten!
                       And that ends my song.

                    2. Choose 10 children to sit in a row, facing the rest of the children.
                    3. Give each child a number card.

4. Ask them to listen for their number in the song. When they hear it, they should jump up and hold the number card high over their heads.

Related books   *Count and See* by Tana Hoban
One Fish, Two Fish, Red Fish, Blue Fish by Dr. Seuss

✚ *Susan Oldham Hill, Lakeland, FL*

Add 'Em Up

addition, counting

Materials
chalk or masking tape
beanbags
chart paper

What to do

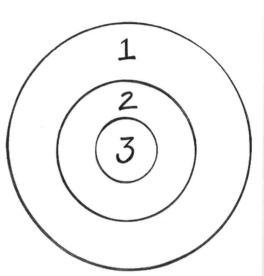

1. Draw a circular target on the ground (with chalk or masking tape) similar to a "bull's eye" target. Start with three concentric circles.
2. In the middle of the inside circle write the numeral 3. In the second circle write the numeral 2, and in the outside circle write the numeral 1.
3. Mark a start line so the children know where to stand to throw the beanbag.
4. The children take turns throwing three beanbags into the target. Help them add up their points depending on where their beanbags land on the target.
5. Record the children's points on a chart.
6. When children are ready, move the start line farther away or add more circles to the target.

3 BEANBAGS   START LINE

✚ *Judy Fujawa, The Villages, FL*

Apple Tree Math

addition, counting

Materials
brown and red poster board
card stock paper
markers
scissors
laminator

Games

What to do

1. Draw a large tree on a piece of brown poster board, and draw 10 medium-sized apples on a piece of red poster board.

2. Draw two large squares side by side on a piece of card stock paper. Color one square blue and the other green. This is the addition mat.

3. Draw a thick black line about 5" below each square.

4. Laminate everything and cut out the tree and apples.

5. Invite two or three children at a time to play this counting game.

6. Place the tree and the addition mat on a low table. Place one apple on the blue square and one apple on the green square of the addition mat.

7. Point to the blue square and ask, "How many apples are on this square?" Point to the green square and ask, "How many apples are on this square?"

8. Ask, "How many apples are there all together?" The children may or may not be able to figure out the answer.

9. Ask the children to count with you as you move the apples from the addition mat to the tree.

10. Continue the game, using varying numbers of apples on each mat. Let the children take turns moving the apples from the addition mat to the tree as they all count together.

11. As the children's skills develop, use a wipe-off marker or crayon to print the correlating numerals on the addition mat on the two thick lines you made.

12. For younger children, you may want to use real apples (some types of apples are very small and easily used for this activity) instead of cutouts. Or use small plastic apples available at any education supply store.

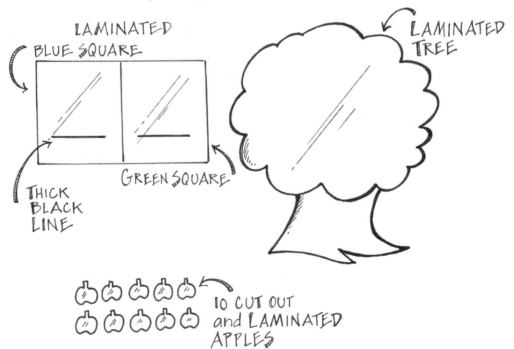

LAMINATED BLUE SQUARE

LAMINATED TREE

GREEN SQUARE

THICK BLACK LINE

10 CUT OUT and LAMINATED APPLES

✚ *Virginia Jean Herrod, Columbia, SC*

Big Dice

counting (adaptable for practicing geometric shapes)

Materials
quart juice boxes or 8 oz. milk cartons (2 of the same size for each die)
scissors
masking tape
markers

What to do
1. Cut off the tops of clean, dry cartons so they are as close to square as possible.
2. Insert the open side of one square carton into the open side of the other carton to create a six-sided cube. If the cartons are not very strong, you may want to stuff one of them with paper before putting them together.
3. Use tape to secure them tightly together. Wrap masking tape around the whole square to make a writing surface.
4. Write a number or shape on each side of the die. If the children are working on numbers above 10, you may want to use six numbers such as 13, 14, 15, 16, 17, and 18. If they are learning about geometric shapes, you might use rectangles, squares, circles, and so on instead of numbers.
5. To play the game, roll the die and give the children a challenge. For example, if you roll a 15, ask them to do a particular task 15 times (jump, clap hands, stomp foot, take 15 steps from a specific location, and so on).
6. If you are using a geometric shapes die, you might ask the children to find a circle in the room and stand by it, or have them use a piece of yarn or pipe cleaner to form the shape determined by the die.

✚ *Bev Schumacher, Racine, W*

Birthday Cake Counting

counting

Materials
Styrofoam circles
permanent marker
birthday cake decorations
birthday candles
old birthday cards with numerals on them

What to do
1. Write a numeral in the center of each Styrofoam circle.
2. Decorate the Styrofoam circles to look like birthday cakes, using little flowers or other birthday cake decorations found in dollar or craft stores.
3. Add birthday candles to each circle to match the numeral on the "cake" (three candles for the numeral 3).
4. Invite the children to "read" the numeral on the card and place it next to the cake.

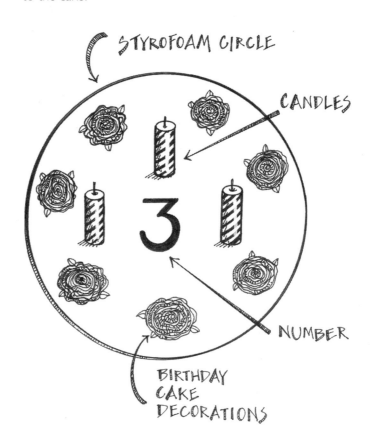

STYROFOAM CIRCLE
CANDLES
3
NUMBER
BIRTHDAY CAKE DECORATIONS

✚ *Jean Potter, Charleston, WV*

Board Sequencing

sequencing

Materials

several smooth pieces of nonstick floor tile
permanent black marker
scissors
cardboard box

What to do

1. On the piece of tile, draw a grid of squares and number them from 1 to 20. Be sure to put dots on each square that match the numerals written on them.

2. Make another identical grid on a separate tile. Number them from 1 to 20 and put the matching number of dots on each one. Cut out each individual square.

3. Mix up the individual number squares in a box, and have the children put them in order on the larger grid.

More to do

Draw jigsaw puzzle-like designs on one square of floor tile, and number each section. Draw identical designs on a second tile, number the bottom of each tile, and cut them out. Invite the children to put the shape puzzle together so the numerals are in order.

 Cookie Zingarelli, Columbus, OH

Bowling

· ·

addition, counting, subtraction

Materials
set of 9 plastic or wooden bowling pins (or make your own)
ball
scoring sheet

What to do

1. If you do not have bowling pins, make your own set by putting sand into plastic soda bottles. Don't make them too heavy or they won't fall down.

2. Place the nine pins in a diamond pattern.

3. Ask the children to count the bowling pins.

4. Invite the first players to take turns rolling a large ball toward the pins. Invite all the children to count the number of pins knocked down each time.

5. Show them how to score in groups of five, putting four ones in a row, then crossing through the set for the fifth number.

6. Each time the pins are knocked down, help the children add and subtract the numbers.

7. Continue playing until everyone has had several turns trying to knock down the pins.

✚ *Anne Adeney, Plymouth, United Kingdom*

Bug Catcher Game

counting, numeral recognition

Materials small butterfly or fishing nets
insect counters
die (if possible, use a die with 1, 2, or 3 dots on the six sides for younger children and a regular die for older children)

What to do
1. This game can be played by two or more children.
2. Each child selects a net and counts out 10 insect counters (20 for older children) and puts them nearby.
3. One child rolls the die.
4. The child counts the number of dots on the side the die lands on and puts that many insect counters from her pile of 10 into the net.
5. The child to her right rolls the die next and adds insect counters to her net.
6. The game continues until one child has all 10 insect counters in her net.

Related books *Bug Safari* by Bob Barner
I Like Bugs by Margaret Wise Brown
The Icky Bug Counting Book by Jerry Pallotta and Ralph Masiello
The Very Grouchy Ladybug by Eric Carle

✚ *Kristi Larson, Spirit Lake, IA*

Butterfly Fun

counting

Materials 50 (or more) 2" squares of colored copy paper, in three or more colors
paper plates

Games

What to do

1. In advance, make butterfly manipulatives by holding on to both sides of the paper square and twisting in the center to form a "butterfly."
2. Draw criss-cross lines on the paper plates to create a "netting" effect.
3. Have the children sit in a circle for this game.
4. Put at least 30 butterflies on a paper plate, and stand in the center of the circle holding the plate of butterflies.
5. Designate a group of children to "catch" the butterflies (for example, children wearing blue shirts, white shoes, and so on).
6. Invite all the children to softly chant three times, "Butterfly, butterfly, fly away."
7. After the final chant, call out, "Catch the butterflies."
8. Launch the butterflies through the air as the selected children use paper plate "nets" to "catch" as many as they can.
9. Invite each child to come forward and count their butterflies aloud as they place them back onto your plate.
10. Repeat the game several times until all children have had a turn to "catch" some butterflies.
11. When finished with the game, place the collection of butterflies in a shoebox along with several color pattern cards (red, blue, red, blue and yellow, red, yellow, red). Invite the children to recite the pattern aloud and then copy the pattern by laying out a row of butterflies to match the pattern on the card.

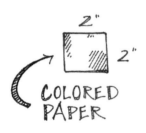

COLORED PAPER

TWIST IN MIDDLE

PAPER PLATE WITH CRISS-CROSS DRAWN ON

+ *Mary J. Murray, Mazomanie, WI*

Buttons

* *

counting, number awareness

Materials
marker
tagboard
scissors or paper cutter
laminator
pocket chart

What to do
1. Make button cards on tagboard of sets of buttons 1–10. Draw 10 buttons on one card, nine buttons on another card, and so on.
2. Print the number names, using a large font, one to ten on another sheet of tagboard.
3. Cut around the number names and button cards so they are all the same size and fit into the rows of the pocket chart. Laminate the cards for durability.
4. Distribute the button cards to the children.
5. Place the number names in the pocket chart, leaving room for the button cards.
6. Invite each child to count the buttons on her card and place it next to the appropriate number name in the pocket chart.

Related book   *The Button Box* by Margarette S. Reid

➕ *Jackie Wright, Enid, OK*

Cat in the Hat Money Game

* *

counting, money

Materials
large aluminum can
various coins
red and white construction paper
tape
scissors
white glue

What to do

1. Trace around the bottom of the can onto red construction paper. Draw tabs pointing in toward the center of this circle.
2. Draw another circle about an inch outside the first circle. This will be the brim of your hat.
3. Cut it out, making sure not to cut off the tabs inside the inner circle.
4. Cut a strip of red construction paper as tall as the aluminum can and wrap it all the way around the can. Glue the strip in place.
5. Use the tabs to glue the brim into the top of the can. Let dry.
6. Cut strips of white construction paper to make the stripes for the hat and glue them around the can.
7. Gather coins to use for the game (two quarters, five nickels, five dimes, and 10 pennies).
8. Place the can on the ground. Put a piece of tape on the ground about 6–8' away from the can.
9. Try to toss the coins into the "cat's hat" from behind the piece of tape.
10. After each child throws all the coins, count the child's change that makes it into the hat. The child whose coins add up to the highest monetary value wins.

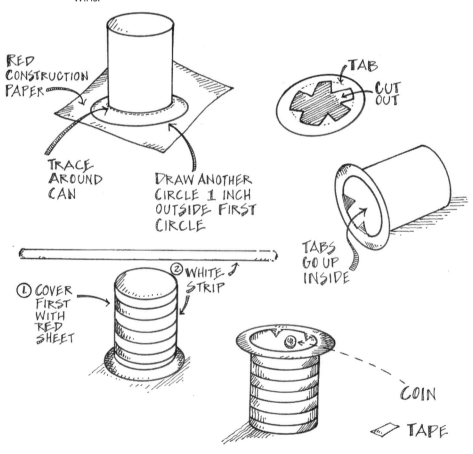

+ *Jennifer Galvin, Stafford, VA*

CD Math

counting

Materials: CDs and CD cases
stickers

What to do   1. With a permanent marker, write a numeral on the outside of a CD case.
2. On the CD, place the same number of stickers to correlate with the case.
3. Separate the cases and CDs on a table.
4. Have the children put the correctly numbered CD into the correct case.

✚ *Wanda Guidroz, Santa Fe, TX*

Clapping Cubes

numeral recognition

Materials   wooden cube with sides numbered 0–5

What to do   1. This game works best with a small group of three to six children.
2. The children sit in a circle and take turns rolling the cube.
3. The child claps the number that the cube lands on.
4. This game reinforces numeral recognition. It is especially good for teaching the concept of zero.
5. Instead of clapping, children can stand and stamp their feet, click their tongue, snap their fingers, or whatever else you choose.
6. Increase the difficulty by adding a second cube with 0 and 6–10.

✚ *Mary Jo Shannon, Roanoke, VA*

Clothesline Math

ordering, matching

Materials
clothesline
basket
clip clothespins (marked with the numerals 1–10)
laminated die-cut shapes or note pad shapes (numbered 1–10)

What to do
1. Hang a clothesline in the room. Place numbered clothespins in a basket near the clothesline.
2. Invite the children to put the clothespins on the clotheslines in the correct order from left to right.
3. Once the children have mastered putting the clothespins in order, put out numbered die-cut shapes. Encourage the children to match the shapes to the clothespins with the same numbers.
4. When all the clothespins and shapes are matched, attach them in order on the clothesline. Ask the children to close their eyes, and have one child remove one or two shapes from the clothesline. The children open their eyes and guess which numbers are missing.

✚ *Sue Fleischmann, Sussex, WI*

Color It In

numeral recognition, sets

Materials
marker
numeral stencils (1–6)
paper
die

What to do
1. Use a stencil to write the numerals 1–6 on a piece of paper. Write two of each numeral. Make a copy for each child.
2. Show the first player how to roll the die and count the dots on top of the die.

3. Ask the player to find a numeral on her paper that matches the number of dots on the die.

Related books *The Art Lesson* by Tomie DePaola
Colors Everywhere by Tana Hoban

✚ *Susan Oldham Hill, Lakeland, FL*

Count It Out

number sense

Materials die

group of 20–25 counters (beads, blocks, plastic eggs, coins) with 3 or 4 counters different from the others in some way (3 red beads in a group of blue beads; 4 dimes in a group of pennies)

What to do

1. Sit on the floor with a small group of children and arrange the counters in a circle on the floor.
2. Have one child toss the die and say the number (or count the dots) on top.
3. Starting at any point in the circle of counters (except for one of the counters that is different), the child counts to that number, touching each counter as she goes.
4. If she stops on a regular counter (for example, a blue bead), she gets to take the counter and have another turn.
5. If she stops on the different counter (for example, the red bead), another child gets a turn. Leave the different counter in the circle.
6. The winner is the player with the most counters when only the different counters remain in the circle.

More to do

Ask the children if they can find other things in the room that are similar but different in some way. Some examples might include a yellow dish among a stack of white dishes in the dramatic play center or a green block in a pile of blue ones.

✚ *Virgina Jean Herrod, Columbia, SC*

Count and See

counting

Materials
large sheet (or a space behind a barrier large enough for a child to hide in)

What to do
1. Ask the children to close their eyes. Choose a child to sneak away and hide under the sheet or behind the barrier so the others can't see her.
2. Ask the child who is hiding to clap her hands a number of times from 1 to 10.
3. Choose another child to count the number of claps and report the correct number. Then ask everyone to clap the number together.
4. Repeat with another child and a different number of claps.
5. As a variation, hold up a number card and have the group clap a specific number of times. Ask the child who is hiding to tell how many claps she heard.

✦ *Susan Oldham Hill, Lakeland, FL*

Counting Cans

one-to-one correspondence

Materials
10 clean, empty frozen juice cans or other identical containers
adhesive dots
45 craft sticks

What to do
1. Place the colored dots on the clean, dry juice cans starting with zero dots on the first can, one dot on the next can, and so on, until you have nine dots on the last can.
2. Give each child a can. Put all the craft sticks in a container where the children can reach them.
3. Ask the children to count the number of dots on their can and put that number of sticks in their can.
4. Let the children help each other. Offer help as needed.
5. Put the cans out during center time play. Encourage the children to explore them and practice their counting skills.

✦ *Virgina Jean Herrod, Columbia, SC*

Counting Jars

counting, estimation

Materials
10 or more clear, plastic jars with screw-on lids (18 oz. peanut butter jars
    work great)
number cards
tape
collection of small objects such as cotton balls, toy cars, crayons, marbles,
    1" cubes, birthday candles, and so on
2 shoeboxes or small tubs

What to do
1. Tape a number card to each jar. (Use numbers according to the children's
   ability level.) Place the jars and lids in one shoebox or tub. Place the collection
   of items in another bucket or tub.
2. Invite the children to practice their counting skills with this fun game for one
   or two players.
3. Put all the jars on the table.
4. The child reads the number on the first jar and then counts out that many like
   objects to place inside the jar (for example, 10 cotton balls into the jar with
   the number 10 card on it).
5. Instruct the child to screw the lid onto the jar.
6. The child continues counting objects for the remaining jars.
7. Children will develop estimating skills as they realize that 10 toy cars will not
   fit in any of the jars, but 10 cotton balls will.
8. Ask the children to remove the lids and empty the jars after completing the
   game so that others may play.

✚ *Mary J. Murray, Mazomanie, W*

Crawl Across

counting

Materials ball or beanbag

What to do
1. Have the children line up at one end of the room.
2. At the command of "Crawl across," children crawl across the room and form a line.
3. Once all the children are standing on the opposite side of the room, pick up the ball or beanbag and stand 3' from the row of children.
4. With all the children facing you, toss the ball to the first person in line and say, "One."
5. As the child catches the ball, she repeats the number and tosses it back to you.
6. Continue with the next child as you say "Two," and toss the ball.
7. After the last child tosses the ball back to you, call out, "Crawl across," and repeat the activity.

More to do Have pairs of children toss a ball or beanbag back and forth and count to 10 or 20 on their own.

✚ *Mary J. Murray, Mazomanie, WI*

Deck of Cards Challenge

counting, number relationships

Materials 2 decks of cards

What to do
1. Gather the children into groups of two or three players per two decks of cards.
2. Remove all face cards (jacks, queens, kings, and aces) and divide the remaining cards in the stack evenly between the players.
3. Place each stack of cards face down. Each player turns over one card and compares them: "Is mine more or less?"

4. The person with "more" takes her opponents' cards and places them in a new pile in front of him. In the event of duplicate cards, everyone turns over a new card and places it on their original card, ignoring the first card. The player with the highest card gets all of the other players' turned over cards.

5. Once all of the original cards have been played, each player counts the cards in her new pile.

Related books
50 Card Games for Children by Vernon Quinn
Card Games for Kids: 50 Fun Games for Your Children by Adam Ward

✚ *Sandra K. Bynum, Blackfoot, ID*

Dog Matching Game

matching

Materials
scissors
magazines with pictures of dogs
cardboard
glue
laminator (optional)
large box

What to do
1. Ask each child to bring in matching dog pictures (from magazines or photos) or provide them with magazines in class to cut out pictures of dogs. Try to find two of each kind of dog.
2. Cut cardboard into squares big enough to fit the pictures.
3. Glue the dog pictures on the cardboard squares and laminate (if possible).
4. Collect the matching pictures from each child and place them in a box.
5. Use the cards to play a matching game.
6. Ask the children to each choose a picture from the box.
7. The children look at their picture and find the person holding the matching picture.
8. Whoever finds their partner first wins. Repeat the game.

✚ *Lily Erlic, Victoria, BC, Canada*

Egg Carton Counting

counting

Materials
several dozen egg cartons
plastic eggs
marker
small items (small enough to put up to 12 of them inside an egg)

What to do
1. Number the slots in the egg cartons and the sets of plastic eggs with the numerals 1–12.
2. Invite the children to fill the eggs with corresponding amounts of the small items, and match the eggs to the numbered carton slots.

✚ *Cookie Zingarelli, Columbus, OH*

Egg Hunt

counting, recognizing differences in number values

Materials
buttons
plastic netting
12 plastic eggs

What to do
1. Loosely wrap different numbers of buttons in pieces of netting. Keep the total number of buttons small (one to five buttons per bag).
2. Place one bag of buttons in each egg.
3. Hide the eggs in the room.
4. When it is time to play the game, explain that you have hidden 12 eggs in the room.
5. As the children find the eggs, have them place them on a table and keep track of them by counting the whole group each time an egg is added.
6. When all the eggs have been found, have one child open one and take out the bag of buttons (without opening it).
7. Ask the child to predict how many buttons are in the bag.

8. The child opens the bag and counts the buttons.
9. Continue until all of the eggs have been opened and all the buttons counted.
10. For a variation, label each egg with a numeral from 1 to 12. Fill 12 bags with buttons (one button in one bag, two buttons in the next bag, and so on to 12). Encourage the children to count the buttons in each bag and put them in the matching egg.

✚ *Virginia Jean Herrod, Columbia, SC*

Feather Fun

counting

Materials
brown lunch bags or decorative gift bags
colorful craft feathers
stuffed beanbag bird

What to do
1. Label the paper bags with the numerals 1–10 (or 1–20 depending on children's ability). Place feathers in each bag according to the numeral on the bag. Place a stuffed beanbag bird inside one bag.
2. Invite the children to sit in a circle. Hand a bag to each child.
3. Play music as the children pass the bags around the circle.
4. When the music stops, invite the children to spill out their bag of feathers and count them aloud.
5. The person who spills the bird from her bag has to "fly" around the circle and flap her wings as she watches her classmates count.
6. Pass the beanbag bird around the circle and invite each child to announce how many feathers she has counted.
7. After the bird has traveled to each child, the children place their feathers back in the bag and continue the game.
8. Stop the music several times until everyone has had several opportunities to count.

✚ *Mary J. Murray, Mazomanie, WI*

Feed the Hungry Bunny

counting, matching

Materials
cardboard
markers
scissors
orange felt

What to do
1. Cut out 10 bunnies from cardboard and write a numeral from 1 to 10 on each one. Cut out 10 carrots from orange felt.
2. Tell the children they are going to feed hungry bunnies.
3. The children give each bunny the number of carrots that is written on each bunny.
4. This game helps children learn to count to 10 and develop matching skills.

Related books
My Little Sister Ate One Hare by Bill Grossman
One Hungry Monster: A Counting Book in Rhyme Board Book by Susan Heyboer O'Keefe

✚ *Renee Kirchner, Carrollton, TX*

Fill the Bucket

classification, sorting, time

Materials
plastic buckets or pails
masking tape
assorted beanbags, crumbled newspaper balls, sponge balls, sock balls, and sponges cut into various shapes or sizes
shoeboxes or baskets

What to do
1. Place the pails randomly around the room.
2. Create a "tossing line" 2' feet in front of each bucket by adhering a 4' length of masking tape to the floor.

3. Place an assortment of beanbags, sponges, and balls in each box.

4. Assign a group of four children to stand behind the line near each bucket.

5. Give each group of children a box of objects to toss into their bucket.

6. Instruct the children to begin tossing the items into the bucket until it is full. Items that miss the bucket can be picked up later and tossed a second time, if necessary.

7. The goal is to be the first group to fill the bucket with objects and sit down.

8. After all the teams have filled their buckets, invite them to sort the objects into groups and talk about how the items are alike or different. Invite the children to count how many objects are in each group.

9. The children move to a different bucket. Repeat the activity several times.

10. Move the bucket farther away or closer to the tape and see what a difference it makes in how quickly the children can fill it.

✚ *Mary J. Murray, Mazomanie, WI*

Frog Pond

counting, one-to-one correspondence

Materials
blue tarp or shower curtain
hot glue gun
light green, dark green, brown, and tan foam sheets
plastic toy flies (found at party supply and novelty shops)

What to do

1. In advance, cut a blue tarp or shower curtain to represent a pond.

2. Also, in advance, cut light green foam sheets in the shape of lily pads. You will need 20 lily pad shapes.

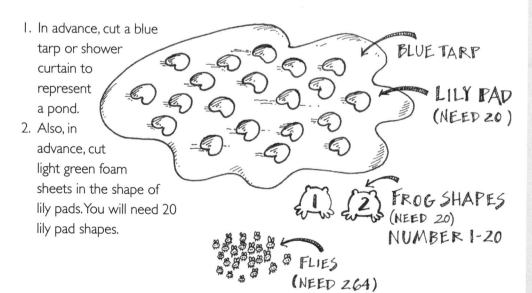

BLUE TARP

LILY PAD (NEED 20)

FROG SHAPES (NEED 20) NUMBER 1-20

FLIES (NEED 264)

3. Hot glue these shapes to the blue pond. Be sure to distribute them evenly throughout the "pond."
4. Cut dark green, brown, and tan foam sheets in the shape of frogs (total of 20), and hot glue one frog to each lily pad.
5. Number each frog from 1 to 20.
6. Provide plastic flies for children to place on the frogs, and invite them to match the number of flies to the numbers on each frog.

✚ *Quazonia J. Quarles, Newark, DE*

The Great Shoe Search

comparison, sets

Materials   shoes

What to do
1. Ask the children to sit in a circle.
2. The children put one of each of their shoes in the middle of the circle.
3. Explain to the children that they will sort the shoes by color, style, and type of shoe.
4. Several children at a time sort the shoes into piles.
5. After they are done sorting, they tell how the shoes in each pile are alike.
6. To make this activity more difficult, the children can put both of their shoes into the pile.

Related books   *Inside the Little Old Woman's Shoe* by Chuck Reasoner
Shoes by Elizabeth Winthrop

✚ *Monica Hay Cook, Tucson, AZ*

Guess the Number

estimation

Materials   none

What to do

1. This is a very simple game that can be played anywhere, needs no equipment, and can be as long or short as you want. It provides great experience in learning numbers.
2. Tell the children you are thinking of a number, which they must guess. The number range will depend on the children's level of math knowledge.
3. Each child has a turn to guess your number. After each turn, give a clue of either "higher" or "lower."
4. When the children are more experienced at the game, let them take turns choosing the number and giving the clues.

More to do   **Language and Literacy:** Play other guessing games, such as I Spy.
Music and Movement: Explore "high" and "low" in music and sound.

✚ *Anne Adeney, Plymouth, United Kingdom*

High Five Shape Pass

shape recognition

Materials   marker
6 colorful tagboard shapes: circle, triangle, square, rectangle, oval, diamond
music

What to do

1. Use a marker to draw a smiley face on both sides of the tagboard circle.
2. Have the children sit in a circle.
3. Hand the six shapes to six children, evenly spaced around the circle.
4. Explain that when the music starts, they pass the shapes around the circle.
5. When the music stops, the children holding a shape stand up and carry their shape to something in the room that matches that shape.

6. Draw the children's attention to the smiley face circle. Explain that whoever ends up with the circle has to travel around the circle and give a high five to all class members before sitting down.

7. Begin the music and invite the children to pass the shapes in a clockwise direction around the circle.

8. Stop the music and wait until each child is standing near her matching shape. Each child holds her shape next to the matching item and explains what shape the object is. For example, "The clock is a circle, like this circle. My earrings are triangles, like this triangle."

9. Always invite the child holding the circle to go last, because she has the special job of giving high fives to the group.

10. After the children return to their place on the floor, begin the music again and continue the game until everyone has had several chances to identify shapes in the classroom.

Note: For younger children, omit the oval and diamond and play the game with the four main shapes.

✚ *Mary J. Murray, Mazomanie, WI*

How Many Windows?

counting, numeral recognition

Materials
poster board (13" × 15 ½")
pictures of houses
scissors
glue stick
computer or marker
laminator
shoelaces
paper drill

What to do
1. Locate six pictures of houses, each with a different number of windows (one to six).

2. Glue these in a vertical line on the right side of the poster board turned horizontally.

3. Print the numerals 1 to 6 in a vertical line. Glue these to the left side of the poster board, opposite the houses.

4. Laminate the poster board for durability and cut out.

5. Make holes next to the six numerals on the left and the six houses on the right.

6. Use a paper drill to cut the 12 holes if a hole punch will not reach.

7. Cut the shoelaces and tie the cut end into knots to keep them from pulling through the holes.

8. From the back side of the poster board, attach the shoelaces through the holes on the left, next to the numerals. The knots will be on the back side of the poster board.

9. The child threads the shoelaces from the numerals on the left through the appropriate holes next to the houses on the right to match the numerals to the correct pictures.

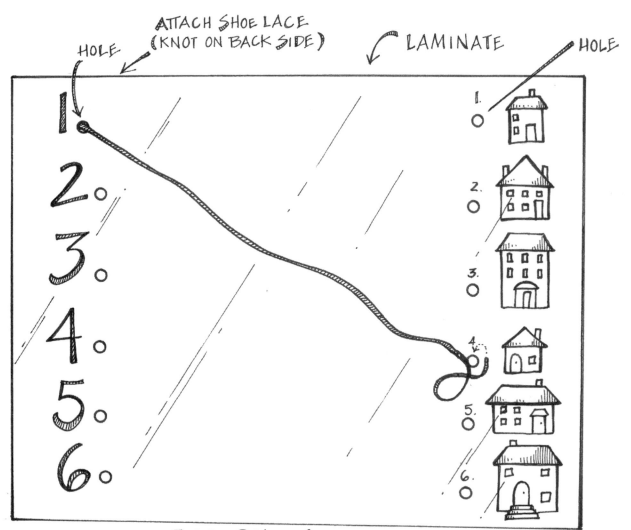

POSTER BOARD (HORIZONTAL)

✚ *Jackie Wright, Enid, OK*

Japanese Shell Game

matching, numeral recognition, representing numbers

Materials
20 large shells (clam shells are ideal)
gold paint
black paint or marker

What to do
This variation of a traditional Japanese game can be made by children or by an adult.

1. Select 10 shells that look identical or almost identical. As the children get more experienced playing the game, add another 10 shells.
2. Paint the inside of the shells with gold paint.
3. When the paint is dry, paint the numerals 1–5 on the inside of five of the shells.
4. Inside the other five shells, paint dots to represent the numbers 1–5. Place the dots as they appear on dice.
5. When dry, place the 10 shells in a spiral shape and play as a traditional memory game.
6. Each player turns over two shells at a time and reads the numbers. If there are dots, she counts the dots on each shell to get the two numbers.
7. If the numbers match, she gets to keep them and take another turn. If they don't match, the player should try and memorize the position of those particular numbers as she turns them over again.
8. The next player turns over two shells and the play proceeds until all the shells are collected.

✚ *Anne Adeney, Plymouth, United Kingdom*

Jump and Tell

patterns

Materials

simple pattern cards showing color or shape patterns
2 stepstools

What to do

1. Place the pattern cards on the floor face down, about 1' apart from each other.
2. Place the two stepstools next to each other in front of the cards.
3. Invite the children to form two single-file lines behind the stepstools.
4. Demonstrate how to play the game. Step on the stepstool, jump off, and pick up a pattern card. Read the pattern aloud (red, blue, red, blue).
5. Turn the card back over and go back into the line.
6. Invite the children to play the game, jumping and naming patterns.

More to do

Display a second set of pattern cards at a table along with an assortment of manipulative such as blocks, linking cubes, beads, and so on. Encourage children to create or copy patterns at the learning center.

✚ *Mary J. Murray, Mazomanie, WI*

Jumpin' Frog Board Game

addition

Materials

egg carton
green tempera paint
large green pompom ball
wiggle eyes
glue
scissors
green felt
marker
paper
dice

Games

What to do

1. Paint the bottom half of an egg carton with green tempera paint. Let it dry.
2. Make a frog using a large green pompom ball. Glue two wiggle eyes on the pompom and add felt feet.
3. Write numerals on small paper circles. These are the lily pads. Glue them into the bottom of the egg carton.
4. Roll the dice and have the frog jump from lily pad to lily pad.
5. Help the children say and add the numbers as they go.

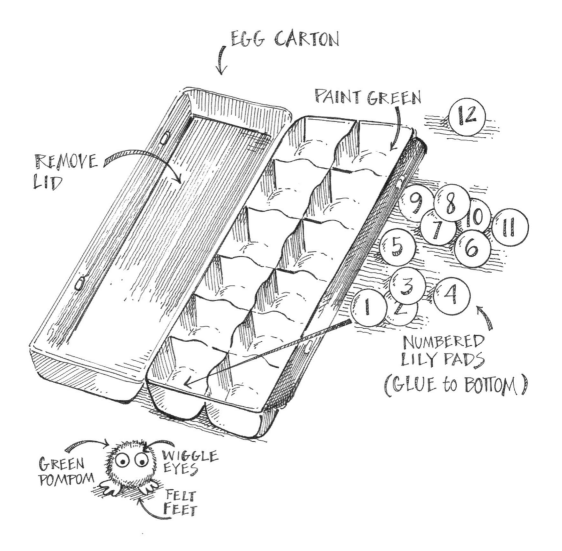

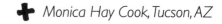 *Monica Hay Cook, Tucson, AZ*

Leaping Lily Pads!

numeral recognition

Materials
10 die-cut frogs
marker
blue plastic round tablecloth or blue butcher paper cut into a circle
10 small green party plates or small cardboard pizza bottoms and green paint

What to do
1. On each frog, draw a number of spots to coordinate with the numerals 0–9.
2. Make lily pads using small green party plates or small pizza bottoms. If using pizza cardboard, paint them green.
3. Number the lily pads from 0–9.
4. Show the children the new "pond." Tell them that each frog is lost and needs help finding her home on the right lily pad.
5. The children match the number of spots on the frogs to the numbers on the lily pads.
6. Let each child take a turn playing the game.

✚ *Shelley F. Hoster, Norcross, GA*

Lift and Say

counting sets, numeral recognition

Materials
6 medium-sized boxes
craft knife (adult only)
6 beanbag animals
twist ties
sets of objects
number cards
plastic hoops
garden/floral wire

What to do

1. Cut the flaps off the boxes so that one side is open.
2. Attach a beanbag animal to the top of each box: Put the open side of the box face down on the floor. Poke two holes in the center of the top of the box, about 2" apart. Attach the animal between the two holes by wrapping a piece of garden wire over the animal and through the two holes. Use a twist tie to attach it securely to the box.
3. Place a set amount of objects or a number card on the floor and cover it with a box.
4. Place a trail of hoops across the floor leading to the boxes.
5. Hold one hoop on its side near the end of the trail for children to crawl through, or attach it to a chair so it will stand on its side.
6. Explain to the class that they have to step inside the trail of hoops and then crawl through the final hoop to get to the special boxes.
7. Once a child travels the course, she lifts one box to see what's underneath. If it's a set of objects, she counts them. If it's a number, she identifies it.

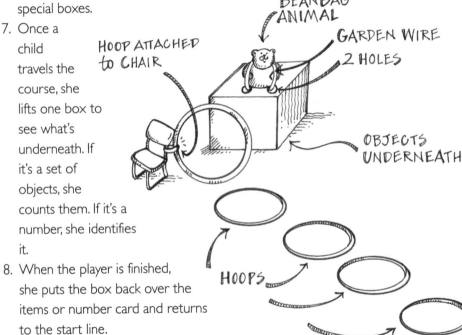

8. When the player is finished, she puts the box back over the items or number card and returns to the start line.
9. Continue the game as players travel the course of hoops and look beneath a different box each time.

More to do

Transitions: Use this activity as part of your daily transition routine. When it's time for children to go home, have them travel the course and peek beneath a box before they get to pack up and leave for the day.

✚ *Mary J. Murray, Mazomanie, WI*

The Match Game

numeral recognition, counting sets

Materials   colored cardstock 3" x 5" (or a size similar to a deck of cards)
markers

What to do
1. In advance, make two sets of cards with the numerals 0–10 on one side. Make two more sets with dots on one side to correspond to the numbers 0 to 10.
2. Shuffle the cards together.
3. Put the deck face down in the middle of the players (two to four children).
4. The first player draws two cards, names the numerals, and counts the dots to see how many are in the set. If these two cards are a matching set, the player places the match face down in a separate area to count later.
5. If the first two draws do not make a set, the next player draws two cards.
6. After all the players have drawn their first two cards, the play continues as players draw only one card after the first round.
7. Players keep the cards in their hand on the table or on the rug in front of them.
8. By showing the cards in their "hands," the other players can help them count correctly and help them recognize a match.
9. Play continues until all the cards have been drawn.

✚ *Susan Oldham Hill, Lakeland, FL*

Matching Hearts

matching

Materials   wallpaper sample books
scissors
markers
heart shape
manila envelope

What to do
1. Cut out two heart shapes from each pattern of wallpaper (make at least 20 hearts in 10 different patterns).
2. On the back, label each heart pair with a numeral and the corresponding number of dots. For example, write a 5 on one heart in the pair and draw five dots on the matching heart. Store the hearts in a manila envelope.
3. Encourage the children to match the pairs based on the numerals and the dots. When they have found a pair, have them turn the hearts over to see if the patterns match.
4. Children can play individually or with partners.

Related books
Bee My Valentine by Miriam Cohen
Valentine's Day by Gail Gibbons
Valentine's Day Is... by Gail Gibbons

✚ *Sandy L. Scott, Meridian, ID*

Matching Keys

matching

Materials
variety of old keys
copy machine
paper or tagboard
laminating film
tray

What to do
1. Make photocopies of keys on sheets of paper or tagboard. Make copies of several different arrangements and number of keys.
2. Write the number of keys on the back of each sheet before laminating.
3. Have the children match the keys to the appropriate key on the sheet.
4. Encourage them to count the number of keys and check their answers on the back of the sheet.

✚ *Sandy L. Scott, Meridian, ID*

Money Dominoes

coin identification, money values

Materials   pattern of a domino (4" × 2" rectangle divided in the middle)
tagboard
colored pictures of various coins
scissors
copy machine
glue stick
laminator

What to do   1. Make a set of dominoes with coins instead of dots.
2. To make a set of money dominoes, copy domino patterns onto tagboard. Make enough so that each child will get one.
3. Glue each coin picture onto separate ends of a domino.
4. Laminate the dominoes for durability, and cut out.

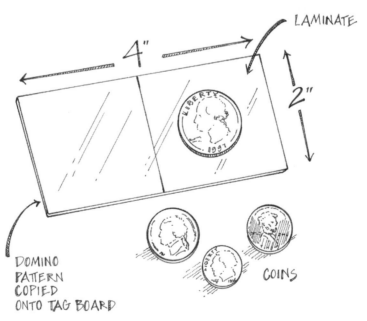

5. Explain that Abraham Lincoln is on a penny, Thomas Jefferson is on a nickel, Franklin D. Roosevelt is on a dime, and George Washington is on a quarter. Discuss what is on the reverse side of each coin as well.
6. To play the game, mix up the dominoes. Place them face down in the center of the table or play area.
7. Have each player choose five dominoes and hold them so the other player(s) cannot see them.

8. Move the extra supply of dominoes to one side.
9. Place one domino face up in the middle of the playing space.
10. The first player tries to match either end of the beginning domino with one from her playing pieces.
11. If the player cannot make a match, then one domino from the supply is chosen by that player and he tries again until a match can be made or until she has drawn three dominoes.
12. Play continues around the table, with each player trying to add a domino to the display. Players build off the ends of doubles as well as at the ends of a domino train.
13. The game ends when one player runs out of dominoes or until no more matches can be made.
14. The player with the fewest dominoes remaining wins the game.

✚ *Jackie Wright, Enid, OK*

Mouse House

· ·

numeral recognition

Materials

construction paper or poster board
scissors
marker

What to do

1. Using a simple pattern or die cut machine, make 10 to 15 simple houses out of construction paper, and write a different numeral on each one.
2. Draw or die cut a mouse out of brown or gray paper. It should be small enough to hide behind the houses without being seen.
3. Place the houses on the floor and hide the mouse behind one.
4. Gather the children and introduce the new game. Tell them that this is a "number neighborhood," and that each house has a different number.
5. Tell them that there is a mouse hiding in one of them and they are to guess which one by calling out the number.

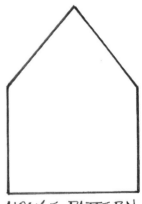

HOUSE PATTERN

MOUSE PATTERN

6. Select the first child to guess which house the mouse is hiding in, and invite all the children to recite the following rhyme:

Little mouse, little mouse,
Are you in the (number) house?

7. Lift up the house and see if the child was right. If not, replace the house and keep guessing and saying the rhyme until the mouse if found. The child who guesses correctly can choose where to hide her next.

✚ *Shelley F. Hoster, Norcross, GA*

Mystery Shape Bag

shape recognition

Materials
poster board or tagboard
scissors
laminator (optional)
paper shopping bag or plain gift bag with handles

What to do
1. Cut out one of each shape from poster board or tagboard. Laminate for durability, if desired.
2. Decorate a paper bag with colored shapes and write "Mystery Shape Bag" on the front, and put the shapes inside.
3. Gather the children and tell them that they are going to play a game. Show the mystery shape bag to the children.

4. Introduce the following song to the tune of "Twinkle, Twinkle, Little Star":

I have the mystery shape bag, look and see.
Inside are some shapes for you and me,
Which one will we pull out? Wait and see.
Can you name this shape? One, two, three!

5. On three, pull out one of the shapes and see if the children can name it.

✚ *Shelley F. Hoster, Norcross, GA*

Numeral Puzzles

printing numerals

Materials
various types and colors of paper (wrapping paper, newspaper, brown bags, copy paper, and so on)
12" × 18" sheets of tagboard
laminator
scissors

What to do
1. Cut a 12" long numeral from each type of paper.
2. Glue each numeral to a sheet of tagboard and laminate.
3. Cut the laminated numerals into two to eight pieces (depending on children's skill level).
4. Keep one piece of each numeral puzzle for yourself and hand out the remaining puzzle pieces to the children. Explain that this is a "silent number game."
5. Put one piece of a numeral puzzle on the floor.
6. The children with the remaining pieces of that puzzle come forward and put the numeral puzzle together without talking.
7. After the first group completes the puzzle, give them a round of applause and have them sit back down in their places.
8. Put out a piece of the next puzzle and continue the game until all the puzzles are complete.

More to do   Store each collection of puzzle pieces in a manila envelope. Invite the children to work independently to put one or more puzzles together. Help the children write their name on the envelope after they complete the puzzle so you can keep track of who has accomplished the task.

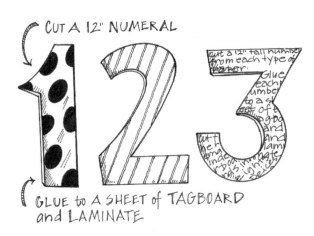

CUT A 12" NUMERAL

GLUE to A SHEET of TAGBOARD and LAMINATE

CUT INTO PIECES

PUT ONE PIECE ON the FLOOR

✚ Mary J. Murray, Mazomanie, WI

Number Toss

* *

numeral recognition, ordering

Materials   5 beanbags labeled 1–5

What to do
1. Ask a child to choose a partner.
2. The child tosses the beanbags to the other child in random order. As the child catches a beanbag, she calls out the numeral printed on the beanbag.
3. When all five have been tossed to the catcher, she puts them in the correct order and counts them again out loud to the first player.
4. For the second part of the game, the catcher becomes the beanbag thrower and repeats the steps with her partner.
5. Increase the challenge of the game by adding five more beanbags with the numerals 6–10 written on them.

✚ Susan Oldham Hill, Lakeland, FL

Games

Object Sort

mathematical operations, sorting

Materials   large container
buttons, bottle caps, old keys, or any other small items

What to do   1. Place the items in a container and give it to a child.
2. Invite the child to sort and classify the items into piles: keys, buttons, and so forth.
3. Then have the child explain how the items in each pile are alike and how they are different. For example, some buttons may be big and some small; some keys may be silver while others are gold.
4. Ask another child to choose one of the piles and organize the items by one characteristic, such as length. The child might put the items end to end and compare and contrast what she sees. For example, how many are short keys? Long keys?
5. Ask another child to use the items in another pile of items to solve a simple math problem, such as:
    ■ If you have 10 bottle caps and give me two, how many will you have left?
    ■ If you have three big buttons and three small ones, how many will you have altogether?
6. For older children, create activities that challenge them to use mathematical reasoning. Ask them, for example, to look closely at items and answer questions such as:
    ■ Is a gold colored key always heavier than a silver colored one?
    ■ Do the big buttons always have more holes that the smaller ones?

✚ *Virginia Jean Herrod, Columbia, SC*

On Top of Spaghetti

counting, sequencing

Materials
cream-colored yarn
red felt
black Velcro dots
brown pompoms
4 plastic plates
3-sided die (1–3)

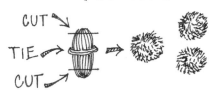

MEATBALL

CUT
TIE
CUT

6" RED CIRCLE (SAUCE)

YARN (SPAGHETTI)
PLATE

What to do

1. Prepare the game pieces by cutting cream-colored yarn into 6" long pieces (spaghetti) and red felt into a 6" circle (for sauce). Attach four black dots to the felt circle (children will use these to attach pompom meatballs).

2. To play the game, each child selects a plate. The object of the game is for the children to take turns rolling a die and selecting one portion of the food, based on a number correspondence. For instance, if a child rolls a one, she puts spaghetti on her plate. If she rolls a two, she puts sauce. If she rolls a three, she puts a meatball on her plate.

3. Explain to the children that they have to roll the foods in order, first the spaghetti, then the sauce, and finally the meatballs.

4. The first player to get the spaghetti, sauce, and all four meatballs (in order) wins.

5. When the children are proficient at the game, start using a six-sided die, and have one and four stand for spaghetti, two and five stand for sauce, and three and six stand for meatballs.

Related books *Cloudy with a Chance of Meatballs* by Judi Barrett
Spaghetti and Meatballs for All by Marilyn Burns

✚ *Kristi Larson, Spirit Lake, IA*

Penny, Nickel, Dime

addition, reasoning, subtraction

Materials

die
pennies
nickels
dimes

What to do

1. Up to four children can play this game with you. Each player rolls the die and says the number.

2. Give the player that number of pennies. Explain that each penny is worth one cent.

3. When a player gets five pennies, replace the pennies with a nickel. Explain that five pennies have the same value as one nickel (five cents).

4. When a player gets five more pennies, replace the pennies and the nickel with a dime. Help the children see that the value of five pennies plus the value of one nickel (five cents) equals 10 cents, which is the value of one dime.

5. The first player to reach a set amount (25 cents, for example) wins.
   Note: Children can be confused by money, often believing that the larger-size coins are worth more. As you play this game, compare the sizes of the coins and point out their value to emphasize that larger does not always mean the coin is worth more.

6. Leave the coins out for supervised use. Notice if the children attempt to sort them or compare their values.

✚ *Virginia Jean Herrod, Columbia, SC*

Photo Task

sets

Materials
family photographs
push pins
bulletin board

What to do
1. Ask the children to bring in one color family photograph.
2. Use push pins to hang the photographs on the bulletin board.
3. Divide the children into groups.
4. Ask one child from each group to count the number of men, women, and children in the photographs. Other options are to ask how many people in the photographs are wearing a particular color, how many are wearing glasses, or another category.
5. A time limit can be set for the task to be completed.

✚ *Shyamala Shanmugasundaram, Nerul, Navi Mumbai, India*

Race Car Track

charting, measurement

Materials
large books
cardboard
blocks
masking tape
measuring tape
small cars
writing paper

What to do

1. On a smooth floor or long table, make a gradual incline out of tiled books or sturdy cardboard by putting blocks underneath them. Use masking tape to make a start and finish line at either end of the track.
2. Measure the length of the inclined "track" with measuring tape.
3. Give each child a toy car to run down the track.
4. Measure the distance from the start line to where each child's car stops on the track.
5. Set up a chart to keep track of the distance each child's car travels on the track, and discuss with the children which cars went the farthest and shortest distances, what the average distance was, and so on.

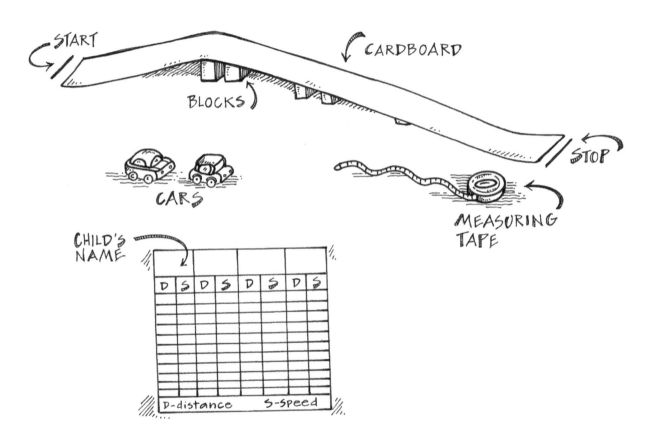

START
CARDBOARD
BLOCKS
STOP
CARS
MEASURING TAPE
CHILD'S NAME

D	S	D	S	D	S	D	S	D	S

D–distance   S–speed

✚ *Kathleen Wallace, Columbia, MO*

Roll a Shape

shape recognition

Materials

small cube or box shaped like a cube
paper shapes
glue
an assortment of small plastic shapes
small containers

What to do

1. In advance, set a limit for the game, either with a timer or by deciding on a number of shapes to collect during the game. Also in advance, tape paper shapes to the sides of the cube to make a shape die.
2. Provide each player with a small container. Spread the assorted shapes on the table or rug.
3. The first player rolls the die and then finds the plastic shape that matches the shape on the die.
4. Repeat with each player in turn.
5. As a variation, ask all the players to choose a matching shape when a player rolls the die.

✚ *Susan Oldham Hill, Lakeland, FL*

Rolling Dice Bingo Game

numeral recognition

Materials

black marker
construction paper
2 dice
several buttons

What to do

1. Make a 9-square grid (3 squares up and 3 squares across) on several sheets of construction paper. Write a numeral from 2–12 in each space on the grid. Do this for all of the grids, writing the numerals randomly to make bingo boards. There are 11 numbers between 2 and 12, so each grid will not have all of the numbers.

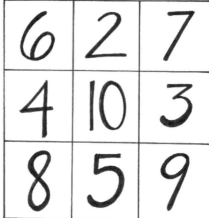

2. Give each child a bingo board. Have them take turns rolling the dice.

3. Call out the number rolled each time. Help the children look to see if the number rolled is on their card. If so, they cover the numeral with a button.

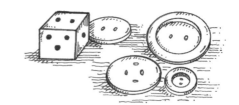

4. When a child has three squares in a row filled (or the entire sheet, depending on how you choose to play), that child calls out, "Bingo!"

5. Continue until all the children have bingo.

✚ *Mary Brehm, Aurora, OH*

The Secret Button

patterns

Materials

buttons of various shapes and sizes

What to do

1. Put out several different kinds of buttons.

2. Talk to the children about the various characteristics of the buttons; for example, discuss the number of holes in the center, the color, size, shape, and material of the buttons.

3. Select one secret button.
4. Invite the children to take turns asking questions about the characteristics of the button.
5. Answer their questions with a "yes" or "no." The children figure out the secret button through the process of elimination.

Related book   *The Button Box* by Margarette S. Reid

✚ *Monica Hay Cook, Tucson, AZ*

Shake It Up

counting, numeral recognition

Materials   egg carton
permanent marker
die
stencils of the numerals 1–6
crayons

What to do   1. In advance, mark the bottom of the cups of the egg carton with the numerals 1–6. Write each number twice so that all the cups have a numeral.
2. Use a stencil to write the outlines of the numerals 1–6 (do not color them in) on a piece of paper. Make at least two of each number. Make a copy for each child.
3. To play, ask the first player to put the die in the egg carton and close it. Demonstrate shaking it gently.
4. Next, the first player opens the carton to see where the die landed.
5. Ask the child to name the numeral on the carton, and then invite her to color in the number on her stenciled numeral sheet.
6. Continue until all the children have had a turn naming and coloring in the numbers.

Related books   *Count and See* by Tana Hoban
Green Eggs and Ham by Dr. Seuss
One Fish, Two Fish, Red Fish, Blue Fish by Dr. Seuss

✚ *Susan Oldham Hill, Lakeland, FL*

The Shape Game

matching, shapes

Materials

markers
tagboard
crayons
small piece of cardboard
scissors
brad
game board markers

What to do

1. Make a board game using a piece of tagboard.
2. Draw double curved lines on the tagboard to create a curvy road.
3. Write "start" at the beginning of the road and "end" at the end of the road.
4. Mark off spaces.
5. Draw shapes (circles, squares, triangles, rectangles, and diamonds) in the spaces. Feel free to use shapes more than once.
6. The children can color in the spaces using crayons.
7. Using a smaller piece of tagboard, make a spinner. Draw a large circle on the board and then divide it into four sections.
8. Draw one of the shapes in each section.
9. Cut out a cardboard arrow and attach it with a brad to the center of the circle.

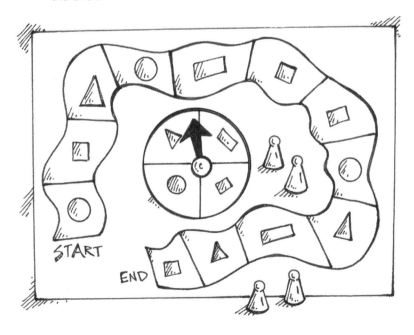

10. Give each child a game board marker. The children place their markers at the start of the road.

11. Have them take turns spinning and moving their markers as indicated on the spinner.

12. The children play until one of the players reaches the end.

Related book   *The Shape of Me and Other Stuff* by Dr. Seuss

✛ *Monica Hay Cook, Tucson, AZ*

Shape and Number Hopscotch

numeral and shape recognition

Materials   plastic hopscotch grid or outdoor hopscotch grid
marker, chalk, or tape
colored beanbags

What to do
1. Use a permanent marker, chalk, or tape to add six new squares to a hopscotch grid.

2. Draw a shape in each added square (see illustration on the following page).

3. Have the children form a circle around the grid.

4. Hand beanbags to several children and invite them to take turns tossing their beanbag onto the grid.

5. Whenever a beanbag lands on a number or shape, the children recite that number or shape in unison.

6. If a child misses the grid completely, the nearest child may pick it up and toss it back to the child.

7. After a child tosses a beanbag onto the grid, she sits down.

8. Once the beanbags have landed on the grid, invite two "helpers" to gather the beanbags and toss them to the children that remain standing in the circle.

9. When everyone is sitting down, invite all the children to stand, join hands, and circle around the grid as they sing a favorite number song.

10. Repeat the activity several times.

More to do

Language and Literacy: Create an assortment of alphabet hopscotch grids on the playground. Invite the children to hop along the grid and name the letters as they land on them.

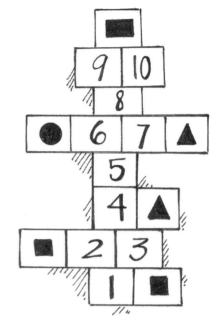

✚ *Mary J. Murray, Mazomanie, WI*

Shapes Bingo

matching, shape recognition

Materials

8 ½" x 11" pieces of heavy card stock paper (one for each child plus one more)
markers
brad
plastic spinner
bingo chips

What to do

■ Prepare the cards:

1. Divide all but one of the cards into six equal sections.
2. Draw a large circle on the remaining card and divide it into six pie-shaped sections.
3. Draw one of the following shapes in each of the pie sections on the circle: circle, diamond, square, triangle, rectangle, and star.
4. Attach the arrow to the middle of the circle with the paper brad.

5. Draw a shape (circle, diamond, square, triangle, rectangle, and star) in each of the six sections of the bingo cards.

■ Play the game:
1. Give each child a bingo card.
2. Let the children take turns spinning the spinner.
3. Encourage the children to name the shape the spinner lands on. If anyone has the shape on their card (all will) they cover it with a bingo chip.
4. Continue until all of the children have covered all of the shapes on their cards. In this game, everyone will win at once!

More to do Encourage the children to look for shapes around them: on the floor, the ceiling, window, doors, clothing, trees, flowers, vehicles, and so on.

Related song **Shapes Are Everywhere** (Tune: "Twinkle, Twinkle, Little Star")
Circle, rectangle, triangle, square,
There are shapes everywhere;
On the ceiling, on the floor,
Keep on looking, you'll find more.
Circle, rectangle, triangle, square,
There are shapes everywhere.

✚ *Virgina Jean Herrod, Columbia, SC*

The Shoebox Game

matching

Materials 10 pairs of shoes
20 shoeboxes
acrylic paint
paintbrushes
smocks

What to do 1. Ask the children to bring a shoebox to class.
2. Have them paint their shoeboxes with acrylic paint.
3. Place the shoeboxes upside down on the floor in five rows, with four boxes in each row.
4. Ask the children to remove their shoes.

5. When the children are not watching, place one shoe under each of the shoeboxes.

6. Let the children take turns trying to find the matching pairs of shoes.

More to do   Play the matching game with pairs of socks, gloves, two decks of playing cards, or cloth napkins.

Related books   *A Pair of Socks* by Stuart J. Murphy
Seaweed Soup by Stuart J. Murphy

✚ *Randi Lynn Mrvos, Lexington, KY*

Signal Station

counting

Materials   flashlights
2 sets of number cards from 1 to 10
box or bag

What to do   1. Choose two children or two groups of children to operate the signal stations in opposite places in the room.

2. Give each group a flashlight and a set of number cards in a box or bag.

3. Turn off the lights and ask one group to draw a card from the bag. They will then signal the other group by flashing the flashlight the correct number of flashes to correspond to the numeral on the card. Remind them to flash slowly so the other group has a chance to count accurately.

4. The children at the other signal station are to count the number of flashes and find the matching number card. If desired, they can either flash back the same number so the first signalers will know the message was sent correctly, or draw a new number and flash out that number.

✚ *Susan Oldham Hill, Lakeland, FL*

Sock Sort

classification, counting, patterns, sorting

Materials
various colors of socks
basket
colored sheets of paper (same colors as the socks)

What to do
1. Invite each child to take a sock from the basket and put it on her right foot.
2. Display the colored sheets of paper on the wall in different corners of the room.
3. On the command of "one, two, three: sort," the children crawl to the corner of the room that matches their sock (red socks go to the red corner, and so on).
4. Call the children back to the circle and have them exchange socks with someone with a different color sock.
5. Place two sheets of colored paper together (black and white or red and blue). Children with red or blue socks (or other two colors) go to the same area and create an AB pattern with their socked foot extended out in front of them.
6. Invite the children to verbalize the pattern in unison.

✚ *Mary J. Murray, Mazomanie, WI*

Spaghetti and Meatballs

counting

Materials
40 12" strands of yellow or white yarn, or rope
4 brown or red sock balls (one sock rolled up and tucked inside the open end)
4-quart cooking pot with lid
4 large plastic bowls
die

What to do
1. Put the spaghetti (yarn strands) and meatballs (sock balls) inside a cooking pot with a lid. Place all the materials together at a table.
2. Invite a child to roll the die and count the number of dots facing up.
3. The child counts out the same number of pieces of spaghetti and places them in a bowl.
4. Let the child repeat the activity for the other three bowls.
5. When the child is finished, she places a "meatball" on top of the bowl of spaghetti.
6. For older children, use two dice. Ask the children to count the total number of pieces of spaghetti and meatballs that are in the pot.

✚ *Mary J. Murray, Mazomanie, WI*

Tagboard Colors

matching

Materials
tagboard in different colors
scissors
wooden clothespins
paint
marker
laminator

What to do
1. Cut out a variety of shapes from tagboard (approximately 4" x 4"). Paint wooden clothespins to match the colors of the tagboard (make several of each color).
2. Write a numeral on the front of the tagboard and laminate.
3. Invite the children to place the correct number of clothespins on the tagboard shape to match the color and numeral.
4. Write numerals on both sides of the tagboard to have twice the fun.

✚ *Sandy L. Scott, Meridian, ID*

Teddy Bear Counting

counting, recognizing sets

Materials
teddy bear counters
paper and marker
large six-sided die, or a spinner with six spaces on it

What to do
1. Prepare a board game by separating a sheet of paper into six equal squares and writing a numeral (1–6) in each square.
2. Choose four children to play the game, and give each of them six counters.
3. The first player rolls the die or spins the spinner and puts the same number of counters on the square of the board that matches the numeral on the die. For example, if she rolls a three, she puts three counters on the 3 square of the game board. That numeral (3 in this case) can no longer be used.
4. Each child takes a turn, and is only able to set her counters down on an open square. The first child to set down all her counters is the winner.

✚ *Iris Rothstein, New Hyde Park, NY*

Throw and Tally (Indoor Snowball Throw)

making tally marks, one-to-one correspondence

Materials
white paper
wastebasket
paper and pencil, or dry-erase board with marker

What to do
1. Group the children into pairs, and help each pair write their names on paper or the dry-erase board.
2. Invite the children to stand about 3' from an empty wastebasket and throw wadded sheets of white paper at the basket, one at a time.

3. Every time one child gets a piece of paper into the basket, the other child makes a note of it on the paper or dry-erase board.
4. At the end, help the children tally their totals to see how many "snowballs" went in the basket.

Related books　*Elmer in the Snow* by David McKee
Snowballs by Lois Elhert

✚ *Sue Fleischmann, Sussex, WI*

Tic-Tac-Toe

counting, logic

Materials　2 sheets of craft foam
scissors
contact cement
10 game pieces

What to do
1. Make your own tic-tac-toe game board using craft foam.
2. Cut an 8" square from black craft foam for the background.
3. Cut out a grid using a contrasting color of craft foam to expose nine spaces.
4. Glue the grid on top of the black background using contact cement.
5. Instead of Xs and Os, use seasonal erasers, craft foam shapes, or thematic objects as game pieces. You will need five game pieces for each player.
6. If all 10 game pieces are alike, have a separate color for each of the two players.
7. Teach the children the rules of the game, and challenge them to consider game strategy as they play.

✚ *Jackie Wright, Enid, OK*

A Valuable Trip

addition, coin identification, money values

Materials
tagboard
color markers
crayons
game markers
real or play money (pennies, nickels, dimes, quarters)
piggy bank or jar
dice

What to do
1. Make a game board using a piece of tagboard. Draw double lines to create a road. Make it curvy.
2. Put an arrow at the beginning and a $ sign, jar, or piggy bank at the end.
3. Mark off spaces.
4. Draw coins and write the values in the spaces, for example, 1¢, 3¢, 5¢, 10¢, and 25¢. You can use the same value more than once.
5. Add other interesting directions in the spaces, such as: go back 1 space, go ahead two spaces, take a rest, and skip one turn.
6. Invite the children to color in the spaces using crayons.
7. Put real coins in the jar or piggy bank.
8. To play the game, the children take turns rolling the dice.

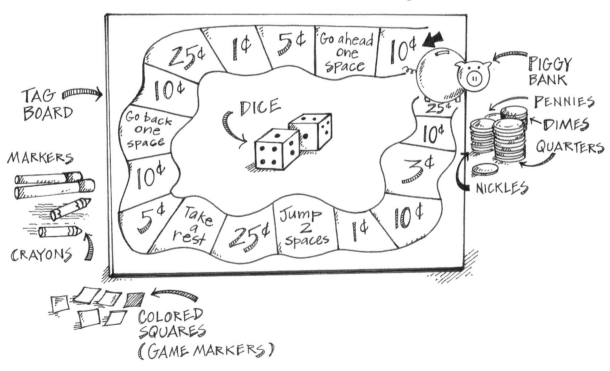

9. When someone lands on a square with cents, they take that many cents out of the jar. Of course, they have to follow what the other spaces say as well.

10. At the end, the children count their coins to see how much money they collected along the way.

11. To make the game more challenging for older children, add spaces where money has to be paid out for things along the way (this offers practice with subtraction).

Related books *The Coin Counting Book* by Rozanne Lanczak Williams
Pigs Will Be Pigs: Fun with Math and Money by Amy Axelrod

✚ *Monica Hay Cook, Tucson, AZ*

We Clap

addition

Materials index cards
marker
2 dice
dry-erase board or sheet of paper

What to do
1. In advance, make a stack of activity cards labeled with movements such as jump, hop, turn around, touch your toes, clap, shrug your shoulders, touch your nose, and shake your hips.

2. Divide the children into two groups.

3. Have the first child from each group roll a die and say what the number is.

4. Write each child's number, spaced apart, on the board.

5. Turn over the top activity card and read what is says, "We're going to clap."

6. The children from the first group use the number that was rolled by their team member (for example, a five) and say, "We clap (one, two, three, four, five) times," while performing the action.

7. The children from the other group go next, using the number their team member rolled.

8. With the help of the children, add the numbers together on a piece of paper or dry-erase board. Say, "Group one clapped five times and group two clapped two times. Together they clapped seven times." Write the equation $5 + 2 = 7$.

9. Have both groups clap seven times together.

10. Repeat so that all get a chance to roll the dice, using a different activity card each round.

More to do

Language and Literacy: Write the numbers as words under the numerals on the board so the children can learn word numbers for the numerals. For example:

$5 + 2 = 7$

five + two = seven

✚ *Susan Grenfell, Cedar Park, TX*

What's Missing?

basic geometry

Materials

dark or thick cloth
four different shapes (from an attribute set)

What to do

1. Introduce the shapes to the children, telling them the names of each one.
2. Cover all the shapes with the cloth, and remove one without the children seeing which one you take away.
3. Pull back the cloth, and ask the children to identify which shape is missing.
4. As the children become proficient at the game, consider removing two shapes at a time, or making the four shapes different colors, and having the children name the shape and the color that is missing.

Related books

My Very First Book of Shapes by Eric Carle
Shapes, Shapes, Shapes by Tana Hoban

✚ *Linda Ford, Sacramento, CA*

What's Remaining? A Problem-Solving Game

problem solving

Materials   5–10 small objects (erasers, assorted crayons, coins, stickers, marbles)

What to do
1. Show the objects to the class and ask them to try and remember each one for a guessing game.
2. Choose five volunteers (one for each object) to come to the front of the room and hide an object behind their back. Move the five children around so the rest of the class will not remember where the objects are.
3. Ask a review question about a concept they have learned prior to this activity. The children who answer correctly may choose one of the five children up front to reveal a hidden object. The child shows it to the class, places it on a visible surface, and joins the rest of the children.
4. Continue asking review questions until only one child is left standing with the "mystery" object still hidden. Ask: "What's remaining?" Encourage the children to look at the objects on the table and use the process of elimination to guess what it is. The child reveals the object after it is guessed.
5. Play the game again until everyone has had a chance to be in front of the class.

Related book   *I Spy School Days* by Jean Marzollo

✚ *Dawnelle Breum, London, ON, Canada*

Birthday Party

counting, numeral recognition

Materials
large balloon
marker
number cards
birthday party hats and blowers
brown paper lunch bags
streamers and extra balloons (optional)

What to do
1. Each time you celebrate a child's birthday, play this fun birthday party game.
2. Blow up a balloon and print the numerals 1–10 and write "Happy Birthday" on it.
3. Give the balloon to the birthday child and let him sit in a special "birthday chair" at the front of the class. (If desired, decorate the chair with streamers and balloons.)
4. Give each child a party hat and blower.
5. Begin to tell a birthday story about the birthday child, incorporating numbers into your story. Display number cards and point to the numerals as you tell the story.
6. Instruct children to listen for the number words in the story. As you say each number, pause and allow the children to blow their party blower the designated number of times. Then continue the story.

   Sample story:
   Sophie turned four years old today. She invited three friends over for cake. Her mother put four candles on the cake. Sophie ate one piece. There were two girls at her party and one boy. Sophie opened five presents that day. Her dad surprised her with two brand new puppies. The children stayed until six o'clock to celebrate with Sophie. Sophie thanked her three friends before they went home.

7. Afterwards, invite each child to give a round of applause to the birthday child as they sing "Happy Birthday" and blow their blowers.
8. Print each child's name on a brown paper lunch bag and on their blower and hat. Store each child's blower and hat in their bag until the next classmate's birthday arrives.
9. Repeat the activity on each child's birthday, telling a different number story each time.

✚ *Mary J. Murray, Mazomanie, WI*

Book of Graphs

comparison, counting

Materials
tagboard
computer or markers
laminator
scissors
page protectors
binding machine
color copies of classroom graphing activities

What to do
1. Make a book to display all your classroom-created graphs.
2. Make a book cover by printing the title "Our Classroom Graphing Activities" on a piece of tagboard. Laminate the front and back covers for durability and cut out.
3. Purchase a supply of top-loading page protectors or make your own from leftover laminating scraps.
4. Bind the page protectors inside the covers using a binding machine.
5. During the year after each graphing activity, make a color copy of the graph results. Take a photo or use your computer to generate and reproduce the graphs.
6. Slide these into the page protectors. At the end of the year, you'll have an organized record of your classroom graphs on many different topics.
7. Place the book in a center for the children to look through during free time.
8. Share the book with parents who visit the classroom for conferences or open houses, or send it home with one child at a time as a "Traveling Book of Graphs" to share with his family.

✚ *Jackie Wright, Enid, OK*

Counting in Context

counting

Materials   none

What to do
1. To raise children's interest in math, give them several examples of when it is helpful to be able to count:

   ■ counting time in line when getting a drink at the water fountain
   ■ waiting for a turn at the swings and counting the number of times each child swings
   ■ knowing how many steps it is to the playground
   ■ scrubbing hands at least 25 seconds when washing
   ■ keeping track of pairs of shoes, socks, mittens, and so on

2. Encourage the children to think of other times it is useful to know how to count.

✚ *Ellen Javernik, Loveland, CO*

Dalmatian Counting Cards

counting, numeral recognition

Materials   10 white 5" x 7" index cards with outlines of dogs on them
black paper circles
marker
glue

What to do
1. Write a numeral from 1 to 10 on each of the dog outlines.
2. The children select a dog outline and count out the corresponding number of dots (for example, three dots on the numeral 3 dog).
3. The children glue the correct number of spots on the dog.
4. Display the counting cards in the math area.

5. Use this concept for other animals, such as cheetahs, zebras, or tigers.

6. This is a great way to involve children in making counting cards to use in the classroom.

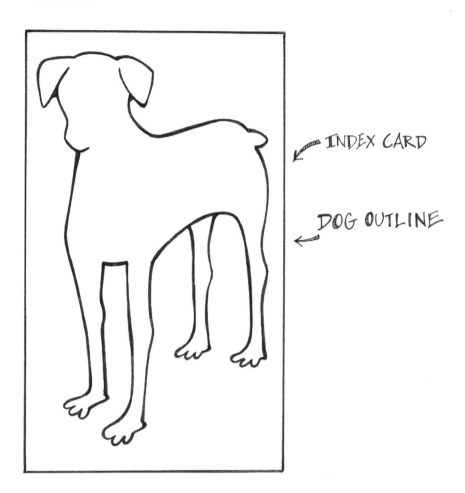

INDEX CARD

DOG OUTLINE

Related books   *101 Dalmatians* by Dodie Smith
Harry the Dirty Dog by Gene Zion
No Dragons for Tea by Jean Pendziwol

✚ *Kristi Larson, Spirit Lake, IA*

Graph Mat

one-to-one correspondence, sorting

Materials

tagboard
computer or marker
laminator
scissors
manipulatives

What to do

1. Make your own computer-generated graph mat by inserting a table with a word processing program to create the desired number of columns and rows.
2. Print the resulting grid on tagboard turned horizontally with the caption "Graph Mat" underneath.
3. Laminate for durability, and cut out.
4. Put the graph mat in a center with manipulatives such as bear counters, farm animals, or rainforest animals.
5. Teach the children to classify and organize the manipulatives by color, shape, or size. Show them how to place one manipulative on each square of the grid.
6. Count and compare the manipulatives.

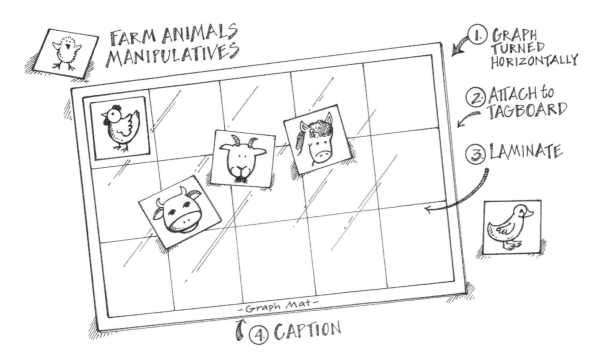

FARM ANIMALS MANIPULATIVES

1. GRAPH TURNED HORIZONTALLY
2. ATTACH to TAGBOARD
3. LAMINATE

—Graph Mat—

4. CAPTION

✚ *Jackie Wright, Enid, OK*

Graph of the Day

graphing

Materials

long white vinyl window shade
permanent marker
small photo of each child
index cards or card stock
clear packaging tape
yardstick

Preparation

1. Roll open the window shade and hold or tape it down on a flat surface for easy drawing.
2. Use permanent marker to draw four parallel lines down the length of the shade, making five columns.
3. Starting at the bottom of the shade, draw lines along the width of the shade until there are a few more spaces than there are children.
4. Starting at the bottom again, skip one row, and begin numbering the rows from 0 to 20 (depending on the number of children in the class).
5. Mount each child's photo on an index card or card stock and cover with a layer of plastic tape. Help the children write their names on the card beneath their photos.

① UNROLL SHADE
② TAPE DOWN ON FLAT SURFACE

22
21
20
19
18
17
16
15
14
13
12
11
10
9
8
7
6
5
4
3
2
1
0

BLANK

yes   no   sort of

What to do

1. Pick a question of the day each day. Use the bottom spaces on the graph as places for response labels (such as a happy face for *yes* or a sad face for *no*).
2. Put the graph on the floor, and ask the children the question of the day. For example, "Did you drink milk at breakfast?" or "Do you have a dog?"
3. Invite the children to respond by placing their picture cards in boxes in the appropriate columns.
4. Discuss the results, using numbers and comparison words like *more* and *less*.

✚ *Ellen Javernik, Loveland, CO*

Graphing

counting, graphing

Materials

large easel paper or dry-erase boards and appropriate markers

What to do

1. To expose children to the concept of graphs, try a simple graphing activity for every lesson or topic you are working on.
2. Choose two or three categories relating to the topic and invite the children to choose one. For example, if the lesson is about apples, ask the children to taste two or three varieties of apples and choose their favorite.
3. Graph the results and then count each column of choices. Talk about the results. "Which apple is the favorite? How do you know?"
4. This graphing technique can be adapted for a variety of experiences. It can make almost any lesson a math lesson.

✚ *Phyllis Esch, Export, PA*

Growth Chart

· ·

measurement

Materials   large piece of butcher paper
markers
measuring tape

What to do   1. This is a great way to chart children's growth throughout the year and teach them about measuring.
2. Tape a large piece of butcher paper to the wall to make a growth chart.
3. Have each child stand with his back against the chart.
4. Mark the child's height and write his name beside the mark using the same color marker.
5. Create a key in the corner with the date and the color of the marker (for example, you might use a green marker in September, a brown marker in November, and so on).
6. Encourage the children to use measuring tape to measure their height on the growth chart.
7. Remeasure the children periodically so they can see how much they've grown since the last time they were measured.

Related book   *In the Tall, Tall Grass* by Denise Fleming

✚ *Monica Hay Cook, Tucson, AZ*

How Many Raindrops?

· ·

counting, numeral recognition

Materials   10 pictures of umbrellas
several raindrop shapes or stickers
glue
markers

What to do
1. Write the numerals 1–10 on each of the umbrella pictures.
2. Let each child select an umbrella. Ask them to count out the corresponding number of raindrops and stick them to the umbrella picture. (The umbrella with the numeral 5 would have five raindrops on it.)
3. Display the counting cards in the math area.

Related books   *Listen to the Rain* by Bill Martin Jr. and John Archambault
Mushroom in the Rain by Mirra Ginsburg
Rain by Robert Kalan

✚ *Kristi Larson, Spirit Lake, IA*

Let's Count How Many

counting

Materials   record-keeping chart

What to do
1. On a regular basis, ask the children to count how many of a particular item there are in the room. You might want to start counting items that are low in number, such as three windows, eight tables, or 10 trucks.
2. Then, start counting items that require more advanced counting skills, for example, 20 markers, 45 stringing beads, 60 pegs, or 104 blocks.
3. Each time you count items, record that number on a record-keeping chart.
4. After the first month of school, continue counting the days. Keep counting until you complete the entire school year. You could add one day to the counting line every day. Keep the chart visible, so that the children will stay aware of the number of days.

✚ *Judy Fujawa, The Villages, FL*

Make Every Day a Math Day

general mathematical skills

Materials none

What to do The following is a list of everyday tips for making math and math talk a part of your regular routines:

1. Younger children sometimes have difficulty understanding that counting means naming numbers in a specific order. To reinforce this simple point, count often throughout the day. Count when you:
   - get ready to move from one spot to another,
   - set the tables,
   - get out or put away small amounts of toys,
   - take attendance, and
   - see that a child has arrived or gone home.

2. Help children practice using math skills throughout the day by asking questions: "How many books are on the bookshelf right now?" "How many more books would we need to have ten?"

3. There are numbers everywhere! Call attention to numbers to point out that they are important and are used for different purposes.

4. Just by playing with the children you can find many opportunities to engage in sorting, matching, comparing, arranging, and counting activities. Think about what you can do in each area of the room.

5. Bring a simple bathroom and/or kitchen scale to the classroom. Let the children weigh each other and various items around the room. This will help prepare them for using equipment in school to weigh and measure.

6. Children can be confused by money. Some think that the larger the coin is, the more valuable it is, so take any opportunity available when the children are playing with real or pretend coins to point out the facts about them.

7. Keep the tone of math activities light and fun. This will increase the likelihood that children will want to do them and make activities seem less of a chore.

8. Use newspapers to help young children learn to recognize numbers in different sizes and kinds of type and to understand that the way a number looks does not change its value. Let children look through newspapers and circle or cut out numbers.

9. As you do cooking activities, call attention to the markings on measuring cups and use their names properly. This will begin to familiarize children with the language they will use when they begin to work with fractions.

10. For older children, call attention to statistical charts in newspapers and magazines and talk with them about what the charts show and why the information is important. Make charts and graphs in the classroom frequently to showcase certain information, such as favorite colors, favored foods, shoes vs. sandals, and so on.

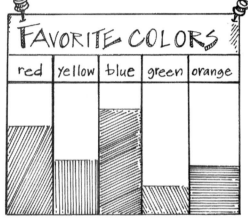

11. Use advertising flyers or newspaper ads to help the children identify, classify and count items. Ask, "How many cans of soup are there?" "What vegetables do you see?" and so on.

12. Keep a collection of grocery items in the dramatic play center, such as cracker boxes, cereal boxes, oatmeal boxes, milk jugs, juice bottles (all cleaned and sealed). Have the children name the shape of each item.

13. Show the children that you use math skills on a daily basis by "thinking out loud" as you do things like measuring, counting, or adding.

14. Children will develop a positive attitude about math if they see that there are fun ways to use math in games and solving puzzles. Do these activities often.

15. Young children can easily confuse letters and numbers. Throughout the day, have them notice and name both, or ask questions such as: "See the sign on that bus? Does it say 5 or E?"

16. When using counters, make sure they are small enough for little hands but large enough to not pose a choking hazard.

17. It is important for children to develop an understanding of the characteristics of numbers, such as odd or even and meaning of the terms such as "more than" and "less than." Use these phrases out loud whenever appropriate during the daily routine.

✚ *Virginia Jean Herrod, Columbia, SC*

Make Math Real

. . . .

measuring time, ordering

Materials   none

What to do   Use real-life, hands-on math activities to introduce young children to numbers and mathematical concepts. Talk regularly about numbers and numerical terms in daily routines with the children to help them learn math concepts naturally and make learning about numbers fun. Here are some examples:

- Time: hours, days, months, years; older, younger; yesterday, today, tomorrow.
- School starts at 9:00, and snack time is two hours later, at 11:00.
- Our class will visit the zoo in three more days.
- Andre is two months older than Janice.
- Yesterday was sunny and warm, but look at the rain today!

(Use a large calendar often to point out or mark special dates, both past and present.)

- Size and portions: large, small; tall, short; thin, thick; wide, narrow; half, whole; full, empty; light, heavy.
- You have made your clay long and thin; Danny's is flat and wide.
- Let's divide the clay into four equal pieces.
- How much water is in this glass?
- Who is taller, John or Chris?

- Shapes and patterns: circle, square, triangle, rectangle, round, sphere, star, cone.
- Let's stand in a big circle.
- This globe is called a sphere. How many other spheres can you find in this room?
- We have square tables and we have rectangular tables.
- If we line up these blocks like this, what shape (or color) comes next?

- Measurement: inches, feet, yards, miles, pounds (or metric system measurements).
- These nametags are 4" wide.
- How many feet can you jump from this line? Let's measure.
- Our rabbit weighs 10 pounds.

More to do **Working with Families:** Create a Parent Guide with tips and ideas for talking about numbers and strengthening math skills at home. Include ideas from a variety of areas such as cooking, home projects, letter writing, household chores, reading aloud, family games, and so on. Encourage parents to talk about numbers that matter most to their child— age, address, phone number, and height and weight. Focusing on these personal numbers helps children learn many important math concepts.

Related books *Big Hand, Little Hand* by Judith Herbst
Measuring Penny by Loreen Leedy
Me Counting Time: From Seconds to Centuries by Joan Sweeney Annette Cable
My First Book of Time by Claire Llewellyn
Telling Time: How to Tell Time on Digital and Analog Clocks! by Jules Older

✚ *Sandra K. Bynum, Blackfoot, ID*

Math Tips

● ●

numeral recognition

Materials none

What to do 1. Before using manipulatives for math lessons, allow the children time to play with them. After the children spend some time exploring the materials, they will be ready to use them for math lessons.
2. When setting up math centers, have each one teach the same concept. For instance, when teaching how to write numerals, have one center with clay, one with salt boxes, one with laminated numerals to trace, and so on. When the children are done with one center, they can move on to another at their own pace, and still be working on the same concept.

✚ *Barbara Saul, Eureka, CA*

Math and Pattern Person

addition, counting, greater than or less than, patterns, sequencing, subtraction

Materials
flannel board
felt numerals
felt dots
felt addition, subtraction, and equal signs

What to do

1. Select a child to be the math person. The children love to do this job, so make sure each child gets a turn at some point.

2. Ask the child if he wants to do patterns, addition, or subtraction. Depending on the theme, consider providing sequencing pictures.

3. If the child picks patterns, start a pattern and have the child finish it, or invite the child to start his own pattern.

4. If he picks addition or subtraction, place felt numerals on the flannel board in an equation (for example, $4 + 1 = $ ___). Explain what an equation is, and introduce the names of the math signs. Encourage the child to put dots on the flannel board to represent each number on the board (four dots + one dot). This helps them to visualize the numbers.

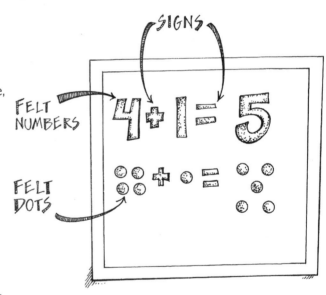

5. Invite the child to answer the question by finding the correct felt numeral to place on the board.

✚ *Wanda Guidroz, Santa Fe, TX*

Number of the Week

numeral recognition, representing numbers

Materials
cornmeal or sand
cookie tray or shallow tray
small die-cuts or stickers
paper
small items such as buttons, coins, jewels, beans, and so on
dry-erase markers and dry-erase board
number books
re-sealable plastic sandwich bag
colored or masking tape

What to do
During the year, take a week to focus on one number at a time. During the week, put out many different activities to reinforce the chosen number. Talk about the number each day at circle time, and set up any of the following activities during center time:

- Fill a shallow tray with cornmeal or sand and ask the children to use their fingers to draw the number of the week in the cornmeal.
- Provide a collection of small die-cuts or stickers and ask the children to count out the number of the week and put the stickers on a piece of paper. Make the pages into a book, if desired.
- Put small items in the sand table and ask the children to find the number of items that matches the number of the week.
- Provide dry-erase markers and a dry-erase board and invite the children to practice writing the number of the week.
- Get out all your number books at a transition time and ask the children to find the number of the week in the books.
- For older children, put small items such as buttons in a plastic sandwich bag that equal the number of the week. Put a piece of tape down the middle of the bag and talk about groups of numbers that add up to the number of the week.

✚ *Gail Morris, Kemah, TX*

Quick Counting!

counting

Materials　　none

What to do　　Teach this simple rhyme to children who are discouraged because they find it hard to master counting. Perhaps they always leave out a number or two while counting, or confuse the order. It can be a very daunting process for them to master counting to 100, so saying this rhyme usually raises a smile.

One, two,
Skip a few,
Ninety-nine,
One hundred!

✚ *Anne Adeney, Plymouth, United Kingdom*

Special Number Day

numeral recognition

Materials　　construction paper
variety of classroom materials

What to do　　1. Every couple of weeks, have a special number day.
2. Ask parents to help their children choose a specified number of items to bring to school to share or to add to the snack.
3. Make special number buttons out of construction paper for the children to wear during the day.
4. Put out the special number of puzzles, or colors of paint.
5. Example of a number 5 day:

　　■ Children might wear five pony tails, five ribbons, five bracelets, or five chains.

- Put out five puzzles, five games, five colors of paint, and five colors of markers.
- Let children create special number 5 buttons to wear.
- Ask each child to bring five crackers to share at snack time.
- Sing songs and fingerplays with the number five ("Five Little Ducks").
- Count by fives during circle time.

✚ *Sandy L. Scott, Meridian, ID*

Tips on Types of Graphs

graphing

Materials

floor graph:
- shower liner
- black electrical tape
- black pen
- yardstick
- large objects for marking the graph

reusable cardboard graph:
- large sheet of colored cardboard
- pen
- yardstick

magnetic graph:
- large magnetic board
- small magnets
- whiteboard markers

What to do

To make a floor graph:

1. Spread the shower liner on the floor.
2. Use a pen and yardstick to measure 12" × 10" rectangles on the liner, creating three to four columns across.
3. Tape over the pen marks, and invite the children to use large objects to mark the graph, such as shoes or stuffed animals.

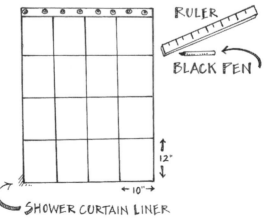

RULER

BLACK PEN

12"

← 10" →

SHOWER CURTAIN LINER

To make a reusable cardboard graph:

1. Measure and mark three to four vertical columns on the cardboard.
2. Mark and divide the columns into 2" sections, and laminate for durability.
3. Provide whiteboard markers to write on the graph. These can be wiped off easily, making the graph reusable.

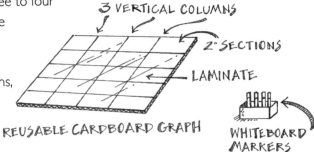

To make a magnetic graph:

1. Mark a T shape on the magnetic board, and write headings on each side of the T.
2. Give the children small magnets to mark preferences on either side.

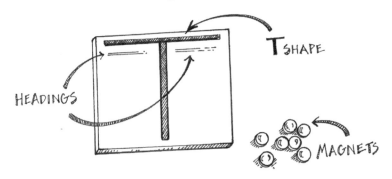

✚ *Barbara Saul, Eureka, CA*

What Comes Next?

time awareness

Materials

tagboard
pictures to illustrate classroom themes
page protectors
laminator
binding machine (optional)

What to do

1. Help the children understand the concept of one month by introducing each new month with a song and short discussion of what themes and events they will experience in the classroom.
2. Make a class book with pages that can be changed as each month approaches. (Top-loading page protectors are great for this.)
3. Bind the pages together between two covers.
4. Write "Classroom Themes" on the cover.
5. Help the children learn what comes next by displaying pictures illustrating each theme for the month.
6. On the last page, be sure to list each child who has a birthday during the month.

✚ *Jackie Wright, Enid, OK*

What Time Is It?

measuring time, ordering

Materials

chart paper
schedule of the day's activities (words or pictures)
paper clocks with minute and hour hands attached with brads
large clock

What to do

1. Use a piece of chart paper to make a daily schedule. Place the words or pictures in order on the chart paper (for example, circle time, snack time, center time, and so on).
2. Attach a paper clock next to each picture or word on the schedule. Place the hour and minute hands to the time the activity begins (circle time: 9:30). Print the time on a piece of paper next to the clock and under the picture.
3. Place a real clock by the schedule.

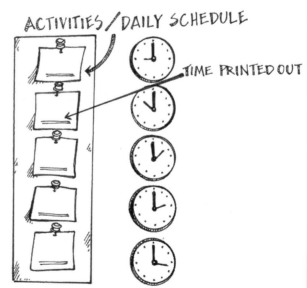

ACTIVITIES / DAILY SCHEDULE

TIME PRINTED OUT

4. When it is time for a new activity, talk about the time on the clock and compare it to the real clock. Look ahead at what will happen at various times throughout the day.

5. Place battery-operated clocks low enough throughout the room so the children can see more clearly the actual time and match it to the paper clocks. The children will begin noticing when it is time to change activities and begin to identify the times.

More to do   **Language and Literacy:** Read *The Grouchy Ladybug* by Eric Carle. Use a paper clock and have the children change the time shown on it to match the pages in the book.

✚ *Sandra Nagel, White Lake, MI*

Winter Count

counting, grouping, sets

Materials   3-dimensional tissue paper snowflakes, 12 large (12") and 12 small (6")
nylon fishing line cut into various lengths (12"–24")
scissors
ornament hangers or opened paperclips

What to do   1. This is a nice winter activity to do in your classroom. The snowflakes can stay up from December through February.

2. Attach fishing line to one end of each snowflake. Attach an ornament hanger or paperclip to the other end of the fishing line.

3. Hang the snowflakes from the classroom ceiling randomly.

4. When the children come in, help them count the snowflakes. Challenge older children to count the snowflakes by themselves. "How many large snowflakes do you see?" "How many small snowflakes do you see?"

✚ *Christina Chilcote, New Freedom, PA*

100 Days Chain

counting backwards

Materials

construction paper
glue
scissors

What to do

1. Children will enjoy knowing when they've attended school for 100 days. Create a paper chain together that will help them count the days.
2. Show the children how to cut construction paper into 100 1" × 8" strips.
3. Loop each paper strip into a circle and glue one end on top of the other.
4. Link the next strip around the first one and glue the ends together.
5. Glue all the strips together to create a chain.
6. Hang the chain at a height in the classroom that the children can reach.
7. Each day the children attend school, remove one strip from the chain until none are left.

Related books

100 School Days by Anne Rockwell
100th Day Worries by Margery Cuyler
Centipede's One Hundred Shoes by Tony Ross
One Hundred Hungry Ants by Elinor J. Pinczes
One Is a Snail, Ten Is a Crab by April Pulley Sayre

✚ *Monica Hay Cook, Tucson, AZ*

Animal Dance

classification, sorting

Materials

vest or jacket with an animal print fabric
piece of fabric with an animal print
4 sheets of 12" × 18" colored construction paper
30 small beanbag animals

What to do
1. Put on the animal print vest or jacket and place the fabric swatch in the pocket.
2. Print one word on each sheet of paper and draw a picture to correspond: household animal (pet), water animal, wild animal, and farm animal.
3. Display the papers in the center of the circle
4. Play an animal sorting game. Give each child a beanbag animal and have the children pass their animals around the circle.
5. Walk around the circle and drop the piece of "animal fabric" in front of a child.
6. Invite that child to identify her beanbag animal and then stand up and role-play how the animal would move and sound. If she is holding a bird, for example, she might flap her "wings" and make an appropriate call.
7. Invite the child to place the animal on the sheet of paper according to where it lives (house, water, wild, or farm).
8. The children continue passing their animals around the circle until you drop the fabric a second time. Repeat this activity until all the animals have been sorted into groups.

✚ *Mary J. Murray, Mazomanie, WI*

At the End of Your Rope

linear measurement

Materials
ropes of various sizes (including three measuring 1", 1', and 1 yard)
ruler
yardstick
poster showing a measured inch, foot, and yard

What to do
1. Pass out the ropes, making sure each child gets one length.
2. Before talking about traditional measurement terms, practice measuring together using only the lengths of the ropes as lengths of measurement. For example, sat, "Let's measure the table with Tommy's rope. How many ropes do we need?" Point out that the shorter the length of rope, the more times they will measure with it.
3. Pair the children with others who have different lengths of rope and send them around the room to measure classroom objects. Encourage the pairs to compare their results.

4. After the children have measured several objects together, call them back into the circle and discuss the experience of measuring with the different lengths of rope. Show them the poster with the inch, foot, and yard.
5. Invite the children to match their lengths or rope to one of the units of measure.

✚ *Ellen Javernik, Loveland, CO*

A Beary Bear Day

counting, ordering, size comparison

Materials   stuffed bears

What to do
1. Invite children to bring stuffed bears from home. Have a few extra for children who do not bring bears in.
2. Line the bears up and together count how many there are.
3. Ask the children to identify the shortest and tallest bears. Compare the bears to confirm.
4. Together, place the bears in a line, from the shortest to the tallest.

✚ *Karyn F. Everham, Fort Myers, FL*

Blocks in Socks

counting

Materials   variety of colorful socks
1" wooden cubes
string

What to do

1. Place a different number of blocks inside each sock. Tie each sock shut with a piece of string and place them in a box or basket.
2. During circle time, invite each child to choose one filled sock from the box.
3. Invite the children to chant the following phrase three times with you as they pass their socks around the circle: "How many blocks are in your socks?"
4. After the third time, each child holds the sock and feels how many blocks are inside.
5. Randomly call on five or six children to share how many blocks are in their socks. Begin the chant again as the children pass the socks again.
6. Continue the game until everyone has had an opportunity to share how many blocks are in their socks.

✚ *Mary J. Murray, Mazomanie, WI*

Body Columns

categorization, greater than or less than, one-to-one correspondence

Materials   none

What to do

1. Choose a category into which you can divide the children into smaller groups. For instance:

   - Who is wearing sneakers, sandals, or shoes with laces?
   - Who has light brown hair, blonde hair, dark brown hair or black hair, or red hair?
   - Who walks to school, rides the bus, or rides in a car?
   - Who likes vanilla, chocolate, or strawberry ice cream?

2. Ask the children to form lines according to their answers.
3. As the children form lines, have them hold hands with children who hold the same ordinal position in the lines next to them (for example, the second child in each line hold hands). Some children may not have someone's hand to hold because their line has more children on it. (For self-esteem purposes, try not to choose a category that puts any child alone.)
4. Ask the children questions about the lines they're in. "Which line has the most children?" "Which line has the fewest children?"
5. See if the children can describe and compare the lines. For example, "Our line has one more person than that line."

✚ *Michelle Barnea, Millburn, NJ*

Body Parts Count

counting

Materials

chart
picture of a person
markers
mirror

What to do

1. Draw or glue a simple picture of a person on a piece of chart paper.
2. Talk to the children about the parts of their bodies. Explain that the group is going to count how many of each body part they have. Provide a mirror.
3. Start by asking the children how many eyes they have, and invite the children to count "One, two."
4. Next, ask the children how many noses they have, and as a group, count "One."
5. Encourage the children to suggest other body parts to count, including hands, feet, legs, fingers on one hand, fingers on both hands, thumbs, toes, and so on.
6. As you count, write the number of body parts a person has on the chart and draw a line to the body part on the person picture. For example, write "2 eyes" and draw a line to the eyes on the picture.

✚ *Sandra Nagel, White Lake, MI*

Body Shapes

shape identification

Materials

large shapes (circle, triangle, diamond, square, and rectangle)
digital or Polaroid camera

What to do

1. Show the children the individual shapes, and ask them how they could make those shapes together in groups of four.
2. Ask each group of four children to lie on their side and hold one another's ankles, so they form a circle.

3. Take photos of the children in this position.
4. Invite the children to move on to making the next shape, and take a photo of them in that position, as well. **Note**: when children make a triangle, one child will need to stand to the side.
5. After printing out the photos, enlarge them and make them into a "human shapes" book.

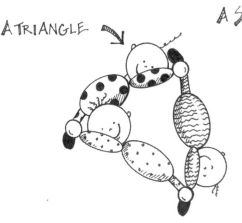
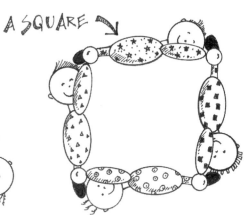

✚ *Kaethe Lewandowski, Centreville, VA*

Button Count

counting, math vocabulary

Materials   large chart paper (approximately 1' x 12')
marker
simple cutouts of children, one per child (from catalogs or paper doll cutouts)
glue stick

What to do   1. In advance, write the numerals 0–15 on the chart paper, widely spaced along the bottom. Write the children's names on the cutouts.
2. Ask the children to count the buttons they have on their clothing. Help the children who have more buttons or buttons on the back of their clothing.
3. Ask each child to use the glue stick to add her cutout to the chart above the numeral showing the correct number of buttons for her clothing that day. A child with three buttons on her shirt, for example, would glue her cutout in the space above the numeral 3.
4. Continue until all the children have glued their cutouts on the chart.

5. Discuss the results. "What is the greatest number of buttons anyone was wearing today?" "What was the smallest number?" "Which numeral has the most number of children on the chart?" "Which has the fewest?" "How many children were wearing no buttons at all?"

Related books   *Brass Button* by Crescent Dragonwagon
The Button Box by Margaret Reid
Corduroy by Don Freeman

✚ *Susan Oldham Hill, Lakeland, FL*

Button Graphing

classification, comparison, math vocabulary

Materials   8 ½" × 11" card stock paper (one for each graph you choose to do)
marker
large buttons (same size) in many different colors
glue

What to do   Children enjoy giving their own opinions or telling facts about themselves. By creating these simple button graphs, you provide a visual representation of these opinions and facts and teach basic math skills.

1. Create a graph by dividing the card stock paper into the appropriate number of rows. For example, if you are going to graph hair color, divide your graph into four rows, one each for red, black, blond, and brown. (For this activity, hair color will be the example.)
2. Ask the children in turn to tell you the color of their hair.
3. Let the children choose a button from the button pile and glue it to the graph in the appropriate row.
4. After everyone has had a turn, ask the children to interpret the graph. Ask, "What does this graph tell us about people with blond hair?"
5. Lead the children to the correct answer for your situation (most of the children have blond hair, no children have blond hair, only a few children have blond hair).
6. Continue until you have had a chance to discuss and focus on each hair color.
7. Leave the graph up in an area where the children can access it easily. Notice if they discuss it with each other.

8. Other button graphing opportunities include: number of brothers and sisters, eye and clothing colors, kinds of pets, height, number of children in class each day, shoe size, favorite foods, favorite colors, favorite storybooks, number of cups of water or sand it will take to fill certain containers, time (in seconds) it takes to run across the playground, and so on. The possibilities are endless!

✛ *Virgina Jean Herrod, Columbia, SC*

Calendar Patterns

patterns

Materials
chart calendar
numerals on two different shapes for the months

What to do
1. Each morning during circle time, look at the calendar.
2. When talking about the day of the week and the date, ask the children to name the next day's date.
3. Create a pattern and ask the children to continue with the pattern each day of the week. For example: In January, use blue mittens and white snowflakes and create the pattern of three snowflakes followed by one mitten. This means that January 1st, 2nd, and 3rd would have snowflakes, the 4th would have a mitten, then snowflakes again on the 5th, 6th, and 7th, and so on.

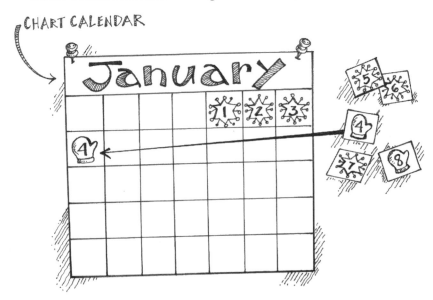

CHART CALENDAR

✛ *Sandy L. Scott, Meridian, ID*

Charting the Weather

addition, comparison, subtraction

Materials
large calendar
pen or pencil
white paper

What to do

1. Set up the calendar in a place where the children can see it easily, and put a sheet of white paper beside it.
2. On the sheet of paper, draw weather symbols. For example, make a C for clouds, or draw a picture of clouds; for the sun, make an S, or draw the sun. Explain all the symbols to the children.
3. Each morning, choose a different child to report the weather and mark the calendar with the appropriate weather letter or symbol.
4. At the end of the month, add up the days: sunny, rainy, overcast, snowing, and so on.
5. Show the children the total number of days in each category, and how those numbers add up to the total number of days in the month. Ask the children how many kinds of weather they experienced through the month, and which was most and least frequent.
6. Remove one type of weather, for example, sunny days, and ask the children how many days there are total now, and which weather types were most and least frequent through the month.

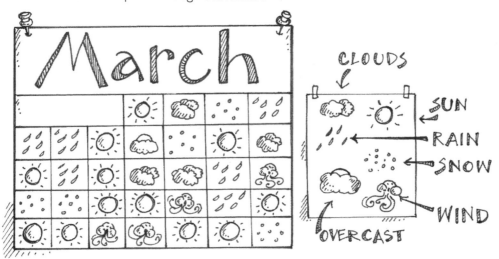

✚ *Ingelore Mix, Gainesville, VA*

Clap It

counting, one-to-one correspondence

Materials markers and paper or magazine pictures
scissors

What to do
1. Cut out pictures from magazines or draw your own.
2. Display four pictures at a time that represent words that have one, two, three, or four syllables. For example: car (one), tree house (two), polar bear (three), and teeter totter (four).
3. Ask a child to clap out the syllables of one of the pictures.
4. The rest of the children guess which word the child clapped.
5. When the children have guessed these four words, select new words with one, two, three, or four syllables. Make sure all of the children get a turn clapping out the syllables.
6. Once the children are experienced with this idea, add words with more syllables.

Related books *Hand Clap!* by Sara Bernstein
Schoolyard Rhymes by Judy Sierra

✚ *Monica Hay Cook, Tucson, AZ*

Count to 100

counting

Materials none

What to do
1. Introduce older children to the different ways it is possible to count: by ones, fives, and tens.
2. Help the children count to 100 by fives and tens.

3. Invite the children to jump, clap, or snap while counting, especially if they get confused about which numbers come next.
4. Have a number line on the wall that you can point to while the children are counting so they can visualize the numbers.

✚ *Sandy L. Scott, Meridian, ID*

Counting Favorite Animals

counting, more and less, one-to-one correspondence

Materials

large sheet of paper, dry-erase board, or chalkboard
marker or chalk

What to do

1. Down one side of the paper or board, write the names of three animals, such as *monkey*, *giraffe*, and *zebra*.
2. Go around the circle and have each child name her favorite animal from the three choices.
3. As each child names her favorite animal, put a mark next to that animal.
4. After all the children have had a turn, count up the marks for each animal and write the numeral next to the animal.
5. Arrange the children into three groups according to the animal they chose as their favorite. Count the children in each group and discuss how the number within their groups corresponds to the number on the chart.
6. Help the children figure which animal had the most votes and which had the fewest votes based on both the numbers and their group size.

✚ *Susan Grenfell, Cedar Park, TX*

Erase It

numeral recognition

Materials
chalkboard or dry-erase board
chalk or dry-erase marker
eraser
.

What to do
1. Write numbers on the board and ask who would like to come up and erase the number you call.
2. Write only a couple numbers at a time. This helps the children who don't know many numbers succeed. For example, write 2 and 7, and ask, "Who would like to come up and erase the seven?"
3. If a child doesn't know a number, let her erase either one and ask if anybody knows what that number is.
4. If you want to challenge the children, write more numbers on the board at one time.

Related books
How Many Blue Birds Flew Away? by Paul Giganti
Ten Little Ladybugs by Melanie Gerth
Ten, Nine, Eight by Molly Bang

✚ *Laura Durbrow, Lake Oswego, OR*

Estimation Station

comparison, counting, estimation, more and less

Materials
clear containers such as plastic mayonnaise jars or cups
items to count, such as math counters, balls, toy erasers, or cubes
chart paper

What to do
1. Place 10 to 15 items (counter bears, for example) in a plastic jar (make it a simple enough number for the children to understand).
2. Gather the children in a large group. Tell them that they are going to play a guessing game.

3. Ask them to guess how many bears are in the jar just by looking.
4. Write the children's guesses on chart paper.
5. When all the children have guessed, count the bears as a group. See who was right or who was the closest.
6. Then, add more bears and ask the children if they think that there are more or less bears this time just by looking.
7. Count again. Compare responses.
8. Next, take most of the items out and ask the children to and estimate again whether this amount is *more* or *less*. Count and compare.

✛ *Shelley F. Hoster, Norcross, GA*

Family Addition

addition

Materials poster board
black marker

What to do
1. Make a sign with the number of people in each child's family.
2. Give the children their signs.
3. Ask them to add one or more children to their family. Ask the class how many they now have.

✛ *Sandy L. Scott, Meridian, ID*

Fast Fingers

addition

Materials pair of white gloves
black fabric or permanent marker

What to do
1. If the children aren't familiar with "high fives," show them how to do it.
2. Have the children practice holding up one, two, three, and four individual fingers and saying the number out loud. Tell the children that this will help them visualize numbers in their minds as they go on to work with numbers later.
3. Quiz the children, asking them to hold up three fingers or four fingers, and see how many they hold up.
4. On one of the white gloves, write a 5 on the palm. On the other glove, write the numerals 6–10 on each fingertip. Put on the gloves. Tell the children that when they think of numbers between 6 and 10 to think of the "high" five.
5. Practice together by asking the children to show you seven or nine fingers, then doing it yourself with the numbered gloves, so they see how to count to 10 on their fingers.

✚ *Ellen Javernik, Loveland, CO*

Fraction Friends

• •

basic fractions, counting

Materials none

What to do
1. Introduce the concept of fractions in a fun, easy-to-understand way. Ask six children to come up to the front of the class. Have them line up in a row.
2. Ask the rest of the class to count the six children.
3. Explain that you want to separate the six children into two equal groups (A and B), stressing the word *equal* and explaining that equal means the same number in each group.
4. Divide the children into two unequal groups (two children in group A and four in group B, for example). Count the children and ask the children if there are an equal number of children in each group.
5. Ask them to tell you who needs to move to a new group.
6. When the groups are equal, tell them that there are three children in group A and three in group B. Explain that by making two equal groups, they have divided the group in half with the same number (three) on each side.
7. Have the class repeat after you, "Half of six is three."

8. Have the six children move back together and invite a new child to come up to the front line. Ask her to divide the group into two equal groups. Repeat the phrase, "Half of six is three."
9. As children begin to grasp the concept, use other fractions.

✚ *Jane Annunziata, Sussex, NJ*

Gift Wrap Match

matching, sorting

Materials   squares of wrapping paper in various colors and patterns
ribbon in a variety of colors
basket

What to do   1. Give each child a square of wrapping paper.
2. Place all the ribbons in a basket. If you don't have ribbons, cut 1" strips or squares from the larger wrapping paper.
3. Pass the basket around and encourage the children to find a ribbon that matches the pattern or color of their paper.
4. Ask each child to tell why she chose a specific ribbon.

Related books   *The Birthday Present Mystery* by Elspeth Campbell Murphy
Birthday Presents by Cynthia Rylant
Mr. Rabbit and the Lovely Present by Charlotte Zolotow

✚ *Kristi Larson, Spirit Lake, IA*

Girls and Boys

comparison, counting

Materials
tagboard
marker
picture of each child in the class
colored card stock, cut into 3" squares
pocket chart

What to do
1. Turn a piece of 7" x 11" tagboard horizontally and write the title "How Many Boys? How Many Girls?" Print "girls" on the left and "boys" on the right, forming two columns.
2. Glue each child's picture on a 3" x 3" square of colored card stock.
3. Laminate the header card and the children's pictures.
4. Place the title card in the top row of a pocket chart.
5. Discuss the meaning of *more, less,* and *equal.* Ask the children, "Are there more girls or boys in our class?"
6. Invite the children to place their photos under the appropriate column to chart the results.
7. Compare the number of girls and the number of boys. Because the pictures are all the same size, the resulting chart is an excellent reference for visual comparison.

✚ *Jackie Wright, Enid, OK*

Graphing Shoes

classification, counting

Materials
butcher paper
marker

What to do
1. In advance, use a marker to divide the butcher paper into three horizontal rows. On the left-hand side of the top row, write "Sneakers." On the left-hand side of the middle row, write "Sandals." On the left-hand side of the bottom

row, write "Boots."

2. Read the names of the three types of shoes with the children. Find an example of each shoe. (Many children may not be familiar with the word "sneaker.")

3. Have each child take off one shoe and, in turn, place it on the chart according to its type. Count the number of shoes in each column.

4. Discuss which row has the most shoes and which has the least. "What would our chart be like in the winter or summer? What if it was snowing?"

5. Return the children's shoes. **Note:** It is important that the children leave one shoe on so that you can easily identify the shoes and their owners.

✚ *Cassandra Reigel Whetstone, Folsom, CA*

Hear the Coins

coin identification

Materials
can with a metal bottom and a plastic, removable top, such as a chip can or baby formula can
paper
glue
scissors or craft knife (adult only)
various coins

What to do
1. Cover the can with paper and glue in place. Cut a slit in the top of the plastic lid.

2. Hold up a penny. Ask the group what it is. After the children name the coin, ask them to listen to the sound it makes as you drop it in the container. Repeat with each type of coin.

3. Ask each child to come up and receive a coin. The child states what the coin is and drops it in the can. Let everyone have a turn.

4. After a few days of doing this, most of the children will know the names of the coins.

✚ *Sandra Nagel, White Lake, MI*

Hocus Pocus Numbers

subtraction

Materials cloth
magic wand (painted dowel)
various items

What to do
1. Put out several items. Count how many there are with the children.
2. Have the children close their eyes. Pretend you're a magician and you are going to make items disappear. Cover the items, tap on the cloth, and say, "Hocus pocus." Take one item away.
3. Remove the cloth and ask the children to open their eyes. Count the items that are left. Ask the children how many items disappeared.
4. If the children have trouble with the subtraction, see if they can tell you what's missing and figure how many disappeared using this method.
5. Gradually make the activity harder by putting out more items and taking more items away.

Related book *Cookie Count* by Robert Sabuda

✚ *Monica Hay Cook, Tucson, AZ*

How Many Days?

multiples of 5 and 10

Materials adding machine paper
pens

Directions
1. Staple a long piece of adding machine paper around the classroom.
2. Each day at group time, write a number on the tape, beginning with one.
3. Every time you add a multiple of five to the tape, write that number in a different color.
4. Every time you add a multiple of 10 to the tape, circle that number.

5. When adding these multiples of five or 10, invite the children to count to that number by fives or tens: Otherwise, help them count to the number by ones.

Related book   *Two Ways to Count to Ten: A Liberian Folktale* by Ruby Dee

✚ *Barbara Saul, Eureka, CA*

How Many Legs Do I Have?

counting

Materials   4 blank sheets of construction paper per child
cutouts of bodies for an octopus, an
    ant, a cow, and a chicken
cutouts of legs for each of the
    animals

What to do

1. Talk to children about animals and ask them how many legs a duck has. "What about a snake? A turtle?"
2. Pass out the construction paper bodies and legs. Ask the children to glue one body on each blank piece of construction paper.
3. Next, have them glue on the legs that go with each body.
4. Talk about how many legs each animal has.

Related book   *How Many Legs: A Book About Counting* by Lori Froeb

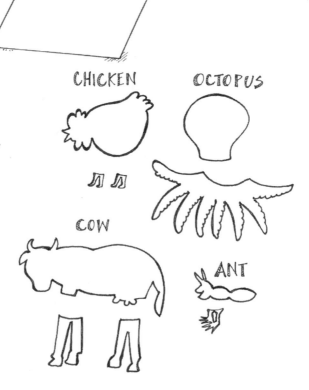

BLANK PIECE
of CONSTRUCTION
PAPER

CHICKEN   OCTOPUS

COW   ANT

✚ *Renee Kirchner, Carrollton, TX*

How Tall Are You?

comparison, estimation, measurement

Materials
flip chart paper
tape measure
2 different colored markers

What to do
1. Encourage the children to guess how tall they are.
2. Chart their guesses with one color marker on a chart and label the children's guesses with their name.
3. Measure each child.
4. Chart the measurements with another color marker on the chart and label the children's actual measurements with their names.
5. Talk about the results. How close were their guesses to their actual height? Is each child's height similar to or different from the others?

Related books
Me and the Measure of Things by Joan Sweeney
Millions to Measure by David Schwartz and Steven Kellogg

✚ *Kristi Larson, Spirit Lake, IA*

Human Knot

spatial awareness

Materials   none

What to do
1. Invite four or five children to stand in a circle, close to one another. (Older children may be able to make a larger group circle). Ask the children to reach across the circle and hold the hands of two different friends.
2. Remind the children to hold hands gently, and tell them not to let go of their friends' hands.

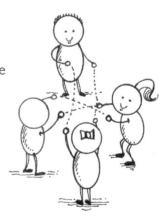

3. Have the children "unknot" themselves, by moving over and under their linked hands to create an untangled circle. For younger children, you will have to direct them on how to move out of the "human knot."

✚ *Michelle Barnea, Millburn, NJ*

I Go Around and Around

counting, numeral recognition

Materials

colored paper
scissors

What to do

1. Trace and cut out one numeral for each child in the class.
2. When children are sitting in a circle, place one numeral behind each child.
3. Select one child to walk around the circle looking for the numeral 1 while the rest of the children recite the following rhyme:

   I go around and go around,
   And pick a number off the ground.
   I pick number (number the child is looking for).

4. When the child finds the numeral 1, she picks it up and sits down.
5. The child who had the numeral 1 behind her then stands up and goes around the circle, looking for the numeral 2.
6. This repeats until each child has a numeral.
7. To transition to another activity, start calling out the numerals in order and have the children line up.

✚ *Ingelore Mix, Gainesville, VA*

I Spy a Shape

shape recognition

Materials   example of one shape (such as a rectangular block)
masking tape

What to do

1. Show the children the example of the shape, and discuss its characteristics to the children, such as number of sides or corners, and so on.
2. Encourage the children to look through the room or in a book to find objects that are of a similar shape.
3. Make a large version of the shape on the floor with masking tape and invite the children to walk in single file along its edge.

✚ *Barb Lindsay, Mason City, IA*

In the Dark

numeral recognition, shape recognition

Materials   flashlight

What to do

1. Invite the children to sit on the floor in the center of the room. Have them sit in a circle formation with their backs to the center of the circle.
2. Make the room as dark as possible so that children are still comfortable.
3. Tell them you will shine the flashlight on a "shape" in the room. When you point the light to the shape, the children should name the shape.
4. Repeat the activity several times.
5. Then shine the light on numbers instead of shapes and continue the activity.

✚ *Mary J. Murray, Mazomanie, WI*

It's About Time

. . . .

measuring time

Materials   calendar
clock
timer

What to do
1. Introduce the children to time concepts.
2. Look at a calendar together. Talk about and count out the days and weeks.
3. Show the children the daily schedule and talk about how much time you have allotted for each activity.
4. Show the classroom clock to the children. Point out the length of a minute, five minutes, half an hour, and an hour.
5. Ask the children questions about time, such as:

   ■ How long does it take you to brush your teeth? Hours or minutes?
   ■ How long does it take you to get to school? Minutes or weeks?
   ■ How long do you sleep at night? Minutes or hours?
   ■ How long does it take for plants to grow? Weeks or minutes?

6. Think of other time concept questions to ask the children.

✚ *Monica Hay Cook, Tucson, AZ*

It's Raining, It's Pouring!

counting, numeral recognition

Materials
white or gray and blue felt
scissors
marker
flannel board

What to do
1. Cut out 10 clouds from white or gray felt.
2. With a permanent marker, number them from 1–10.
3. Cut out raindrops from the blue felt.
4. Place the clouds and the raindrops in a basket next to the flannel board.
5. Ask a child to choose a cloud and say the number on it.
6. Next, have the child count out the number of raindrops and put them under the cloud on the flannel board.
7. Continue by having a different child choose another cloud and repeat the game.

Related books
It's Raining It's Pouring by Andrea Spalding
Rabbits and Raindrops by Jim Aronsky

✚ *Shelley F. Hoster, Norcross GA*

The Key to Math

counting, sorting

Materials
keys
coffee can
Post-it notes
copy machine

What to do

1. Send a note home asking families to collect old keys that they no longer use. Attach an envelope for them to put the keys in.
2. Place the collected keys in a coffee can. (Place some keys on the copy machine and use the copies to cover the can). As you add to the collection each day, count the number of keys and write the new amount on a Post-it note on top of the lid.
3. Ask the children to close their eyes and listen as you drop the keys into the can, counting with their eyes closed as they hear each one drop.
4. Invite the children to use the keys for counting and sorting.

More to do

Collect key rings and make one ring for each number. The first key ring holds one key, the second holds two, and so on.

Dramatic Play: Use key rings full of keys to add to the dramatic play opportunities in the housekeeping area.

Related books

Cars, Trucks, and Things That Go by Richard Scarry
Duck's Key—Where Can It Be? by Jez Alborough
Lilly's Purple Plastic Purse by Kevin Henkes

✚ *Laura Durbrow, Lake Oswego, OR*

Kid Clocks

measuring time

Materials

clear or white shower curtain
marker

What to do

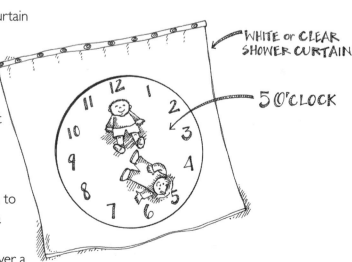

WHITE or CLEAR SHOWER CURTAIN

5 O'CLOCK

1. Prepare a shower curtain by drawing a large clock shape on it (make a circle and numbers, but no hands).
2. Introduce the children to the manner in which a clock keeps time, explaining that whenever a

new hour begins, the minute hand is on the 12, and the hour hand is on whichever hour is beginning.

3. Place the shower curtain clock on the floor and tell the children that they will be playing a clock game.

4. Start naming different times, for example, 4:00. Have the children lie down two at a time: one as the minute hand, one as the hour hand.

5. When one pair of children gets the time right (help them, as needed), ask a new pair of children to lie down and be the clock's hands.

Related book   *The Going to Bed Book* by Sandra Boynton

✚ *Sue Fleischmann, Sussex, WI*

Kid Patterns

classification, patterns

Materials   none

What to do

1. Based on the makeup of the group, pick a rule for your "Kid Pattern" (boy/girl, long hair/short hair, pants/dresses, sneakers/sandals, and so on).

2. Tell the children what kind of pattern they will be making, such as boys and girls.

3. Have the children come up one at a time and stand in an ABAB pattern (boy, girl, boy, girl). Use some or all of the children.

4. If there are extra children who don't fit into the pattern, for example, three extra girls, they can be the "pattern callers."

5. Have the children "read" the kid pattern: "Boy, girl, boy, girl." If you have callers, they can walk by the children and point or gesture to each child as the pattern is called. If appropriate, introduce the idea of ABAB patterns and have them call out "ABABABAB."

6. Have the children sit down and try another pattern rule, such as arms up/arms down, standing/sitting, hair color, or clothing color.

7. When the children have practiced the ABAB pattern, try grouping them into more complex patterns, such as ABCABC or ABBABB.

✚ *Cassandra Reigel Whetstone, Folsom, CA*

Let's Find Out

counting, one-to-one correspondence

Materials
2 groups of 10 objects of different shapes and/or colors such as cube blocks, linking rings, or red and white bingo chips

What to do
1. Place two groups of five objects in front of the children. Say, "Find out if there is the same amount or number in each pile."
2. Let them experiment with different ways they can find out if the number is the same in both piles. The children may arrange the items so they match in one-to-one correspondence or they may count each group to determine if they are equal.
3. Count the items in each group with the children to confirm their answers.
4. Continue the activity, placing one more item in each pile each time until you reach a total of 10 items in each pile.
5. Leave the activity out during center time for individual exploration.

More to do
Cleanup: While cleaning up after an active day of play, encourage the children to sort small manipulative items by color and then compare the piles. Which has more? Less? The same amount?

✚ *Virginia Jean Herrod, Columbia, SC*

Look Who Is Here in Class Today

counting, number awareness

Materials
tagboard
camera
laminator
scissors
basket
pocket chart

What to do
1. To prepare, take a head shot of each child in your class.
2. Mount each photo on a separate piece of tagboard with the child's first name below the picture.
3. Write the title "Look Who Is Here in Class Today" on a piece of 7" x 11" tagboard turned horizontally.
4. Laminate the title card and children's photos, and cut out.
5. Display the title card in the pocket chart. Place the photos in a basket nearby.
6. Have a volunteer take attendance by placing the photos of the children who are present in the pocket chart.
7. How many children are present? How many are absent?

✚ *Jackie Wright, Enid, OK*

Making Shapes

shapes

Materials
very long piece of string or ribbon

What to do
1. Cut a very long piece of string or ribbon that is big enough for all of the children to hold in a large circle.
2. Begin with two children holding the string or ribbon between them. Ask the children: "How many ends are there?" Explain that when there are two ends, the string makes a line.
3. Have another child join them. Give one child both ends of the string to hold and ask the other two children to hold the string taut with their fingers while creating a triangular shape.
4. Ask the children how many sides there are now (3). Ask how many children are holding the string. Ask them what shape this makes.
5. Have another child join them in holding a point of the string and create a new point to the shape. Help the children form a square. Ask them how many sides there are, how many children are holding the string, and what shape they made.

6. Continue to add one child at a time to create the following shapes:

5 children = a pentagon (some children may call it a "house")
6 children = a hexagon
7 children = a heptagon
8 children = an octagon (or a STOP sign)

7. Now have all the children join in the activity to create a circle.

✚ *Michelle Barnea, Millburn, NJ*

Math and Me

counting, printing numerals

Materials   markers
tagboard

What to do   1. During circle time, tell the children they are going to learn more about
themselves by making a chart about themselves.
2. Give each child a piece of tagboard.

3. Help them select and write column headings, for example, my body, my family, and so on.
4. Have each child count her body parts: head, eyes, nose, mouth, ears, hands, fingers, legs, feet, and toes.
5. The children write the numbers of each body part on their chart.
6. Ask other questions. "How old are you?" "Do you have any brothers or sisters? Pets?" Write the answers on the chart.
7. When finished, the children have a poster that tells important things about themselves.

Related book   *From Head to Toe* by Eric Carle

✚ *Monica Hay Cook, Tucson, AZ*

More, Less, Fewer, Same

math vocabulary, number sense, shape recognition

Materials   flannel board or magnet board
10 of each flannel board or magnet board shapes (circle, square, triangle, rectangle)

What to do   1. Set up a flannel or magnet board with many shapes on it.
2. Put up two groups of shapes.
3. Ask questions, such as: "Are there as many circles as squares?" "Red circles as blue circles?" "Which group has more?" "How many circles are there?" "How many squares are there?"
4. Allow time for the children to answer each question before moving on. The children can point, tell with words, or move the pieces around to show the answers.
5. As you talk with the children, use proper math terms to reinforce their answers. For example: Yes, this group of squares has *fewer* in it than the group of circles. This group of blue circles has *more* in it than the group of red circle. There are *fewer* blue triangles on the board than anything else.

More to do   **Snack:** When setting the table for snack, have the materials (cups, spoons, plates, napkins) in an easily accessible area. Say, "Let's find out if we have enough _____ for everyone." Give the children ample time to discover ways to find out if they have enough. If they have trouble, suggest they count or match.

✚ *Virginia Jean Herrod, Columbia, SC*

More or Less

comparison

Materials   many small items such as pennies, buttons, and so on

What to do   1. Make two piles of pennies, one large and one small.
2. Ask the children, "Which pile has *many* pennies?" "Which pile has just a *few?*" "Which pile has *more?*" "Which has *less?*"
3. Repeat with different items.

Related book   *How Much Is a Million?* by David M. Schwartz

✚ *Sandy L. Scott, Meridian, ID*

Moving to the Beat

counting

Materials   none

What to do   1. Begin by inviting the children to clap and chant the numbers one to 10, then stamp feet and chant from 11 to 20, and pat legs and chant from 21 to 30.
2. Do this in groups of 10 until you reach 100, or as high as the children are able.

✚ *Barbara Saul, Eureka, CA*

My Favorite Number

matching, number sense

Materials   two sets of large numerals (1–5 or 1–10)

What to do
1. Place one set of numerals on the chalkboard or a bulletin board.
2. Ask the children to name the numbers.
3. Show the children the second set of numerals.
4. Show them how to match numeral 1 to the numeral 1 on the board.
5. Ask, "Can you show me what number matches with the number on the board?"
6. Ask them to choose their favorite number.

More to do   Place the large numerals on the table. Ask the children to find objects around the room to match the number. For example say, "How many objects do you need for the number five?" The child may find five objects and then place them below the numeral 5 on the table.

✚ *Lily Erlic, Victoria, BC, Canada*

Number of the Day

counting, numeral recognition, number sequence

Materials   a variety of small beanbag animals
large number cards (1–10 or 1–20)

What to do
1. Display the animals about 1' apart from each other, along the chalk tray at the front of the room (or on a table).
2. Prop each number card in order next to an animal.
3. Invite the "helper of the day" to walk along the row of animals, back and forth, as the rest of the class sings softly to the tune of "London Bridge Is Falling Down."

What's the number of the day,
Of the day, of the day?
What's the number of the day?
Tell us now!

4. At the end of the song the child stops walking, announces the number she has chosen, and picks up the animal and number card and holds them high in the air.

5. Write the number the child is holding on the chalkboard, and invite the children to sing the response in unison,

_____ *is the number of the day,*
Of the day, of the day.
_____ *is the number of the day.*
I can write it.

6. After the number is written, everyone gives the child a round of applause.

More to do

Writing Center: Set up a learning center where children can use various mediums to practice writing the "number of the day." Stock the center with modeling clay, manipulatives, crayons, watercolor paints, and more.

✚ *Mary J. Murray, Mazomanie, WI*

Number Walk

● ●

counting, numeral recognition

Materials

large cutout numerals or large number flash cards

What to do

1. Have the children stand in a circle. Place a numeral in the middle of the circle. Talk about what number it is. Ask the children to say the name of the number name and count to that number.

2. The children start walking around the number on the floor while singing the following song to the tune of "Here We Go 'Round the Mulberry Bush."

Walk around the number _____, the number _____, the number _____.
Walk around the number _____, so early in the morning!

3. After the children have sung the song, have them call out the number and then count to that number.
4. Change the numeral each time the children sing the song.

✚ *Shelley F. Hoster, Norcross, GA*

Perfect Graph

charting, surveying

Materials

window roller shade
markers
graphing items

What to do

1. Create a generic, reusable graphing chart. Because it lays flat and can be rolled up and stored easily, the window shade is a perfect pull out and put away item. Make horizontal and vertical lines to create a graph.
2. If you have a die cut machine, cut out a variety of shapes to stimulate charting activities. Put small amounts of tape on the back of shapes when using them to help them stay put, but also be easily removed.
3. Introduce the graph at group time to help children learn graphing skills. They may conduct their own surveys during choice time.
4. Start with simple, fun surveys, such as who has pets and what kinds, favorite foods, ice cream flavors, favorite learning centers, and so on.

✚ *Bev Schumacher, Racine, W*

Pizza Chart

counting

Materials blank graph paper with four columns
pictures of pizza ingredients

What to do 1. At the bottom of the chart put a picture of cheese, pepperoni, sausage, and black olives. Write numerals going up the side of the chart, using as many numbers as you have children in your class. Laminate the chart so you can re-use it.
2. Ask children what their favorite kinds of pizza are.
3. Using a colored marker, shade in the number of children that like each kind of pizza.
4. Ask the children questions about the chart. "Which kind of pizza do most children like?" Or, "Which kind of pizza is the least favorite?"

Related books *Pete's a Pizza* by William Steig
Pizza Counting by Christina Dobson
Pizza That We Made by Joan Holub

✚ *Renee Kirchner, Carrollton, TX*

Ribbon Cups

comparison

Materials 16 oz. plastic cottage cheese or sour cream containers, with lids
spools of ribbon in a variety of colors and widths
scissors

What to do 1. Cut the ribbon into lengths of 2", 4", 6", 8", 10", 12", 14", 16", 18", and 20" to make sets of ribbons in different sizes.
2. Place one set of ribbons in each container and place the lid on top.
3. Have the children sit in pairs for this activity and give each child a container of ribbons.

4. Invite the children to sing the following song to the tune of "Mary Had a Little Lamb."

Take a ribbon from the cup,
From the cup, from the cup.
Take a ribbon from the cup.
Whose is longer now?

5. At the end of the song, each child pulls one ribbon from her cup and lays it on the floor.
6. Partners compare the lengths of their ribbons. The person with the longest ribbon raises her hand.
7. Continue the activity until all 10 ribbons have been drawn from the cup and their lengths compared.
8. To add to the activity, invite the children to put all 10 of their ribbons in order from shortest to longest. Or, invite them to put their ribbons end to end and compare the total lengths.

✚ *Mary J. Murray, Mazomanie, WI*

Riddle Me This

* *

counting, numeral recognition

Materials   large number cards, 1–6

What to do
1. Display the number cards in random order.
2. Read the following riddles and choose a child to point to the correct card.

I'm the number of toes you have on one foot.
I'm the number of knees you have.
I'm the number of necks you have.
I'm the number of noses you have.
I'm the number of eyes you have.
I'm the number of hands and the number of feet you have.
I'm the number of ears and the number of heads you have.
I'm the number of thumbs you have.
I'm the number of elbows and the number of tongues you have.
I'm the number of fingers you have on one hand.
I'm the number of mouths you have.
I'm the number of noses and the number of feet you have.

More to do   **Music:** Sing "Head, Shoulders, Knees, and Toes" with the children.

Related books   *Here Are My Hands* by Bill Martin, Jr. and John Archambault
The Skeleton Inside You by Philip Balestrino

✚ *Susan Oldham Hill, Lakeland, FL*

The Three Little Pigs Find Their Homes

one-to-one correspondence

Materials   design paper in the following designs: straw, sticks, bricks
3 small identical square blocks
3 small identical triangular blocks
hot glue gun (adult only) or glue dots
small plastic or fabric pig dolls
yarn

What to do
1. Cover each block with a piece of design paper. If you can't find design paper, make your own using a computer and commercial software. Most computers have a program with graphics such as straw, sticks, and bricks. Layer the graphic over a single page on the computer and print. **Note**: If desired, you can skip steps 1 through 4 and simply use a picture of a straw house, stick house, and brick house.
2. Cover the triangular blocks with black paper. Add a paper chimney for effect.
3. Use hot glue or commercial glue dots to attach one triangular block to each square block to form a house shape.
4. Add a black rectangular paper to the front of each house to represent a door.
5. Set the houses up on one side of a small table. Set the pigs up across from the houses.
6. Show the children how to use the yarn to make a path from each pig to its respective house. To do this, put the yarn down at the pig's feet and stretch it across the table until it reaches a house. Repeat for the other two pigs and houses.

7. Ask the children, "Who are these young fellows? Is there a house for each pig?"
8. Use your finger to trace the route from each pig to its house. Say, "Yes, this little pig has a house" each time.
9. Confirm the idea by saying, "The three little pigs have three little houses."
10. Tell or read the story of the "Three Little Pigs."
11. Leave the display up for use during center time.

More to do **Dramatic Play:** Add a wolf doll and let the children use the props to take turns telling the story of "The Three Little Pigs."

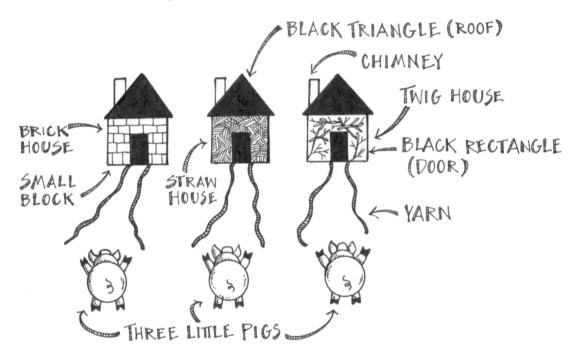

Related fingerplay **Run Home, Little Piggies** (tune: "My Little Red Wagon")
One little, (hold up one finger)
Two little, (hold up two fingers)
Three little piggies (hold up three fingers)
Built three homes, (pretend to swing a hammer)
Bricks, straw, and twiggies. (hold up three fingers in sequence)
Scared by the wolf, (make a frightened face and hold up both hands as if to ward off the wolf)
He's sure a biggie. (gesture up to indicate the wolf's height)
Run home, little piggies, run home. (hold up three fingers and move hand quickly behind your back)

✚ *Virginia Jean Herrod, Columbia, SC*

Two By Two

matching

Materials
flannel board or magnet board
pairs of objects represented by felt or magnetic pieces (two hearts, two triangles, two puppies, two circles)

What to do
1. Place several pairs of felt pieces on the flannel board or magnets on the magnet board.
2. Point to each pair in turn and ask, "What are these?" "How many are there?"
3. Let the children touch and count the items in each group to determine the answer.
4. Say, "Yes, there are two of each one. They are in groups of two."
5. Ask the children to look at their own bodies to see what they have that comes in twos, such as arms, legs, eyes, and ears.
6. Ask the children to look around the room for other groups of two.
7. Mix up the flannel board items. Ask the children to sort through the items to find groups of two.
8. Leave the materials out for exploration during center time.

More to do

Transitions: When moving from one area to another, have the children move in groups of two. Ask them to find a friend with whom to walk. Say, "Now, we are moving two by two; we are moving in pairs."
Music and Movement: While outside, sing "The Ants Go Marching" and have the children act out the verses by marching around the area in ones, twos, threes, and so on.

✚ *Virgina Jean Herrod, Columbia, SC*

Vote for Your Favorite Color

counting

Materials
4 containers
construction paper cutouts of crayons in 4 different colors
flannel board in 4 sections
tape

What to do
1. Put the crayon cutouts in the four separate containers, divided by color.
2. Ask the children to choose their favorite color of crayon and attach it to its designated section of the flannel board, making a visual representation of the colored crayons.
3. When complete, help the children count the number of crayons in each color.
4. When done, ask the children which color has the most crayons, which has the least, and so on.

Related book
Crayon Box That Talked by Shane DeRolf

✚ *Deborah Hannes Litfin, Forest Hills, NY*

What Am I?

shape identification, size identification

Materials
variety of food packages and cans

What to do
1. Display several different kinds of food packages.
2. Ask one child to select one of the packages without saying which one she picked.
3. She describes one thing about the package (shape, color, and so on).
4. The other children try to guess which package the child is describing.
5. When the item has been guessed, select another child to describe a package.

✚ *Monica Hay Cook, Tucson, AZ*

What's Today?

calendar, days of the week, recognizing dates

Materials

large, blank calendar
names of the months, in large print
cutout numerals (1–31) that will fit into the calendar spaces

What to do

1. Staple the large calendar where the children can reach it.
2. Every day, invite the children to pick the correct numeral and put it in its correct space on the calendar.
3. Announce to the children, "Today is (day's date)."
4. Teach the children the following rhyme:

   Sunday, Monday, Tuesday, Wednesday, Thursday, Friday,
   Saturday, and let's begin again.
   Sunday, Monday, Tuesday, Wednesday, Thursday, Friday,
   Saturday and that will be the end.
   Today is _____!

✚ *Barbara Saul, Eureka, CA*

What's Your Vote?

counting, more and less

Materials

chalk and chalkboard or chart paper and pencil

What to do

1. Set out several books.
2. Ask the children to think about which book they would like to hear that day. Tell them to raise their hands for the book they would like read.
3. Hold up each book and count the number of votes for each book.
4. Write the results on the chalkboard. Talk about which book received the most votes, the least votes, and so on.
5. Read the book with the most votes.

More to do

Snack: Give the children choices of what they would like to eat that day. Ask them to vote for their favorite choice. Whichever food receives the most votes is the snack that day.

Related books

Duck for President by Doreen Cronin
Vote! by Eileen Christelow

✚ *Monica Hay Cook, Tucson, AZ*

Zero the Hero

counting

Materials

roll of adding machine paper
marker
puppet
small prizes

What to do

1. Each day add a number to the roll of paper to indicate how many days the children have been in school.
2. Whenever you reach a number that ends in zero, the children get a visit from "Zero the Hero" (this can be a puppet or stuffed character).
3. Use the character to give each child a small prize. The prizes can be simple items such as stickers. It is nice if the prizes correspond to the season, a particular activity, or the classroom theme.
4. Children enjoy counting and looking forward to special days.
5. On the 100th day of school, have a special party. Ask the children to bring in 100 of an item to show their classmates (such as pennies, paperclips, marbles, cards, and so on).

✚ *Sandy L. Scott, Meridian, ID*

Apple Seed Counting Book

counting

Materials   red, green, and yellow construction paper for each page of apple book
scissors
markers
stapler
glue sticks
apple seeds or black construction paper "seeds"

What to do   1. Cut out apple shapes from the colored construction paper. Cut out several for each child. Explain to the children that they will be using the apple-shaped paper to make apple books.
2. Help each child write "_____'s Apple Counting Book" on an apple shape. Let the children decide if they want their books to have only one color of apple, or two, or all three, depending on their preference of apple.
3. Help the children staple the pages together to make a book.
4. On the first page of each book, help the children write "one," then write "two" on the second page, and so on, and help them glue the corresponding number of seeds or paper seed cutouts on each page.

Related books   *Apples and Pumpkins* by Anne Rockwell
Dappled Apples by Jan Carr
Ten Red Apples by Pat Hutchins

✚ *Cookie Zingarelli, Columbus, OH*

Big Fat Hen

number sequence

Materials   card stock or construction paper
markers
yarn
Big Fat Hen by Keith Baker
hole punch

What to do

1. Using the cardstock or construction paper, make 15 signs.
2. Write or trace and color the numerals 1–10 on each of 10 signs. On the other five, draw or glue pictures of a shoe, a door, sticks in a pile, sticks in a row, and a big fat hen.
3. Punch two holes at the top and string the yarn through so that the signs can be worn around the children's necks.
4. Gather the children in a circle and give each child a sign. If there are more than 15 children in your class, make extra signs so that everyone will hold one.
5. Tell them that you are going to read a story about numbers and chickens.
6. As you read *Big Fat Hen*, have the children listen for the number or object that they are wearing and stand up as you read about it.
7. See if the children can put themselves in order according to the popular rhyme. Chant it aloud and have them run to their places as you call it out.

One, two, buckle my shoe!

CARD STRING HOLE

✚ *Shelley F. Hoster, Norcross, GA*

Chick, Chick Count

addition

Materials

I Bought a Baby Chicken by Kelly Milner Halls
simple chick pattern
assorted sheets of colored felt (yellow, black, tan, red, white, brown)
flannel board

What to do

CHICK PATTERN

1. Using felt, cut out one yellow chick, two black chicks, three tan chicks, four red chicks, six white chicks, seven brown chicks, and 32 other chicks of different colors.
2. Hand out the sets of chicks to specific children (one yellow chick to one child, two black chicks to another child, three tan chicks to a third child, and so on).
3. Pass out a few assorted chicks (the 32 assorted chicks) to the rest of the children. Ask the group to listen to the story so they know when to add their chicks to the flannel board.
4. Read *I Bought a Baby Chicken*. Pause after each page so the children can add their chicks to the flannel board.
5. After finishing the story, help the children count the total number of chicks on the flannel board, and invite them to count the chicks based on color. Also ask the children to identify how many sets of like-colored chicks there are.

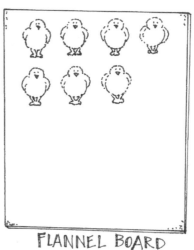

FLANNEL BOARD

Related fingerplay

Four little chicks went, "Peep, peep, peep." (hold up four fingers)
Three little chicks went, "Cheep, cheep, cheep." (hold up three fingers)
Two little chicks went, "Coo, coo, coo." (hold up two fingers)
One little chick went, "Cock-a-doodle-doo!" (flap arms like wings)

 Christina Chilcote, New Freedom, PA

Class Scrapbook

counting, numeral recognition, patterns

Materials
digital camera
tagboard or construction paper
glue sticks
markers
scrapbooking supplies: stickers, paper shapes, rubber stamps, stamp pads

What to do
1. Create a classroom scrapbook to help teach math skills to the children.
2. Take several photographs of various groups of children in the classroom. Make sure that everyone is included in one or more pictures.
3. Paste the pictures on pieces of tagboard or construction paper and then decorate each page using the stickers or other scrapbooking materials.
4. Write numerals, number words (one, two, and so on), or patterns (ABAB) on the pages accordingly. For example, if there are two children in one picture, write a "2" or a "two" on the page.
5. Place the scrapbook at a special table. Invite the children to "read" the scrapbook. Encourage them to count the number of children in each picture, identify patterns, recognize numerals, and so on.
6. Add to the scrapbook as the school year progresses. By the end of the year you will have a special record and keepsake that children and parents can enjoy for years to come.

Note: Invite two or more parents with scrapbooking experience to work on this project together. Invite parents to donate some of the scrapbooking materials.

✚ *Mary J. Murray, Mazomanie, WI*

Corduroy's Graph

comparison, counting, graphing

Materials

chart paper
80 to 100 3" bear cutouts
markers
glue
small bag or box
lined chart tablet
Corduroy by Don Freeman

What to do

1. Ahead of time, prepare a piece of chart paper with a grid of 4" squares. Make 11 horizontal squares and 11 vertical squares.
2. Along the left vertical side, write the numerals 0–10, one numeral per square, with the 0 in the top square, a 1 in the next square, and so on to 10.
3. Also ahead of time, mark the front of each bear with a numeral from 0 to 10.
4. Make sure to have an uneven number of some of the numerals (for example, write a 7 on five bear cutouts, and 3 on seven cutouts). This ensures that some numerals on the graph will have more than others.
5. Read the book *Corduroy* to the children.
6. Shuffle the bear cutouts and drop them into a small bag or box.
7. Ask the children to draw one out and glue it on the correct place on the grid, starting with the empty square closest to the numeral on the chart that matches the one shown on the bear.
8. Continue until everyone has a turn or until no bears remain in the bag.
9. Discuss the completed graph with the children. "Which numeral has more bears?" "Which has the fewest?" "Are any of the two the same?" "Is there one without any bears at all?"
10. Ask the children to dictate a story about the graphing process. Write their sentences on the blank chart paper and reread it with them.
11. Display the graph and the experience chart in the classroom.

Related books

A Pocket for Corduroy by Don Freeman
Where's My Teddy? Jez Alborough

✚ *Susan Oldham Hill, Lakeland, FL*

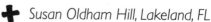

Experiencing Fractions

counting, division

Materials
construction paper
scissors
markers
clear contact paper or laminate
The Doorbell Rang by Pat Hutchins

What to do
1. Cut out 24–36 circles and decorate as cookies. Laminate or cover them with clear contact paper to make them more durable.
2. Read *The Doorbell Rang* for children to become acquainted with the events in the story.
3. Invite the children to role-play the characters in the story: Mom has a plate with 12 cookies. Divide the cookies between the children as they appear in the story.
4. At the end of the story, have "grandma" come in with a tray of another 12–24 cookies.
5. Divide the cookies between children. Talk about how many cookies each child has each time the doorbell rings.

✚ *Phyllis Esch, Export, PA*

Find It!

numeral recognition

Materials
empty food or soap boxes, cans, and bottles

What to do
1. Place several empty boxes, cans, and bottles on a low table. You might want to use a cereal box, a can of soup, and a bottle of dishwashing liquid.
2. Sit with the children and point out one or two numerals on each item. Numerals can be found in the names of some products, as well as listed in the contents and addresses found on the labels. Point to single digits, not a large number such as a zip code.

3. Point to one of the items and say a numeral that is easy to see. Ask the children to find it. Have them look for that numeral on other items.
4. Ask the children to choose a numeral for you to find on one of the containers.
5. This is a great way to use environmental print for a math activity.

More to do   Use the labels from the products to create a number book. Mount each label on a 5" × 7" piece of construction paper. Create a front and back cover and bind the pages into a book.

✚ *Virginia Jean Herrod, Columbia, SC*

Friends Counting Book

counting

Materials   camera
small photograph albums (one per child)
note cards
markers

What to do
1. Take pictures of each child alone, pictures of two children, three children, and so on. Print the pictures.
2. Give each child a photo album. Help them put a photo of themselves on the cover, and on a sheet of paper below the photo, write "_____'s Friends Counting Book."
3. On the first page of the book, show the children how to insert the same picture from the cover, and write "one friend" at the bottom of the page with a numeral 1 beside it.
4. On the next page, have the children add photos of themselves and one other person, and insert the text "two friends" with a numeral 2 beside it.
5. Repeat this until each child has a photo of the entire class on the last page of their book.

✚ *Kathleen Wallace, Columbia, MO*

How Big Is Your Bait?

measurement, sorting

Materials
Inch by Inch by Leo Lionni
rubber worms in a variety of sizes
small bucket or other container
pails in three different sizes
ruler or measuring tape

What to do
1. Read *Inch by Inch* to the children.
2. Have the children take worms from the small bucket and sort them by sizes into the corresponding size pail.
3. They can use the ruler or tape measure to measure the worms.

Related book
Wonderful Worms by Linda Glaser

➕ *Kristi Larson, Spirit Lake, IA*

How Many Caps for Sale?

counting, number sense

Materials
Caps for Sale by Esphyr Slobodkina
one checkered cap
several blue, brown, gray, and red baseball caps

What to do
1. Read *Caps for Sale* to the class.
2. Ask families to bring caps to the classroom.
3. Invite a parent to come to class and act out the part of the peddler while you tell the story again. As you tell the story, invite the children to place hats on their parents' heads.
4. Ask the children questions. "How many checked hats did the peddler have?" "How many are red? Blue? Brown? Gray?" "Which is more, one or a bunch?"

➕ *Karyn F. Everham, Fort Myers, FL*

Hungry Caterpillar!

counting

Materials   *The Very Hungry Caterpillar* by Eric Carle
flannel board
felt cutouts of 1 caterpillar, 1 leaf, 1 butterfly, 1 apple, 2 pears, 3 plums, 4 strawberries, 5 oranges

What to do
1. Read *The Very Hungry Caterpillar* to the class.
2. Read the story again and invite the children to help put the felt cutouts on the flannel board as you get to them in the story.
3. Encourage children to count out loud the number of pieces of fruit eaten by the caterpillar.

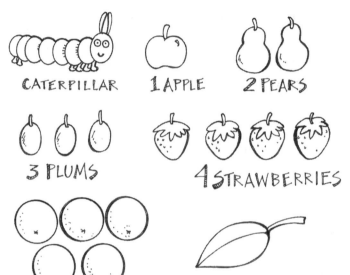

CATERPILLAR   1 APPLE   2 PEARS

3 PLUMS   4 STRAWBERRIES

5 ORANGES   1 LEAF

1 BUTTERFLY

✚ *Karyn F. Everham, Fort Myers, FL*

If You Give a Mouse a Cookie

counting, numeral recognition

Materials

If You Give a Mouse a Cookie by Laura Joffe Numeroff
laminated large brown circles (numbered)
laminated small black circles
toy oven
cookie sheets
timer

What to do

1. Read *If You Give a Mouse a Cookie* to the children.
2. Put the numbered brown circle cookies on the cookie pans.
3. Invite the children to place the correct number of "chocolate chips" (small black circles) on the cookies. For example, a child would put five chocolate chips on the numeral 5 cookie.
4. When they are done, encourage them to "bake" the cookies in the toy oven.
5. Tell the children to place the oven on 350 degrees and place cookies in the oven. Invite them to set the timer for the appropriate length of time.

✚ *Wanda Guidroz, Santa Fe, TX*

In the News

number sense, numeral recognition, sequencing

Materials

newspaper
scissors
pencils or crayons
glue
paper
hole punch
yarn

What to do

1. Give the children a newspaper and a set of numbers to look for. (1–5 is a good range to start with; 1–10 for children familiar with larger numbers.)
2. Invite the children to cut out the numbers and glue them in numerical order on a large piece of paper.

3. Call the children's attention to any ways in which the numbers differ. For example, some will be in a bigger font than the others, and some will be in italics or bold type.
4. Ask the children to read the numbers to you. Encourage them to practice counting the numbers.
5. Next, make a counting book using pictures the children cut from the newspaper.
6. Give each child seven pieces of paper. Have them write the page numbers (1–5) at the bottom of each of five blank pages.
7. Have the children paste one item on page one, two items on page two, and so forth. Explain that all the things they put on one page must be in some way related, such as all animals, all basketball players, all cars, and so on.
8. Help them print the name of each item on the appropriate page.
9. Have them create a front and back cover for the book using the other two pieces of paper.
10. Punch holes in all the pages (including the front and back covers) and have the children thread the yarn through the holes to bind the pages together into a book.

✛ *Virginia Jean Herrod, Columbia, SC*

Inchworm and a Half

measurement

Materials

Inchworm and a Half by Elinor Pinczes
playdough
rulers

What to do

1. Read the story to the children.
2. Talk about all the things the worms measured in the story.
3. Show the children the inch markings on a ruler and talk about how we use inches to measure things. Count the number of inches on the ruler. Show them where the half-inch markings are as well.
4. Give the children playdough and ask them to make inchworms.
5. Put out rulers and invite the children to measure their inchworms. Ask the children questions: "Whose is the longest?" "Shortest?" "How many inches long are they?"

✛ *Shelley F. Hoster, Norcross, GA*

Judging Sizes

comparison

Materials   10–20 groups of 3 of the same items in varying sizes

What to do
1. Collect 10–20 groups of three of the same items in different sizes. For example, a small, medium, and large block; a small, medium, and large pencil; a small, medium, and large bowl, and so on.
2. Invite the children to make patterns of the different objects (large, medium, small; or large, small, large, small; and so on). For example, they might make a pattern like this: small ball, large ball, small eraser, large eraser; small cup, large cup, and so on.
3. Ask the children to describe aloud the size patterns they are making.

✚ *Iris Rothstein, New Hyde Park, NY*

Jump, Frog, Jump!

subtraction

Materials   *Jump Frog Jump!* by Robert Kalan
plastic frogs
paint
butcher paper

What to do
1. Read *Jump Frog Jump!* by Robert Kalan.
2. Do the fingerplay "Five Little Speckled Frogs" with the children to reinforce the concept of subtraction and the numerals 0–5.
3. Make "frog track" pictures with the children by dipping the plastic frogs in paint and jumping them across butcher paper.

✚ *Shelley F. Hoster, Norcross, GA*

Legs!

counting, addition

Materials   none

What to do
1. Explain to the children what a riddle is.
2. Tell them the traditional riddle "Legs!"

   Legs
   Two legs sat upon three legs,
   With one leg in his hand;
   In comes four legs,
   Runs away with one leg;
   Up jumps two legs,
   Catches up three legs,
   Throws it after four legs,
   And makes him bring back one leg.

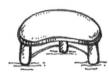

3 LEGS

2 LEGS

3. Encourage the children to try and work out what each number of legs represents (two legs: man; three legs: stool; four legs: dog; one leg: chicken leg or leg of lamb).

4 LEGS

4. Add up the number of legs in the riddle.

1 LEG

✚ Anne Adeney, Plymouth, United Kingdom

Like and Different Dinosaurs

comparison

Materials   container with a variety of small plastic dinosaurs (or any other creature of interest, such as insects or jungle animals)

What to do
1. Have each child select two dinosaurs from the container.
2. Ask each child to describe one way his dinosaurs are alike, and one way they are different.
3. If a child chooses the same dinosaur, he can choose a different dinosaur.

Related books   *Dinosaur Roar* by Paul and Henrietta Stickland
How Do Dinosaurs Count to Ten by Jane Yolen
Saturday Night at the Dinosaur Stomp by Carol Diggory Shields

✚ *Kristi Larson, Spirit Lake, IA*

Make a Counting Book

classification, counting, reasoning

Materials   colorful newspaper ads (found in newspaper inserts)
magazines
glue sticks
paper
scissors
markers or crayons

What to do
1. Give each child a piece of white paper, a glue stick, and a pair of scissors. Place several newspaper ads and magazines in the center of the table for the children to browse through.
2. Explain to the children that they will be making counting books by gluing pictures of similar items on different pages.
3. The children begin by cutting out one picture of an object to glue on page one. Help them write the numeral 1 somewhere on that page.

4. As they complete page one, give them another piece of paper. Ask them to glue a picture(s) of two similar objects on the page. They might use pictures of two dogs, two animals, two stuffed toys, and so on. Let the children decide how "similar" the items should be. This helps them learn to categorize while also encouraging creative thinking.

5. Help them write the numeral 2 on the page.

6. Continue until each child decides she is finished (perhaps five pages). Older children may want to work on their books for several days and make 10 pages.

7. Encourage the children to dictate a story about the items they chose for each page and how they are similar. Help them to write the name of the item at the top or the bottom on the page. For younger children, it sometimes helps to write the word on a separate piece of paper for them to copy.

8. Help the children create covers for their books. On a piece of construction paper, help them write "My Counting Book," "My Book of Numbers," or whatever they want. Let them write their names at the bottom of the cover.

9. Punch two holes in the cover and the pages of the book on the left side. Use brads or yarn to bind or tie the pages together.

✚ *Sandra K. Bynum, Blackfoot, ID*

Making a Measuring Book

counting, measurement, number order

Materials

library books
rulers
paper
crayons and markers
stapler (adult only)

What to do

1. Ask each child to choose a favorite library book. Ask them to draw a picture of the most exciting part of the story. Make sure the paper is held horizontally so they will all fit into a class booklet.

2. Help the children write the title of the book on their page, below or above the drawing.

3. Show the children how to position a favorite library book as though they were ready to read it, and use a ruler to measure from the left side of the book to the right side.

4. Demonstrate how to hold one edge of the ruler even with the left edge of the book, and how to look at the other side of the ruler to read the number of inches.
5. Help them write the number of inches on their drawing.
6. At circle time, spread out all the drawings and ask the children to put them in order by the number of inches written on the pages.
7. Add a front and back and staple the pages together.

✚ *Susan Oldham Hill, Lakeland, FL*

Measuring Feet

measurement

Materials   *The Foot Book* by Dr. Seuss
black coloring pencil
colored paper
scissors
plastic inchworm counters
glue

What to do   1. Read *The Foot Book* to the children.
2. Give each child a black colored pencil and two different colors of paper.
3. Help each child trace a bare foot on one piece of paper.
4. Help them to cut out their footprints.
5. Have the children glue their footprints on the other piece of paper.
6. Using plastic inchworms as a standard of measurement, help them measure their footprints. Write the number of inchworms underneath the footprint.

Related book   *Inchworm and a Half* by Elinor J. Pinczes

✚ *Quazonia J. Quarles, Newark, DE*

Menu Journal

days of the week, sequencing, time awareness

Materials

Today Is Monday by Eric Carle
7-day weekly calendar
small pictures of string beans, spaghetti, soup, roast beef, fresh fish,
    chicken, and ice cream
glue
scissors

What to do

1. Read *Today Is Monday* by Eric Carle.
2. Afterwards, review the days of the week and sing the song *Today Is Monday*.
3. Give each child a 7-day calendar and pictures of the food mentioned in the story.
4. Encourage the children to cut out the pictures and glue the food that was eaten on the specific day of the week.

✚ *Quazonia J. Quarles, Newark, DE*

The Mitten

counting

Materials

The Mitten by Jan Brett
photographs of the types of animals that climb into the mitten

What to do

1. Before reading the story, ask the children to guess how many animals they think can fit in a mitten.
2. Pass out the animal pictures to eight of the children.
3. Read *The Mitten* to the children. As you read, have the children holding the correct animals stand up with their pictures when their animals are introduced (the mole, snowshoe rabbit, hedgehog, owl, badger, fox, bear, and meadow mouse).

4. At the end of the story, ask the children if they know how many animals fit inside the mitten. Count the children holding the pictures of the animals.

5. Remind the children who didn't get a turn to stand that they will have a turn with another story.

✚ *Sandy L. Scott, Meridian, ID*

The Monster Countdown

counting

Materials   *Seven Scary Monsters* by Mary Beth Lundgren

What to do
1. Read *Seven Scary Monsters* to the class.
2. Read the story a second time, and ask the children to help tell the story, calling out the appropriate number.
3. Invite the children to join in "The Monster Countdown," calling together:

   Seven, six, five, four, three, two, one!
   Monsters, please come back!

✚ *Karyn F. Everham, Fort Myers, FL*

My Ocean Counting Book

addition, counting

Materials   paper or card stock
markers or crayons
hole punch and rings or stapler

What to do

1. This is a great book to make when doing an ocean theme, but it works well with many classroom themes.
2. Give each child six pieces of paper or card stock.
3. On the first piece of paper or card stock, the children write the numeral 1 and then draw one item related to the ocean. Help them write what the item is on the page.
4. On the next piece of paper, they write the numeral 2, draw two of an item related to the ocean, and write what the items are.
5. Continue doing this with the numerals 3, 4, and 5. Five is a good amount for children's attention spans, but the project can be spread out over multiple days.
6. When the children finish, have them create a cover page.
7. Help the children assemble the books and staple together.

Related books   *One Giant Splash* by Michael Dahl
Over in the Ocean: In a Coral Reef by Marianne Berkes
Somewhere in the Ocean by Jennifer Ward and T.J. Marsh

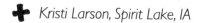 *Kristi Larson, Spirit Lake, IA*

The Number Three

number awareness

Materials
magazines or catalogs
tagboard
marker
laminator
scissors
binding machine (optional)

What to do
1. Locate pictures of animal families (adult male, female, and baby) in magazines or old educational catalogs. Use the pictures to construct a book for your classroom.
2. Mount the pictures on tagboard with three animals to a page.
3. Label the adult male's name, the adult female's name, and the baby's name. For example: stallion, mare, colt; bull, cow, calf; and so on.
4. Make a cover for the book with the title "Animal Families and Babies."
5. Laminate the covers and pages for durability, and cut out.
6. Bind the pages between the covers using a binding machine, if available.
7. Discuss the number three with the children. Lead them into listing the animal families with father, mother, and baby names with which they are familiar.
8. Introduce the book to the class. Place it in the classroom library for reference.

✚ *Jackie Wright, Enid, OK*

Numbers on the Tree

counting, numeral recognition

Materials
Chicka Chicka 1, 2, 3 by Bill Martin, Jr., Michael Sampson, and Lois Ehlert
dark brown, green (light and dark), and red construction paper
scissors
large white poster board
glue
laminator
large letter-size envelope
assorted foam colored sheets or foam numerals
Velcro

What to do

1. In advance, make a large tree using various shades of green construction paper for the leaves of the tree and dark brown paper for the trunk and branches. The tree should be the size of the poster board.
2. Glue the tree to the poster board and laminate for durability.
3. Cut out red and green apples (the size of golf balls) from red and green paper. Laminate apples for longevity and add Velcro to the back.
4. Attach 20 pieces of Velcro throughout the leaves of the tree.
5. Cut out two sets of 2" numerals (0–10 or 0–20) from foam sheets or, if available, use purchased foam numerals.
6. Seal the envelope shut and cut in half. Laminate and slit the side open to form a pocket. Attach the pocket to the trunk of the tree using Velcro.
7. During group time, read *Chicka Chicka 1, 2, 3*.
8. After reading the story, display the poster board tree and foam numerals. Explain to the children that they are going to count the apples on the tree.

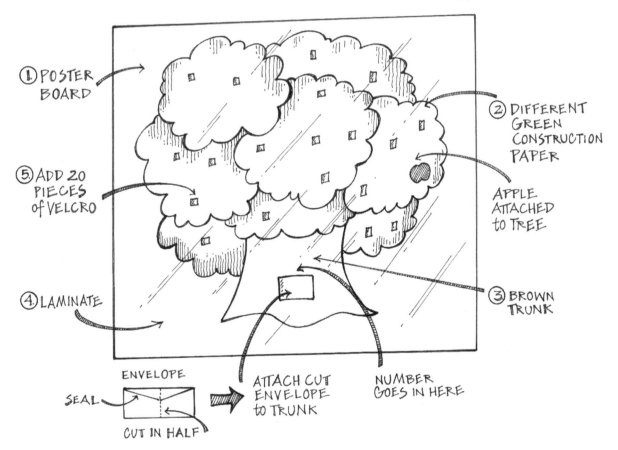

9. Attach the desired number of apples to the tree, for example, eight.
10. From one of the sets of numerals, choose the corresponding numeral (8) to the number of apples on the tree and hide it in the envelope.
11. After the children count the apples encourage a volunteer to pick the number of apples represented from the other set of numerals.
12. Reveal the hidden number after the child chooses his number to see if they have counted correctly.
13. Continue to play a few more times.

✚ *Quazonia J. Quarles, Newark, DE*

One to Ten in Chinese

· ·

numbers in another language

Materials   *Count Your Way Through China* by Jim Haskins
Eyes of the Dragon by Margaret Leaf or *Silk Peony, Parade Dragon* by
    Elizabeth Steckman
white poster board
broad-tipped black felt marker
red and blue medium-tipped washable felt markers

What to do   1. Use the book *Count Your Way Through China* to make a chart number chart. List the numerals 1–10 on the left side of the poster board. List the symbols for 1–10 in Chinese on the right side (see illustration on the following page).
2. Learn the pronunciation of the numbers in Chinese in advance.
3. Read *Eyes of the Dragon* by Margaret Leaf or *Silk Peony, Parade Dragon* by Elizabeth Steckman to the group.
4. Show the chart, explaining that numbers are written and pronounced differently in many other countries, such as China.
5. Pronounce the names of the numbers in Chinese, pointing to each number. Have the children repeat after you several times.
6. Sing the numbers 1–10 in English with the children. Try singing the numbers 1 to 10 in Chinese with the children.
7. Offer to write each child's age on the back of their hand in Chinese with their choice of red or blue washable marker.

Note: For younger children, you may only want to count from one to five.

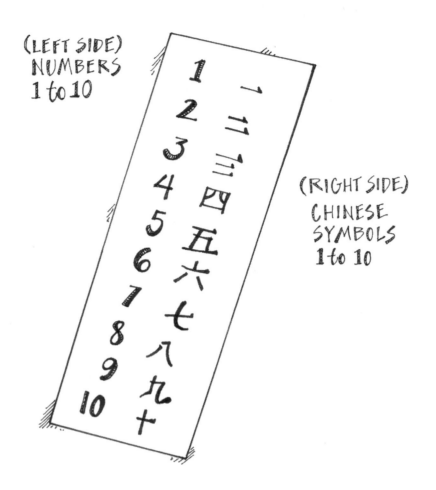

(LEFT SIDE) NUMBERS 1 to 10

(RIGHT SIDE) CHINESE SYMBOLS 1 to 10

Related books   *Count Your Way Through Japan* by Jim Haskins
Count Your Way Through Korea by Jim Haskins
Count Your Way Through Russia by Jim Haskins
Red Eggs and Dragon Boats: Celebrating Chinese Festivals by Carol Stepanchuk

✚ *Christina Chilcote, New Freedom, PA*

Pairs

. . . .

sorting

Materials   *A Pair of Socks* by Stuart J. Murphy
color copy machine
paper
scissors
laminator

What to do
1. Use the endpapers of the book *A Pair of Socks* by Stuart J. Murphy to enlarge several pairs of socks on paper using a color copy machine, or simply draw pairs of socks.
2. Laminate the socks and cut them out.
3. After reading the book aloud to the class, have the children match the corresponding pairs and place them together.

➕ *Jackie Wright, Enid, OK*

A Pet's Week

measuring time, days of the week

Materials
Cookie's Week by Tomie dePaola and Cindy Ward
blank week-long calendar
crayons

What to do
1. Read *Cookie's Week* and review with the children what Cookie did each day. (Cookie fell into the toilet on Monday, knocked over a plant on Tuesday, and so on.)
2. Give each child a blank week-long calendar to take home. Ask the children to draw one thing their pet does each day. Send home a note with the calendars asking parents to write down what their child says about each day's drawing. For children who do not have pets, have them observe a class pet, a neighbor's pet, or an outside wild animal (like a squirrel or bird).
3. Place an enlarged version of the calendar and pictures of Cookie's daily adventures one of the classroom centers. Encourage children to place the pictures under the correct day.
4. Invite the children to share calendars the following week.

Fluffy played with his catnip toy.

Monday

Fluffy watched a bird.

Tuesday

Fluffy sat in a bag.

Wednesday

Fluffy slept in the sun.

Thursday

Fluffy got on top of our table.

Friday

Fluffy hid under my bed.

Saturday

Fluffy watched bugs.

Sunday

✚ *Quazonia J. Quarles, Newark, DE*

Post-It Number and Word Game

numeral recognition

Materials   marker
              Post-It notes

What to do
1. Write the numerals 1–10 on separate Post-It notes (not the sticky side).
2. On the opposite (sticky) side, write five simple words the children know or can learn easily. Start with the children's names or simple words such as *stop, go,* and *ball.* Write each word on two Post-Its with numerals that aren't adjacent (for example, write "ball" on Post-Its 1 and 7).
3. Stick the Post-Its on a wall in two or three rows.
4. The children take turns calling out two numbers at a time.
5. Turn over the Post-It notes corresponding to the called numbers.
6. When the words on two Post-Its match, remove the numerals from the board.
7. If there's no match, return the Post-Its to their places and give the next child a turn.
8. When the children have matched all the words, play again with the same words or use new words.

Related books   *Rock It Sock It, Number Line* by Bill Martin, Jr. and Michael Sampson
                   Ten Puppies by Lynn Reiser

✚ *Monica Hay Cook, Tucson, AZ*

Seasonal Number Books

counting from 1–5, numeration

Materials unlined drawing paper
stapler

What to do
1. Staple together five 5-page booklets for each child, with one number written at the bottom of each page in numerical order.
2. Invite the children to draw a corresponding number of seasonal objects on each page. For example, in the winter, the children could draw one snowball, two hats, three mittens, four earmuffs, and five coats. For the spring, the children could draw one rainbow, two drops of rain, three flowers, four worms, and five snails. For summer, the children could draw one sun, two fish, three seashells, four sun hats, and five sand buckets and shovel sets. For fall, the children could draw one tree, two apples, three pumpkins, four leaves, and five birds.

✚ *Barbara Saul, Eureka, CA*

Set Me Right

number sequence

Materials old children's books or magazines
staplers

What to do
1. Divide the class into groups.
2. Remove the staples or binding from the magazines and jumble up the pages.
3. Ask each group to arrange the pages in the book in ascending or descending order. Help them staple the pages together.

✚ *Shyamala Shanmugasundaram, Nerul, Navi Mumbai, India*

Shape Flip Book

number sequence, shape recognition

Materials
construction paper
scissors
tagboard
glue
strips of paper
marker
clear contact paper or laminator
hole punch
2 binder rings

What to do
1. Cut out one of each shape from different colors of construction paper (circle, square, triangle, star, oval, diamond, and rectangle). Each shape should be a different color.
2. Glue each shape to a piece of tagboard or sturdy paper. Put each shape on a separate page. Number each page at the bottom right.
3. Write the name of each shape on a strip of paper. Glue each strip under the shape on the page.
4. Laminate the pages, using contact paper or a laminator.
5. Punch two holes at the top of each page (top left and top right) and string the rings through to hold the pages together.
6. Gather the children for circle time.
7. Hold up the new book and tell them you have a new book about shapes.
8. Go through the book with them once, and see if the children can name all the shapes in the book.
9. Read the book again and point out the page numbers at the bottom of each page.
10. Take the book apart and invite the children to put the pages in order according to the page numbers.

✚ *Shelley F. Hoster, Norcross, GA*

Shapes, Shapes, What Do You See?

shape recognition

Materials

white construction paper
colored construction paper
4 basic shapes (circle, square, triangle, rectangle)
scissors
markers
stapler

What to do

1. Write the following questions or answers on separate sheets of white paper as indicated.

   Page 1: *Round circle, round circle, what do you see?*
   Page 2: *I see a square looking at me.*
   Page 3: *Square box, square box, what do you see?*
   Page 4: *I see a triangle looking at me.*
   Page 5: *Triangle, triangle, what do you see?*
   Page 6: *I see a rectangle looking at me.*
   Page 7: *Rectangle, rectangle, what do you see?*
   Page 8: *I see all the shapes looking at me.*

   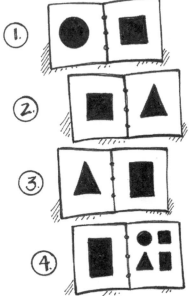

2. Make enough copies for each child to have all eight pages.
3. Help each child cut out three of each shape from the construction paper.
4. Ask the children to identify which shapes are associated with each page of text. Have them glue the shapes to the appropriate pages, and one of every shape to the final page.
5. When the glue dries, help the children staple the pages into a book.

✚ *Kaethe Lewandowski, Centreville, VA*

Small, Medium, and Large Friends Book

classification, sorting

Materials
camera
copy machine or computer and printer
paper
glue
stapler or hole punch and rings

What to do
1. Take photos of each child in the class.
2. Use a copy machine or software to make each photo three different sizes (by enlarging and reducing each picture).
3. You can either cut out the photos, or span the project over several days and let the children cut out a few.
4. Create a page with three sections, labeled "Small," "Medium," and "Large." Make several copies of the page.
5. Let the children sort the pictures of their friends by size and glue them in the corresponding sections.
6. When all of the pages are complete, assemble the pages into a book by stapling them together or using a hole punch and rings.

Related books
Bear's New Friend by Karma Wilson and Jane Chapman
Do You Want to Be My Friend? by Eric Carle
How to Lose All Your Friends by Nancy Carlson

✚ *Kristi Larson, Spirit Lake, IA*

Spider Count

counting

Materials
large butcher paper
marker
plastic spiders
pie tin

What to do
1. Write the words to the song "Itsy, Bitsy Spider" on a piece of butcher paper and hang it so children can see.
2. Invite the children to recite it with you.
3. Encourage the children to count the number of times the word "spider" appears in the rhyme. Point to the words on the butcher paper.
4. Sing the song again and place a plastic spider in a pie tin each time the children say "spider."

Related book   *The Itsy Bitsy Spider* by Iza Trapani

✚ *Sandy L. Scott, Meridian, ID*

Swimming in a Row

patterns

Materials
One Fish, Two Fish, Red Fish, Blue Fish by Dr. Seuss
assorted colors of plastic fish
small die-cut fish or fish stickers
orange, yellow, red, blue, and green construction paper
large bowl pattern
white paper
blue crayons

What to do

1. Prepare one fish bowl pattern per child using white paper and either make fish die-cuts out of orange, red, yellow, blue, and green paper or provide fish stickers of the same colors mentioned.
2. After reading the story *One Fish, Two Fish, Red Fish, Blue Fish* make a pattern using the plastic fish.
3. Create an ABBCD pattern to go with the title of the book [*One Fish* (A) *Two Fish* (BB), *Red Fish* (C), *Blue Fish* (D)] or create a much easier AB pattern (red and blue fish) or ABB (one fish, two fish).
4. Encourage the children to come up with their own patterns using fish die-cuts or stickers. Invite them to glue fish on their white fish bowl pattern. Provide blue crayons so they can add water to the fish bowls.
5. Help them add a description under their patterns.
6. Discuss the children's patterns as a way to review patterning.

✚ *Quazonia J. Quarles, Newark, DE*

Ten Black Dots

counting to 10

Materials
Ten Black Dots by Donald Crews
black construction paper
scissors
paper
glue
crayons or markers

What to do

1. Cut out enough circles from black construction paper for each child to have 10.
2. Set out paper, glue, and drawing materials at the art center.
3. Gather the children in a circle.
4. Show the children the 10 black circles. Talk about the circles and let them know that circles can also be called dots, as they are in the story that they are about to hear.

5. Sing the following song (tune: "Little Red Wagon"):

Ten Black Dots
One little, two little, three little black dots,
Four little, five little six little black dots,
Seven little, eight little, nine little black dots.
What can we make with ten black dots!

6. Read *Ten Black Dots* by Donald Crews. After the story, let the children make pictures using their black "dot" circles, following the examples in the story. They can choose how many dots they would like to use. Make sure they count their dots while they are working.

7. Write "_____ black dots make a _____" on the children's papers as they dictate to you how many circles they chose to use and what they made with them.

✚ *Shelley F. Hoster, Norcross, GA*

There Were Ten in the Bed

counting backwards, subtraction

Materials
Ten in the Bed book (any author)
tagboard
computer or marker
laminator
scissors
rubber cement
felt
blank cassette tape
tape player
flannel board

What to do
1. Locate a book version of the song "Ten in the Bed." There are several books available, including one by Jane Cabrera and several by Penny Dale. Photocopy the illustrations on each page, reducing them if necessary.

2. Mount the pictures on tagboard. Use a computer or a marker to print captions under each picture: "There were _____ in the bed." (In each blank, list 10, 9, 8, and so on to 1.)
3. Laminate the pictures for durability, and cut out.
4. Use rubber cement to glue felt on the backs of the pictures for flannel board use.
5. Make a cassette recording of the children singing "There Were Ten in the Bed."
6. Place the pictures and recording of the song in a center with a flannel board and tape player.
7. Allow one child at a time to visit the center and put the appropriate pictures on the flannel board and sing along with the cassette as the song counts down from 10 to one.

✚ *Jackie Wright, Enid, OK*

This One Is Just Right

comparison, ordering

Materials   *Goldilocks and the Three Bears* by James Marshall
construction paper cutouts of 3 bowls, 3 chairs, and 3 beds in small, medium, and large sizes

What to do   1. Read *Goldilocks and the Three Bears* to the children.
2. After finishing the book, invite the children to sort the cutouts from largest to smallest, asking them which size of bowl, chair, and bed Goldilocks would like.

Related book   *Berenstain Bears Big Bear Small Bear* by Stan Berenstain

✚ *Renee Kirchner, Carrollton, TX*

The Three Little Pigs: A Story About Counting

addition

Materials none

What to do **Note:** This activity is better for older children.
Tell the children the following version of the "Three Little Pigs," asking them the questions as noted:

Once upon a time, there lived three little pigs, age two, three, and four. What is the total age for all three pigs together? (9)

Every morning for breakfast, the pigs ate eggs (no bacon!). One pig ate one egg, the second pig ate three eggs, and the third pig ate five eggs. How many eggs did they eat in all? (9)

One day, after eating all those eggs, the three pigs decided to take a walk. The first pig walked one mile, the second pig walked three miles, and the third pig walked two miles. How many miles did they walk total? (6)

After all that walking, the three little pigs decided to go back home. Each pig's four feet were very sore. How many sore feet were there in all? (12)

Now, the wolf was very hungry. It took him three puffs to blow down the first pig's straw house, and five puffs to blow down the second pig's stick house. However, after six puffs, he couldn't blow down the third pig's house. How many puffs does that make? (14)

✚ *Geary Smith, Mexia, TX*

Twelve Little Girls in Two Straight Lines

counting, multiplication

Materials   *Madeline* by Ludwig Bemelmans

What to do
1. Read *Madeline* to the class.
2. Invite the children to recite all the lines in the book about the 12 girls who went about their day "in two straight lines."
3. Choose 12 children to do the following:

   ■ Form two straight lines standing (as in book).
   ■ Form two straight lines sitting at a table.
   ■ Form two straight lines "brushing teeth."
   ■ Form two straight lines "in bed."

4. Continue the activity with other children, so that everyone gets a chance to participate.

✚ *Karyn F. Everham, Fort Myers, FL*

What Is It?

geometric shapes

Materials   *Seven Blind Mice* by Ed Young
glue
geometric shapes to create an elephant (see activity below)

What to do
1. Read *Seven Blind Mice* by Ed Young. In this story, the seven mice try to figure out what creature is at their pond. Each mouse provides a different opinion, until the seventh mouse puts all the pieces together.

2. Prepare the following shapes beforehand, or provide a drawing of the elephant for children to color or paste in the shapes:

- ■ 1 large rectangle for the body
- ■ 4 long, narrow rectangles for legs
- ■ 1 long, narrow oval for the trunk
- ■ 1 large circle for the head
- ■ 1 large triangle for the ears
- ■ 1 short, narrow rectangle for the tail

3. Using the geometric shapes or a coloring/pasting guide sheet, discuss the shapes (circle, rectangle, triangle, and oval).
4. Invite the children to guess which shapes will be used for which parts.
5. Color or make the elephant with the children.

✚ *Theresa Callahan, Easton, MD*

What Next?

sequencing

Materials
If you Give a Mouse a Cookie by Laura Numeroff
wax paper
Popsicle sticks
1 plain cookie per child
icing
small edible pieces (M & Ms, raisins, sprinkles, and so on)

What to do
1. Ask children questions about getting dressed in the morning. What do they put on first, second, and third?
2. Read *If You Give a Mouse a Cookie* by Laura Joffe Numeroff and ask the children to predict what might happen in the story as you read it.

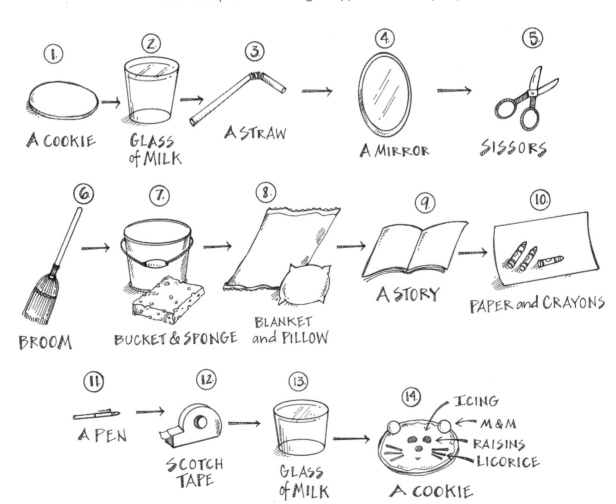

1. A COOKIE
2. GLASS of MILK
3. A STRAW
4. A MIRROR
5. SISSORS
6. BROOM
7. BUCKET & SPONGE
8. BLANKET and PILLOW
9. A STORY
10. PAPER and CRAYONS
11. A PEN
12. SCOTCH TAPE
13. GLASS of MILK
14. A COOKIE — ICING, M & M, RAISINS, LICORICE

3. Ask comprehension questions regarding the sequence of events in the story.

4. Explain that they are going to create their own mouse with the cookie.

5. In a small group, children frost their cookies using Popsicle sticks and decorate them as they wish to look like mice.

6. Ask the children to retell the story in the proper sequence.

7. Save the cookies for snack!

✚ *Dr. Geraldine Jenny, Grove City, PA*

The Wide Mouthed Frog

counting

Materials
The Wide Mouthed Frog by Keith Faulkner
green construction paper frog cutouts
pipe cleaners
glue
Velcro strips
pencil
white sheet of paper
string

What to do

1. Ask the children what they know about frogs. "What do they like to eat?" "What makes a frog a good flycatcher?"

2. Read the book *The Wide Mouthed Frog* to the children. Encourage them to say the repeated text and ask what the surprise was at the end of the story.

3. After reading the story, ask how a frog's tongue works.

4. Have the children work in pairs to make a frog. Give each pair a paper frog cutout. Show them how to glue on a pipe cleaner tongue and attach a piece of Velcro to it.

5. Then invite the children to cut out a fly from white paper and attach a piece of Velcro to it. Help them attach string to the fly.

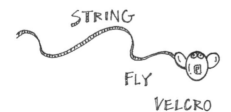

6. Encourage the children to practice trying to catch a fly with their frog's tongue. One child holds the string of the fly while the other child uses the frog to catch the fly. The child holding the fly may move it to make it more challenging.

7. Ask the children how many flies they could catch in a minute if they were frogs.

8. Write down their predicted numbers on a piece of paper and then time the children for one minute each while they try to catch flies.

9. After the first child in a pair tries, have them switch roles and repeat the procedure.

10. Ask why they think they got better at fly catching and if their predictions were correct about how many flies they thought they would catch.

SAMPLE DATA SHEET

Trial	Prediction	Actual
1.		
2.		
3.		

Dr. Geraldine Jenny, Grove City, PA

Beanbag Fun

counting, measurement, positional relationships

Materials   small beanbags (one per child)
CD or tape player
CD or tape of any kind of music

What to do
1. Invite the children to pick up a beanbag and find a space in the classroom to stand.
2. Play music and invite the children to dance around the room with their beanbags. After about one minute call out various positional directions. Ask them to move around the room with the beanbag *above* their head, *under* their body, *beside* their body, and so on.
3. Ask the children to sit on the floor with their beanbags. Instruct them to place their body *on top* of the beanbag, *underneath* the beanbag, and *next to* the beanbag.
4. Have the class practice counting by stacking the beanbags into sets of threes, sets of twos, and so on.
5. Incorporate measurement into the activity. Invite the children to place the beanbags end to end to see how long the "train of beanbags" grows. Have the children lie beside the beanbag train to see if they are taller or shorter than the train.
6. Encourage groups of children to use the beanbags to form shapes or numbers on the floor.

✚ *Mary J. Murray, Mazomanie, WI*

Clap a Pattern

patterns

Materials   none

What to do
1. Gather the children in a circle on the floor.
2. Clap a pattern for them to repeat, beginning with a simple "One, two." (Do not say the words.)
3. If the children can do this successfully, clap hands on the first beat and tap your knees on the second beat.

4. Add a third beat and accent the first: "*One*, two, three; *one*, two, three," clapping hands on one, knees on two and three.
5. Vary the pattern, increasing the difficulty as the children progress.
6. Clap the syllables in words and the children's names, letting the rhythm indicate accented syllables (hi-ber-nate; E-liz-a-beth).
7. As a variation, use clapping to accompany nursery rhymes. For example:

One, two, (clap hands twice)
Buckle my shoe. (tap knees)
Three, four, (clap hands)
Shut the door. (tap knees)

➕ *Mary Jo Shannon, Roanoke, VA*

Color Search

matching, numeral recognition

Materials
small index cards
markers or crayons

What to do
1. Make matching color cards by putting a certain number of colored dots on one card and printing the number of dots in the same color on another card. For example, put four dots on one card in blue and write "four" on another card in the same shade of blue.
2. Give each child a color card. Ask her to look at it and hold it to her chest with the number or dots facing out.
3. Play music as the children walk around the room.
4. When the music stops, the children try to find their "color partner" by matching colored dots to the matching word.

➕ *Jean Potter, Charleston, WV*

Cool Math Moves

numeral recognition

Materials   none

What to do   Sing the song with the children and follow the instructions for each line.

> *Now let's dance, let's real-ly move!*
> *Take one step forward to find the groove!*
>
> *Take two steps back to make some space.*
> *Then hop three times in just one place.*
>
> *Take four steps left, then five steps right;*
> *Now jump six times! You're doing just right!*
>
> *Make seven loud claps, they sound so great.*
> *Wiggle eight times: 1-2-3-4-5-6-7-8! (count numbers in double time to keep the beat)*
>
> *Stamp hard nine steps; no, make it ten.*
> *Turn in a circle and start again!*

Related book   *Cool Cats Counting* by Sherry Shahan

✛ *Theresa Callahan, Easton, MD*

Count and Do

numeral recognition

Materials   die (preferably with numbers, not dots)
card stock
pictures of various actions or markers

What to do

1. Glue or draw pictures of various actions, such as jumping, clapping, snapping, pointing, touching toes, and patting head on 4" × 6" (or other size) card stock to make movement cards.

2. Introduce the movement cards to the children, and invite them to act out each movement as a group.

3. Place all the movement cards face down on the floor or on a table.

4. Let the children take turns rolling the die and picking an activity card. The children act out whatever movement is on the card the number of times showing on the die.

✦ *Linda Ford, Sacramento, CA*

Counting Piano Notes

counting

Materials

electronic keyboard or xylophone

What to do

1. Play a note on the keyboard or xylophone. (If these aren't available, substitute a drum or recorder.) Explain to the children that when they hear a note, it is a signal to stop what they are doing and listen. Practice this with them.

2. Play two notes and explain that when they hear two notes, they are to sit down.

3. Play three notes, and explain that this is the signal to clap three times.

4. Practice the one-, two-, and three-note sequence with the children.

5. At different times throughout the day, play the three-note sequence.

6. As children get used to the three-note sequence, play four- and five-note sequences to cue different responses, such as jump four times.

✦ *Karyn F. Everham, Fort Myers, FL*

Do the Number Hop

numeral recognition

Materials   sidewalk chalk

What to do
1. On the floor or in the outdoor play area, draw large numerals from 1 to 10.
2. Call out a number, and encourage the children to run to the correct numeral.
3. As a variation, consider playing music and having the children walk from numeral to numeral, similar to musical chairs. When you stop the music, the children yell out the numbers they are standing on.

✚ *Barbara Saul, Eureka, CA*

Feel the Beat

counting

Materials   chart with the numerals printed on it

What to do
1. Count with the children and have them tap their thighs.
2. Repeat counting, and say, "Now as we count to ___, we are going to clap our hands."
3. Ask the children to suggest things they can do with their bodies as they count. Some ideas include: stomping feet, clapping knees together in and out, jumping, tapping head, and moving arms up and down.
4. Have the children do this with the days of the week and the months of the year.

✚ *Sandra Nagel, White Lake, MI*

How Many Taps or Claps?

counting

Materials
2 decorative bags, baskets, or boxes
index cards
markers or glue and pictures

What to do
1. Draw or glue pictures of different movements on index cards and write the movement next to it. Movement ideas include *tap, clap, bounce, stamp, turn, hop*, and so on.
2. Make number cards by writing the numerals 1–10 in big, bold print on 10 index cards, one numeral per card.
3. Place the movement cards in one bag and the number cards in the other bag.

4. Ask one child at a time to pull out a movement card from one bag and a number card from the other bag.

5. Encourage the children to act out the movement as many times as indicated on the number card.

✚ *Judy Fujawa, The Villages, FL*

I Know My Phone Number

numeral recognition

Materials
paper or sentence strips
marker
toy phone or old cell phone (optional)

What to do
1. Write each child's phone number on a piece of paper. If available, sentence strips work well for this activity.

2. Hold up one phone number at a time, and sing the following song to the tune of "This Old Man."

I Know My Phone Number

555-123-4567 ha! ha! ha! (insert the phone number you are holding)
I know my phone number,
And I'm telling you,
I know my phone number.
Yes, I do!

(If you don't need the area code where you live, substitute "Hey, hey, hey!" for the first three numbers.)

3. You may want to provide a toy phone or old cell phone for the children to practice finding the numbers on the keypad.

Related books
Martha Speaks by Susan Meddaugh
Toni's Topsy Turvy Telephone Day by Laura Ljungkvist

✚ *Laura Durbrow, Lake Oswego, OR*

Leap Frog

• •

counting

Materials   green lily pad shapes cut from felt (enough for each child in the class)
buttons
thread and needle
CD or tape player
CD or tape of lively music

What to do   1. Sew a different set of buttons on each lily pad. (Ask parent volunteers to sew the buttons on the lily pads or for a quick alternative, simply draw flowers on each lily pad with a permanent marker.)
2. Display the lily pads randomly around the room (pond).
3. Play lively music as the children pretend to be frogs hopping around the pond.
4. When the music stops, the "frogs" hop to a lily pad and pick it up.
5. Each frog touches and counts the "flowers" (buttons) on their lily pad and places it back on the floor.
6. Continue the game for several minutes or until the frogs tire of hopping.

More to do   **Games:** Put the lily pads in a row down the length of the room. Invite children to play "leap frog" with a partner. The children "leap" over one another and identify the number of "flowers" on each lily pad, or count the lily pads as they go.

✚ *Mary J. Murray, Mazomanie, WI*

Let's Get the Rhythm

• •

patterns

Materials   musical rhythm instruments (optional)

What to do   1. Clap a short rhythm with your hands. For example: clap two times fast and two times slow, or clap three times fast and two times slow.

2. Repeat the rhythm three times for the children to hear, and then ask them to clap the rhythm with you.

3. After the children have demonstrated that they can clap the rhythm correctly, ask them to walk around the circle to the beat of the rhythm. (If you clap two times fast and two times slow, the children take two quick steps followed by two slow steps.)

4. Invite the children to move their bodies to the rhythm. For example, have them stand on their tiptoes two times and then bend their knees and bounce on their legs two times. Or have them put their hands up in the air two times and then touch their knees two times.

✚ *Michelle Barnea, Millburn, NJ*

Listen for a Number

counting, recognizing number words

Materials

colorful plastic eggs
permanent marker
popcorn kernels
transparent tape

What to do

1. Use a permanent marker to print the numerals 1–10 on each plastic egg.

2. Create a rhythm instrument called a shaker egg with the children, and then have some fun using the shaker egg to improve their counting and number recognition skills.

3. Help each child count out 10–20 kernels.

4. Give each child a plastic egg. Ask them to open the egg, place the kernels inside one half of an egg, and put the egg back together.

5. Help them seal their eggs tightly by taping the seam.

6. Encourage the children to explore the noises their eggs make, as well as the eggs of the children around them.

7. Once the children are familiar with the sounds of their eggs, tell them they are going to play a number game. Ask them to listen carefully as you say various words. If they hear a number word, they shake their eggs.

8. Recite a list of familiar words to the children, inserting number words every now and then. For example: *swing set, ball, five, blocks, two, mom, seven, three, tree, leaves, ketchup, six,* and so on.

9. After several minutes, invite one child to lead the game by naming words.

10. Keep the shaker eggs handy for other rhythm activities.

More to do   **Music:** Invite the children to use their shaker eggs to keep the beat while you play their favorite marching or counting song.

✚ *Mary J. Murray, Mazomanie, WI*

Move Like Me

numeral identification

Materials   index cards
markers

What to do   1. Make up musical task cards. Write number directions on each card for the children to follow. For example:

Click your tongue 2 times.
Stomp your feet 4 times.
Skip around your chair 1 time.
Clap 6 times.
Snap your fingers 3 times.

2. Ask a child to select a card.
3. The child follows the action pictured on the card. Then the rest of the children follow the action.
4. Another child selects a card and the game continues, until everyone has had a turn.

Related book   *From Head to Toe* by Eric Carle

✚ *Monica Hay Cook, Tucson, AZ*

Moving in Patterns

patterns

Materials none

What to do

1. After children are familiar with the concept of patterns, talk about making patterns with one's body. The group's first movement pattern can be an easy-to-follow AB pattern: tap legs, clap, tap legs, clap, tap legs, clap, and so on.

2. Introduce a few more AB patterns:

   - clap, stomp (your foot), clap, stomp, clap, stomp
   - head, shoulders, head, shoulders, head, shoulders
   - snap (fingers), clap, snap, clap, snap, clap

3. Invite the children to think of a few patterns for the group to follow.

4. After the children seem to be doing well with the AB patterns, change to more complex patterns each month (ABC, ABCD, AABAAB, and so on). For example:

   - clap, jump, tap (thighs), clap, jump, tap, clap, jump, tap
   - head, shoulders, knees, toes, head, shoulders, knees, toes, head, shoulders, knees, toes
   - head, head, knees, head, head, knees

5. Again, invite the children make up patterns for the group to do. You might want to divide them into groups to make up patterns and practice them.

✚ *Sandra Nagel, White Lake, MI*

Musical Number Hoops

counting, numeral recognition

Materials large hula hoops
music
number cards

What to do

1. Place six hoops in a large space.
2. Divide the children into six groups, and write numerals on six cards that add up to the total number of children.
3. Place one card inside each hoop.
4. Play music and have the children move from hoop to hoop, as though they are playing musical chairs.
5. When the music stops, have the children gather in the hoops in groups that match the numerals written on the cards inside. (If whole bodies don't fit together in the hoops, just have the children put their feet inside the hoops.)
6. Change the numerals each time you stop the music, so the children always have to look at the numeral in the hoop and figure out if there is room for them inside.

HULA HOOP

CARD WITH NUMBER

✚ *Audrey Kanoff, Allentown, PA*

Number Parade

counting

Materials   ½" wooden dowels cut into 12" pieces (2 per child)
marching music

What to do   Turn on the music and invite the children to march around the room, tapping the dowels together, counting up to 10 or 20 tap by tap.

Related book   *Parade* by Donald Crews

✚ *Barbara Saul, Eureka, CA*

Number Scramble

number sequence

Materials
index cards
markers
CD player or tape player
music tape or CD

What to do
1. Write numerals on index cards, beginning with the numeral 1. Continue writing numerals (2, 3, 4, 5, and so on) until there is one for each child.
2. Ask the children to line up.
3. Give each child a card to hold.
4. Play music and invite the children to move around the room.
5. When the music stops, the children get back into the line in sequential order according to the numeral they have on their index card.

More to do
Music and Movement: End the activity by playing freeze dance. The children dance until they hear the number 10, then they all freeze.

Related book
Rock It Sock It Number Line by Bill Martin

✚ *Monica Hay Cook, Tucson, AZ*

Pattern Clapping

counting

Materials
none

What to do
1. Clap your hands in a pattern and encourage the children to try to follow the pattern. An example would be to clap two times fast and two times slow, then wait for the children to respond.
2. Extend the pattern by stomping your feet, snapping your fingers, or clapping

on other parts of your body such as your head or knees.

3. Once the children become familiar with the activity, let them take turns leading the pattern.

✚ *Sandy L. Scott, Meridian, ID*

Pattern March

directionality, patterns

Materials   marching music
CD or tape player

What to do   1. Play marching music and invite the children to stand up and begin marching.
2. Have the children repeat numbers while marching. Begin with a 1-2 pattern, then a 1-2-3 pattern, and finally a 1-2-3-4 pattern.
3. Add other number patterns as the children are ready for them.
4. Add directions, such as skip to the right, take two steps to the left, and so on.

✚ *Monica Hay Cook, Tucson, AZ*

Pattern Path

patterns

Materials   laminated pieces of colored construction paper
masking tape

What to do   1. Laminate enough pieces of colored construction paper to go around your classroom or open area.
2. Begin to tape down the laminated pieces of colored construction paper on the floor in a pattern to make a path around your classroom.
3. The children follow the path and recite the pattern out loud.
4. Leave room for the children to finish the pattern and the path around the

room.

5. To make the game more of a challenge, use shapes to make the path.

✚ *Ally Langmead, Walpole, MA*

Shape Hop

shape recognition

Materials

12" x 18" construction paper
scissors

What to do

1. Cut out large shapes from 12" x 18" construction paper (squares, triangles, circles, and rectangles), one shape per piece of paper. Make enough so that you have at least one of each shape per three children.
2. Place the paper shapes on the floor.
3. Explain that when you call out the name of a shape, children walk, hop, or wiggle to the shape. No running! Tell them that more than one child may stand on a shape.
4. Call out a movement and a shape, such as "walk to a square," "hop to a circle," or "wiggle to a rectangle."
5. Check that all the children are standing on the correct shape before calling out the next direction.
6. Allow the children to take turns calling the shapes.
7. To make this game more challenging, cut out shapes in different colors and play the game with two variables—color and shape. For example, "Walk to a green triangle," "Hop to a red square," and so on. Use no more than three colors and three shapes the first time you try this variation.

✚ *Cassandra Reigel Whetstone, Folsom, CA*

Shape Songs

shape recognition

Materials

masking tape
large space on the rug or floor

What to do

1. Ahead of time, use tape to make a large circle on the rug, big enough for four or five children to stand inside it.
2. Teach the children this simple song to the tune of "Someone's in the Kitchen with Dinah."

   Someone's in the circle with Jason,
   Someone's in the circle, it's true-uuu.
   Someone's in the circle with Jason,
   Waiting for a friend like you!

3. Choose a child to stand in the circle and sing the song with the children. Then ask the child inside the circle to choose a friend to join her. Continue until several children have a turn and then choose a new leader.
4. Repeat with a large square, triangle, and so on.
5. As a variation, collect items from the classroom that are the same shape to place into the large masking tape shape on the rug.

   ✚ *Susan Oldham Hill, Lakeland, FL*

Show Me Shapes and Sizes

shape recognition, shape words

Materials

What to do

1. Explain that when you say, "Show me _____," they should act out the word. For example, if you ask them to show you tall, they might stand on their tiptoes and stretch their arms up high.

2. Ask the children to show you shapes and sizes such as: tall, short, wide, narrow, circle, flat, tiny, huge, bent, straight, and round.

3. Invite the children to work in groups to form different shapes and figures, such as a circle, line, or square. It may help to put masking tape patterns on the floor for more difficult shapes such as a square or triangle.

TALL

WIDE

STRAIGHT

✚ *Cassandra Reigel Whetstone, Folsom, CA*

Ten Purple Elephants

subtraction

Materials   11 chairs

What to do
1. Select 10 children to be the elephants.
2. Set up 11 chairs one behind the other. Have the 10 "elephants" stand in a line near the chairs. Stand with them.
3. Invite the children to recite the following rhyme, having them move into their seats as the song suggests:

Ten purple elephants standing in line,
Waiting for bus number nine.
The bus arrives and goes to the mall.
Two get on, and that's all. (two elephants sit on the chairs)

How many elephants are there now?

Eight purple elephants standing in line,
Waiting for bus number nine.
The bus arrives and goes to the store,
Four get on, but no more. (four elephants sit on the chairs)

How many elephants are there now?

Four purple elephants standing in line,
Waiting for bus number nine.
The bus arrives and goes to the zoo,
Four get on, and I do, too! (remaining elephants and you sit on the chairs)

Are there any elephants left?

✚ *Ingelore Mix, Gainesville, VA*

What Did I Do?

counting

Materials   none

What to do
1. Ask the children to imitate an action you perform, such as stomping your feet.
2. Tell the children to watch carefully and count the number of times you stomp your feet.
3. After completing the action, ask the children for their answers.
4. Repeat with other actions such as waving, clapping, scratching, wiggling your fingers, tapping your nose, and so on.
5. Have the children take turns performing actions and counting the number of times the action is completed.

Related book   *From Head to Toe* by Eric Carle

✚ *Monica Hay Cook, Tucson, AZ*

ABC Line Up

classification, counting

Materials   sidewalk chalk

What to do
1. Draw a line on the blacktop and write each letter of the alphabet on the line using large letters.
2. Have the children stand on one side of the ABC line. Sing the "Alphabet Song" and step on each letter as you say it.
3. One at a time, ask the children to say their name and identify the first letter of their name. As they identify their letter, they stand in rows behind that letter in the line.
4. When all of the children are standing in rows, count how many are standing behind each letter.
5. Discuss which letter has the most children and which has the fewest.
6. Do the activity again using last names.

Related books   *Alison's Zinnia* by Anita Lobel
Chrysanthemum by Kevin Henkes
The First Thing My Mama Told Me by Marie Swanson

✚ *Cassandra Reigel Whetstone, Folsom, CA*

Around the Clock

numeral recognition

Materials   clock
blacktop area
sidewalk chalk
foam water noodle
beanbags

What to do

1. This activity will help get young children familiar with the standard clock. Display a real clock. Point out the numbers and hands on a real clock.

2. Take the children outdoors to a blacktop area. Draw a very large circle and write numbers on it like a real clock. Put a foam water noodle in the middle (like one hand of a clock). Remind children that a real clock has two hands, but for this game, the clock has only one hand.

3. Gather the children around the "ground clock." Explain that they are going to play a game called Around the Clock to help them learn their numbers.

4. Have the children line up at the twelve. Give each child a beanbag.

5. Set the noodle "hand" on the clock so that it points to a number.

6. The children run around the clock and drop their beanbags on the number the noodle is pointing to. As they drop the beanbag, they say "_____ o'clock" (according to the selected number).

7. They run around the clock a second time to pick up their beanbag and recite the time again as they pick up their beanbag.

8. Continue the game, pointing the clock hand to a different number each time.

✚ *Mary J. Murray, Mazomanie, WI*

The Big Catch!

counting

Materials
small plastic containers
crayons
plastic fish (from dollar or novelty stores).
small children's plastic pool
small fishing nets
timer

What to do
1. Give each child a small plastic container ("bucket")
2. Fill a regular size children's pool with water and plastic fish.
3. Provide small fishing nets for the children to retrieve the fish.
4. Set the timer for two minutes and encourage the children to pick up as many fish as they can.
5. Instruct the children to fill their buckets until the timer sounds.
6. Then ask the children to count the fish in their buckets.

Related book *Fish Eyes* by Lois Ehlert

✚ *Quazonia J. Quarles, Newark, DE*

Bouncing Counting

counting

Materials playground balls

What to do
1. Give each child a ball.
2. Together as a group, count out loud and have the children count by bouncing the balls.
3. For more outdoor counting, encourage the children to keep track of the number of times they jump in a row.

✚ *Barbara Saul, Eureka, CA*

Bubble Blowing

counting

Materials   jar of bubble solution

What to do
1. Dip a bubble wand into the bubble solution.
2. Give one child a turn to blow bubbles with the wand.
3. Count the number of times the child blows through the wand to create bubbles. Ask the children to try and count the bubbles. This will be a challenge!
4. Dip the wand into the bubble solution and give other children turns.

Related book   *Bubble Bubble* by Mercer Mayer

➕ *Jackie Wright, Enid, OK*

Carry Me Light

weight

Materials   hammock
objects with different weights (feathers, leaves, books, paper, boxes, pillows)

What to do
1. Tie the two ends of a hammock to two poles or two trees. (If a hammock is not available, use a canvas tarp or heavyweight plastic sheeting.)
2. Ask the children which objects dropped onto the hammock would make it sag in the middle.
3. Let each child take a turn dropping an object on the hammock.
4. Discuss what happens to the hammock with each object.
5. Let the children take turns sitting on the hammock and see what happens when more children are added.

➕ *Shyamala Shanmugasundaram, Nerul, Navi Mumbai, India*

Carton Countdown

addition, counting

Materials
10 2-quart orange juice cartons
paint
paintbrushes
kick ball

What to do
1. Have the children paint the cartons. Let dry.
2. Play this game in a large outdoor play area.
3. Arrange the cartons like bowling pins, with one carton in the front, two behind the first one, three behind the second row, and four in the back row.
4. Have the children stand about 10 feet away from the cartons and knock them over with a kick ball. Each child gets two turns.
5. Ask the children to count the number of cartons they knock down.
6. As a challenge for older children, number the orange juice cartons from 1 to 10 with a black marker or black paint. Set them up like bowling pins. Have the children roll a kick ball to knock them down. Ask them to write the numbered cartons they knocked down on a piece of paper (for example, 5, 7, and 8). Help them to add the numbers together to get the sum.

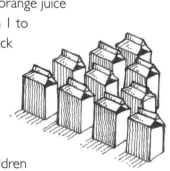

✚ *Randi Lynn Mrvos, Lexington, KY*

Changing Times

recognizing numeral positions on a clock

Materials chalk

What to do This is an energetic game for 13 children to play together.
1. Draw a giant clock on an outdoor blacktop area, writing the numbers in their appropriate places.
2. Have one child stand in the center of the clock (the hands), while each of the other children stand beside a number.
3. The child in the center stretches out his arms (like the hands of a clock) to two different numbers.
4. He calls out the numbers loudly, "Four and nine, change times!"
5. The two children standing at the 4 and 9 have to try and run across the clock and change places before the "hands" can run into one of their empty places.
6. The child without a place becomes the "hands" and calls out two more numbers. The children standing by these numbers switch places.
7. Remind the children to check their number each time because if they switch numbers with another child, they might forget which number they are standing next to.
8. After playing this game a few times the children will be more familiar with the positions of numbers on the clock face.

✛ *Anne Adeney, Plymouth, United Kingdom*

Circle Time

shape recognition

Materials

paper
scissors
circular items (ball, round cake pan, hat)

What to do

1. Cut out at least two different sizes of circles from paper.
2. Show the children the circles and ask them to name the shape.
3. Show examples of circles, such as a ball and the inside of a hat.
4. Ask the children what circles they can see in the room (toys, art work, eyes, clock, and so on).
5. Go on a circle walk to look for circles outdoors. Encourage the children to identify circular shapes. Look for balls, bike wheels, rocks, parts of flowers, acorns, and so on.
6. Return to the classroom and list the circles they found.
7. Repeat the activity another day using a different shape.

✚ *Cassandra Reigel Whetstone, Folsom, CA*

Clock Face Race

recognizing numeral positions on a clock

Materials

chalk (on concrete) or long rope (on grass)
large numerals (1–12), preferably on stand-up boards like a photo frame

What to do

1. Mark a large circle on the ground using chalk or rope. The size depends on how many children are playing the game, but it should be at least 30' in diameter. Clearly indicate which is the top and bottom of the clock.
2. Mark a long line beneath the clock, about 3' away from it.
3. Place the numerals around the circle, so they are clearly visible.
4. Children stand on the line beneath the clock face, facing 12 o'clock.

5. Stand in the center and call out a time, using your arms like clock hands. Hold out an outstretched arm for the minute hand and bend your elbow toward your body for the hour hand.
6. All the children have to run to the appropriate place on the clock face.
7. Have them return to the line underneath the clock face each time, so they are always looking at the clock the right way up.
8. Once the children are familiar with the position of the hours, you can progress to half and then quarter hours.

✚ *Anne Adeney, Plymouth, United Kingdom*

Colorful Number Line

counting, number sense, numeral recognition

Materials sidewalk chalk

What to do
1. Draw large numerals in order from 1–10 (or 20) on the sidewalk or blacktop (one large 3' numeral per square or space).
2. Draw the numeral with a bold outline so that the inside may be colored or decorated.
3. Assign two or more children to each numbered space. Let them decorate the numeral using the colored chalk.
4. Invite the children to draw sets of objects within the sidewalk square.
5. Have the children line up at the beginning of the colorful "number line."
6. Give specific directions for children to follow (hop, skip, jump, crab walk, and so on) as they travel along the number line and say each numeral aloud.
7. Children will enjoy moving along the number line as they admire each other's artwork.
8. Older children may draw their own number line using the colored chalk. Invite the children to draw a straight line and then print the numerals 1–10 (or higher) down the length of the line.

✚ *Mary J. Murray, Mazomanie, WI*

The Counting Path

counting, numeral recognition

Materials

washable paint
chalk

What to do

1. Paint a series of circles (resembling a path) on the pavement or blacktop. The circles should be about 10" in diameter and placed about 5" apart. The number of circles will depend on the space that you have available. Paint them right outside the door, next to a fence, or in an open space somewhere in the play yard.
2. Draw numerals inside the circles, starting with 1 and marking the circles in ascending order.
3. Indicate a place to start as children begin their walk on the path.
4. Ask the children to call out the numeral as they step on it. This is a fun way for them to identify numerals.
5. Change and rearrange the numerals as often as you like. You can even repeat numerals, to add a little twist.

More to do

Change what's inside the circles depending on your focus each day, for example, write the letters of the alphabet, different shapes, and colors.

✚ *Judy Fujawa, The Villages, FL*

Down the Slide

shape and numeral recognition

Materials

shape and number cards
slide
sandbox or tub of sand

What to do
1. Use this fun movement activity to get the children excited about shapes and numbers.
2. Have the children line up behind the steps to the slide.
3. Stand at the front of the slide with the shape and number cards in hand.
4. Invite the children to climb the ladder and slide down one at a time.
5. As each child reaches the bottom of the slide, he names the shape or number card as you display it.
6. As the child correctly identifies the shape, he gives you a high five and then moves to the sandbox to form that number or shape in the sand.
7. Instruct the child to make his shape or number quickly and then smooth out the sand so the next child can form his shape or number.
8. Repeat this activity several times so the children have numerous opportunities to climb and draw.

More to do

Sand Table: Provide plastic numeral and shape molds along with a tub of wet sand so children can form numerals with the molds.

✚ *Mary J. Murray, Mazomanie, WI*

The Egg and Pebble Hunt

counting, numeral identification

Materials
plastic eggs (5 times the number of children in the class)
pebbles
5 large plastic containers

What to do
1. Fill the eggs with one, two, three, four, or five pebbles.
2. Label the containers 1, 2, 3, 4, and 5.
3. Hide the eggs on the playground.
4. Invite the children to find eggs. Show them the containers and explain that they should remove the pebbles inside the egg and put them into the appropriate container.

✚ *Karyn F. Everham, Fort Myers, FL*

Find the Shape That Matches

matching, shapes

Materials   cardboard shapes
scissors
chalk

What to do

1. From the cardboard, cut out four circles, four squares, four triangles, and four rectangles. The shapes should be about 8"–10" across.
2. On the pavement/blacktop outdoors, trace around the shapes with chalk. Draw three of each shape. Place them in random order.
3. Distribute the cardboard shapes to the children and ask them to find the matching shape on the blacktop.
4. When the children begin, let them take their time. After a while, start to time how long it takes for them to finish. Also, consider letting one child at a time match all of the shapes by himself.

More to do

Add variety to this activity by cutting the shapes into three different sizes (small, medium, and large). Count the shapes at the end of the activity and ask the children questions, such as "How many are small? How many are medium? How many are large? How many are there all together?"
Depending on the age of the children, add more complicated shapes (octagon, diamond, and parallelogram).

✚ *Judy Fujawa, The Villages, FL*

Flying Sizes

comparison

Materials   different types of kites
different length of streamers
strings

What to do   1. Attach different lengths of streamers to the kites and fly them outdoors.
2. Initiate a discussion with the children about the kite with the longest or
shortest tail, and the kite flying the highest, lowest, nearest, and so on.

➕ *Shyamala Shanmugasundaram, Nerul, Navi Mumbai, India*

Here We Go

counting

Materials   items to set up an obstacle course, such as tumbling mats, chairs, old tires,
and barrels
markers
tagboard

What to do   1. Set up an obstacle course with items listed above or other available items.
2. Make signs for each station that tells the children what to do as they move
through the course. For example:

- Roll over two times on the mat.
- Crawl around the chair four times.
- Take five giant steps through the flattened tires.
- Crawl through the barrel one time.

3. A daily obstacle course is great for the children. Make one inside as well as outside. Play Follow the Leader using the obstacle course.

Related books *Follow the Leader!* by Emma Chichester Clark
Follow the Leader by Erica Silverman

✛ *Monica Hay Cook, Tucson, AZ*

Hoopla

counting, movement

Materials plastic hoops (1 per child)
colorful fabric scraps or bandanas (1 per child)

What to do 1. Disperse the hoops randomly around the playground.
2. Place the fabric scraps randomly near (but not inside) the hoops.
3. Ask each child to stand inside a hoop.
4. When you say, "It's time to count to ____," each child runs and grabs a fabric scrap, raises it high in the air, and waves it around while "whisper counting" to the designated number.
5. When a child finishes the quiet counting, he drops the fabric and runs to a new hoop.
6. Once every child has found a new hoop, continue the game. Play for several minutes.

More to do **Movement:** Have pairs of children stand inside a hoop together and hold it at waist height. Invite the pair to run from a designated start line to a select place (while inside their hoop together) to pick up a fabric scrap. Once the pair has the fabric in hand, they count in unison to 10 or 20 and then return to the starting line.

✛ *Mary J. Murray, Mazomanie, WI*

Hopscotch

counting, numeral recognition

Materials

sidewalk chalk
beanbag

What to do

1. Use sidewalk chalk to make squares of a hopscotch board. Write the numerals 1–10 in the squares.
2. Demonstrate how to hop on one foot and two feet to jump in the squares. Have the children say the numerals as they jump in the squares.
3. Show children how to play traditional hopscotch by tossing the beanbag onto a numeral, hopping and jumping to the square with the beanbag on it, bending to pick it up, and continuing along the grid.
4. For younger children, draw shapes in the squares instead of numerals and have them just jump with no hops.
5. Use numbers greater than 10 for children who are ready to practice recognizing larger numbers.

More to do

Language and Literacy: Substitute letters for numerals.

✚ *Sandra Nagel, White Lake, MI*

How High Is that Kite?

counting, measuring distance

Materials

kite string
brightly colored stickers
yardstick
kite

What to do

1. On the playground with the children, unroll kite string. Ask how long they think the string is. At 3' intervals, attach a sticker, noting the length. Together, count the number of yards of string.
2. Roll up the string and fly the kite, counting the yards of string as they unfurl.
3. When the kite falls, put the entire length of unfurled string on the ground. Together, count the number of yards "high" the kite flew.
4. With the string unfurled, invite each child to lie on the ground, head to toe, to find the number of children needed to reach as high as the kite.

✚ *Karyn F. Everham, Fort Myers, FL*

Jump Rope Math

numeral recognition and formation

Materials

jump ropes (1 per child)

What to do

1. Show the children how to use the jump ropes to form numerals on the ground.
2. Encourage the children to make the numerals 0–9, then have them pick up the ropes and jump that many times. For example, if a child makes the numeral 7, he would jump rope seven times.
3. If the children cannot jump rope, have them place the ropes on the ground and jump over them instead.

✚ *Barbara Saul, Eureka, CA*

Make It Whole!

fractions, matching

Materials
sidewalk chalk
tagboard in various colors
scissors
balance beam

What to do

1. Cut out large shapes, such as a circle, square, rectangle, oval, diamond, and triangle from tagboard. Make one shape for every two children in the class. Cut the shapes in half.
2. Draw shapes on the blacktop or sidewalk to correspond with the tagboard shapes (you might want to trace them).
3. Have the children line up at one end of the balance beam.
4. Give each child half of a shape.
5. Have the children walk the balance beam and find the shape on the ground that matches their shape half.
6. Invite the children to put their shape half on the chalk drawing and wait until another player comes along to "make it whole."
7. Ask the children to exchange their shapes with another child and then play the game again.
8. If you don't have a balance beam or as a variation, invite the children to run around the playground holding a shape half. When you blow a whistle, the children find a partner with a matching shape half. The two children hold hands and walk around to find the matching shape on the ground. Once they find their shape, they place their pieces on it to make it whole, and sit down.

More to do

Snack: Cut an assortment of food items in half. Invite the children to work with a partner to make each item whole by matching like halves. Then let the children eat the food fractions.

✚ *Mary J. Murray, Mazomanie, WI*

Number Jumps

numeral recognition

Materials
expanse of sidewalk about 7' long
sidewalk chalk

What to do
1. Ahead of time, draw a hopscotch board on the sidewalk, putting the numerals 1–10 in the spaces.
2. Ask the children to call out the names of the numerals as they jump on the squares.
3. To vary the game, draw the numerals in random order, or call out a numeral and have the child jump to that particular square.
4. For a fun cleanup, provide water and brushes for the children to wash off the sidewalk.

✚ *Susan Oldham Hill, Lakeland, FL*

Number Line Fun

counting, number sequence, numeral recognition

Materials
sidewalk chalk
four 3' plastic hoops
beanbags (optional)

What to do
1. Draw a number line on the sidewalk or blacktop. Print the numerals 0–10 along the line, 2' to 3' apart.
2. Place the plastic hoops at the end of the number line.
3. Have the class form a single-file line at the beginning of the number line. Draw their attention to the zero as the start line.
4. Invite the children to move down the number line by jumping as they count from zero to ten.
5. When a child reaches the numeral 10, he steps inside a plastic hoop, lifts it to his waist level, and holds onto it as he runs back to the start line.

6. When the child returns to the start line he puts the hoop on the ground and gets back in line.
7. Direct one or two "helpers" to be in charge of returning the hoops to the end of the number line after the runners set them down.
8. Continue this activity several times, calling out a different form of movement each time such as skip, hop, crab walk, dance, run, gallop, and so on.
9. Extend the number line to 20 for older children.
10. For an added challenge, see if the children can balance a beanbag on their heads as they walk down the line.

✚ *Mary J. Murray, Mazomanie, WI*

Number Run

numeral recognition

Materials chalk
4 plain colored 2' squares of fabric
thick-line permanent marker

What to do
1. Print large numerals 1–10 (or 1–20) at one end of the playground area.
2. Use the permanent marker to print the same numerals on the fabric squares.
3. Have children line up in pairs on the opposite side of the playground from the numerals.
4. Have the first several pairs of children hold a fabric square between them.
5. On the command: "Go to __ (fill in the numeral)," each pair of children runs across the playground and around the numeral they are assigned, without letting go of the fabric square.
6. When the first pair is halfway there, send another pair to a different numeral.
7. When the children return, they go to the end of the line.
8. Continue the game as the children run around each numeral and back.

More to do
Draw shapes or groups of objects on the playground instead of large numerals. Have the children identify the shape or count to objects as they run around it.

✚ *Mary J. Murray, Mazomanie, WI*

Obstacle Course

counting

Materials
16" lengths of ribbon or crepe paper
plastic traffic cones
plastic hoops
cardboard boxes

What to do
1. Create an obstacle course that requires children to run around cones, jump over boxes, step inside the hoops, and so on.
2. Invite five children to line up at the end of the obstacle course and hold a hand high in the air, ready for a "high five."
3. Invite the rest of the class to stand at the beginning of the obstacle course.
4. Hand each runner a ribbon.
5. Demonstrate how to complete the course, holding your ribbon high in the air. When you get to the end of the course, jog past the five children and give each one a "high five" as you count from one to five.
6. Invite the children to line up and take turns running the course one at a time.
7. When the first child completes the obstacle course, he runs past all the other children in line, giving them high fives and counting to five, then gets at the end of the line and begins to give the children coming behind him high fives.
8. Allow children to run the course several times.
9. For added counting practice, have the children count the hoops and cones as they pass them.

✚ *Mary J. Murray, Mazomanie, WI*

Over/Under Pass

shape recognition

Materials
various objects of different shapes

What to do
1. Ask half of the children to form a line on the playground. The rest of the children are the audience.
2. Hold up an object. The audience shouts out the name of the shape.

3. The children in line pass the object over their heads or under their legs to the person behind them. (Older children will be able to play this game in an over/under pattern. Younger children may just want to pass it under their legs to the next person.)
4. Each child in line identifies the shape as he passes it to the child behind him.
5. When the object reaches the end of the line, the last child holds it up high and shouts out the shape.
6. Repeat the activity several times using other shape objects.
7. Have the audience switch places with the children in line and repeat the activity several more times.

More to do
Games: Make this a relay game. On the command of "one, two, three, go!" two rows of children pass objects at the same time. When the last person in line receives the object, he races to a designated finish line. The first person to reach the finish line and place the object in a laundry basket wins that round of the game.

✚ *Mary J. Murray, Mazomanie, WI*

Paint a Shape

shape recognition

Materials
buckets of water (1 for every 2–4 children)
2" paintbrushes
sidewalk chalk

What to do
1. Draw a shape on the playground about 2' in size.
2. Invite the children to identify the shape.
3. Change the colors of chalk and draw several more shapes, one or two per child.
4. Invite each child to choose one or more shapes to "paint." Help them print their names (with chalk) inside the shape they want to paint.
5. Provide children with buckets of water to share and paintbrushes.
6. Invite the children to "paint" their shapes and watch their names and shapes disappear.
7. Invite the children to create their own chalk shapes and paint them with water.

✚ *Mary J. Murray, Mazomanie, WI*

Scavenger Hunt

one-to-one correspondence

Materials   chart with numbered images of the desired items (see illustration)

What to do
1. On a sheet of paper, create a visual scavenger hunt sheet.
2. If children can count to nine, for example, divide the paper into nine sections, number each section, insert a picture of the item to find, and write the word under the picture.
3. You can also draw the number of items (for example, three trees) and have the children cross them off the paper.
4. As a way to extend the activity, make a scavenger hunt using items the children may encounter on their way home from school, such as a mailbox, a truck, a stop sign, and a house. Have them make a mark in the block each time they see one of these items.
5. The next day, tally how many of each item the children saw to discover which item was most common to their experiences. Discuss.

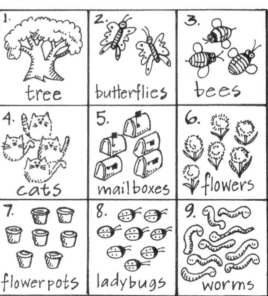

SCAVENGER HUNT

1. tree
2. butterflies
3. bees
4. cats
5. mailboxes
6. flowers
7. flowerpots
8. ladybugs
9. worms

✚ *Theresa Callahan, Easton, MD*

Shapes in the Neighborhood

counting, geometry, shape recognition

Materials
paper
pen or marker

What to do
1. Take the children outdoors for a walk. Before you leave, ask them which shape they think they will see most frequently. Write the shapes on a piece of paper to start a tally sheet.
2. Walk around the school and neighborhood, looking for shapes.
3. As the children see shapes and call them out, write them down (for example, square windows, rectangle doors, circle wheels, and so on). Be creative! Look at nature objects to find shapes (tree rings, rocks, leaves, and so on).
4. When finished, return to the classroom and compare your results with the prediction.

More to do
Circle Time: Have the children sit in a triangle or rectangle instead of a circle. Call them to "Triangle Time."

Related books
The Shape of Things by Dayle Ann Dodds
Shapes, Shapes, Shapes by Tana Hoban
When a Line Bends, a Shape Begins by Rhonda Gowler Greene

✚ *Kristi Larson, Spirit Lake, IA*

Sidewalk Fun

numeral and shape recognition

Materials
buckets of water
paintbrushes
sidewalk chalk

What to do

1. On a nice day, take the children outside to practice writing numerals and drawing shapes.
2. Demonstrate how to use the water and a brush to make a numeral. Demonstrate how to draw a circle with the sidewalk chalk and then paint over it with a brush and water. The children love watching the numerals disappear!

Note: Some of the children in your class may be more independent than others. Young children may just put the chalk in the water and it will dissolve. In these situations it would be better to draw shapes on the sidewalk and just have the water and the brushes available for the children.

✚ *Sandra Nagel, White Lake, MI*

Sidewalk Sets and Numerals

counting, numerals, sets

Materials

long expanse of sidewalk
sidewalk chalk

What to do

1. Ahead of time, plan the sidewalk sets and numerals.
2. Ask the children to think of items to draw on the sidewalk for each numeral 1 through 10.
3. On a sunny day, go out to the sidewalk to start the project.
4. Divide the children into 11 groups. Depending on the size of your class, their may only be one child in some or all of the "groups."
5. Give them the numeral they are to work on, and ask them to draw a big numeral on the sidewalk with the chalk.
6. Next, ask them to draw the items previously discussed in the classroom, making sure they are drawing the right number of items to match the numeral.
7. When the sidewalk mural is completed, invite other classes outside to see it.
8. At the end of the day, provide water and wide paintbrushes to wash everything away.

✚ *Susan Oldham Hill, Lakeland, FL*

Sports Connections

Venn diagrams

Materials
equipment for several different games or sports (skates, various sports balls, tennis racket, baseball bat, football helmet, hockey helmet, protective pads, sun visor, baseball cap, types of sports shoes, and so on)
large chalk or wide tape

What to do
1. With the chalk or tape, make a Venn diagram (interlocking ovals) on the ground or floor.
2. Discuss pairs of sports, encouraging the children to put all the items for one sport on one side of the diagram, and all the items for another sport on the other side.
3. Ask the children to put items they find in common in the middle, interlocking space. Here's an example of tennis and baseball equipment:

- Tennis: ball, racket, tennis shoes, net, sun visor, white clothes
- Baseball: bat, glove, hat, ball, base, uniform
- Interlocking section: head coverings, balls, athletic clothing

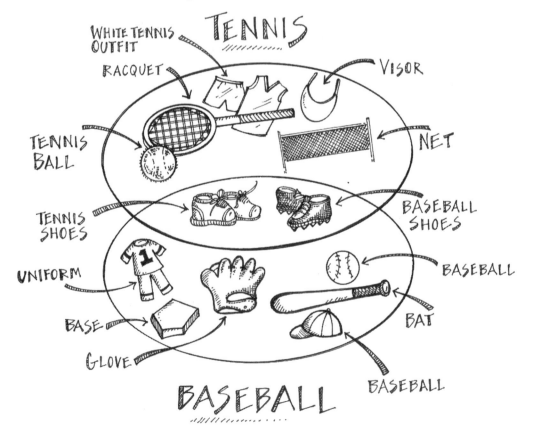

4. Discuss how the sports' equipment and rules are both similar and different (such as tackling or not touching, team vs. individual games).

Note: This activity can be adapted by using pictures of the articles in place of the actual items and taping the pictures on a Venn diagram drawn on a board.

Related book　*H Is for Home Run* by Brad Herzog

✚ *Theresa Callahan, Easton, MD*

Steps Count

counting, numeral recognition

Materials　inexpensive pedometers

What to do
1. Purchase inexpensive pedometers (available at most dollar stores) that simply count steps. Fasten one to several different children and encourage them to run or walk around the playground.
2. The children will enjoy running and then counting how many steps they have taken. It doesn't matter how accurate the pedometers are; simply wearing them as they run helps get them moving and interested in numbers.
3. After the children have worn the pedometers for a specified time, ask them to give their pedometers to other children.

More to do
Math: Write down the numbers that are on the pedometers and make a graph.
Working with Families: Send home a note telling parents how many steps the child took outside that day. Ask parents to encourage their children to take as many steps as they can each day to stay healthy.

Related books　*I Went Walking* by Sue Williams
Silly Sally by Audrey Wood

✚ *Laura Durbrow, Lake Oswego, OR*

Throw It Far

measurement

Materials assortment of balls (footballs, crumbled paper balls, sponge balls, rubber balls, sock balls, and playground balls)
measuring tape
plastic traffic cones

What to do

1. Take the children outdoors for this activity.
2. Put the assortment of balls along a start line.
3. On the command of go, invite the class to pick up the balls and throw them as far as possible, all in the same direction.
4. Invite several children to help you measure the distance from the start line to where the farthest ball landed.
5. Mark the place where the farthest ball landed with a cone. Challenge children to get a ball to go farther than the cone during the next round of play.
6. Then measure the distance from the start line to where the closest ball landed.
7. Ask the children to think about why some balls will go farther than others. Explain that a variety of things affect how far the ball will go, such as the weight and shape of the ball, the experience of the thrower, and so on).
8. Ask the children to gather up all the balls.
9. Repeat the activity several times.

More to do

Language and Literacy: Display numbers, letters, or sight word cards randomly around the "throwing area." Invite the children to identify the letter, number, or word nearest to where their ball landed.

✚ *Mary J. Murray, Mazomanie, WI*

Walk and Count

counting, estimation

Materials   none

What to do
1. Take the children for a walk. Walk in the community around the school or just in the playground or even around the school on a rainy day.
2. As you walk, ask the children to do silly things. For example:

   - Take two big steps and three little steps.
   - Take three little steps, hop one time, and take three big steps.
   - Take one little step, and turn around two times.
   - Hop four times, and turn around one time.
   - Take three big steps forward and two big steps backward.

3. Count aloud as the children perform each action.
4. Let the children take turns telling the group silly things to do as you walk.
5. For older children, expand the activity by asking them to estimate how many steps it will take to get from one spot to another (such as from a particular tree in the playground to the edge of the sandbox). After they make their estimates, have them count the steps to see how close their estimates were.
6. Next ask them to estimate how many of your steps it will take. Will it take you more steps or fewer to go the same distance? Why? Again, have the children count your steps to see if they are correct.

✚ *Virginia Jean Herrod, Columbia, SC*

Water Fun

numeral recognition, writing numerals

Materials   4 or 5 plastic swimming pools
marbles
small rubber ducks
rubber canning rings
permanent marker
sponges
gallon milk jugs

What to do

1. Fill the pools with 3" of water.
2. Pour a couple of bags of marbles into the first pool. Let a few children at a time remove the marbles with their toes. Ask them to keep track of how many they pull out. Record the numbers.
3. Write numerals on the bottom of the ducks and put the ducks in the second pool. Invite the children to toss canning rings around the ducks. When a child gets a ring on a duck, he reads the number on the bottom of the duck.
4. Put out several sponges along with gallon jugs. Encourage the children to fill the gallon jugs by plunging the sponges into the pools, then squeezing them out into the gallon jugs.

➕ *Ellen Javernik, Loveland, CO*

Wheel Walk

addition, counting, observation

Materials

paper
pencil

What to do

1. Go for a walk outdoors. Ask the children to look for objects that have wheels.
2. When the children find an item with wheels, have them count the number of wheels they see. Write down the object and the number of wheels it has.
3. Look for more objects with wheels.
4. When you return to the classroom, count the total number of wheels you saw on your Wheel Walk.
5. Next time you go for a walk, pick something else to count.

Related book   *One Wheel Wobbles* by Carole Lexa Schaefer

➕ *Monica Hay Cook, Tucson, AZ*

Bottles, Bottles Everywhere

estimation

Materials
assortment of plastic bottles
sand and water table
measuring cups

What to do

1. Show the children an assortment of bottles and talk about the different sizes. Ask them which bottles might hold the most or the least sand and water. Ask them if they think any might hold the same amount of water even if they are different shapes.
2. Put the bottles in the sand and water table and let the children experiment with filling them. Have them pour each bottle into measuring cups to determine if their estimations were correct.
3. Explain that different size bottles may hold the same amount of liquid or sand because one bottle may be taller and thin while the other is shorter but wider.

Related book   *Each Orange Had Eight Slices* by Paul Giganti, Jr.

✚ *Barbara Saul, Eureka, CA*

Buried Treasure

counting

Materials
9 pictures of treasure chests
markers
sand table
play coins
sifters

What to do

1. Cut out or draw nine pictures of treasure chests. Write a different numeral on each one (1–9).
2. Bury play coins in the sand table and invite the children to sift through the sand to find them.
3. Show the children the different treasure chests, and have them place the correct number of coins on the treasure chests.
4. Help count the coins with the children to check their accuracy.

✚ *Wanda Guidroz, Santa Fe, TX*

Container Comparisons

comparison, estimation, measurement

Materials

empty containers in different shapes (yogurt cups, margarine tubs, juice boxes with tops cut off, baby food jars, pie tins)
tray with raised edges (to contain spills) or sand and water table
popcorn kernels
water
felt-tip marker
masking tape
paper

What to do

1. Clean and dry all containers. Let each child select a container. Help the children write their names on masking tape and stick it on their containers.
2. Choose a "container of the day." Invite the children to discover which containers hold *more than*, *less than*, or *the same as* the container of the day by filling the day's container with water and popcorn kernels and then pouring the substance from that container into their own container.
3. Ask the children, "Is the container full, not full, or overflowing?" "Does this mean the second container holds more than the first, less, or the same?"
4. Ask questions to encourage comparison, estimation, and thinking about measurement.
5. Put all the containers that hold more in one spot, those that hold less in another, and those that hold the same in yet another. Label the areas "more," "less," and the "same."

6. After the children have sorted the containers, ask them if there are more containers that hold more, less, or the same. Help them count the containers in each category.

7. Continue the process of predicting, filling the containers, and comparing how much each will hold, giving each child an opportunity to select a container to start with. (You might want to repeat the activity over a period of several days.) This activity allows children to experiment with measurement without worrying about exact answers.

Related book   *Sorting* by Henry Arthur Pluckrose

✚ *Sandra K. Bynum, Blackfoot, ID*

Cup Chart

comparison, counting

Materials   large piece of poster board
markers
sand and water table
large plastic pitcher
large plastic cylindrical container (about the size of an oatmeal container)
large plastic bowl
large square plastic box
1-cup measuring cup
many cutout pictures of a 1-cup measuring cup
glue

What to do   ■ Prepare the chart:

1. Divide the poster board into five columns. The first column should be half the width of the other four. The other four should be equal widths.

2. Draw a line across the bottom of the chart about five inches from the bottom.

3. Draw a simple representation of each container in each of the second through fifth columns: for example, draw the cylindrical container at the bottom of the second column, the bowl at the bottom of the third column, the pitcher at the bottom of the fourth column, and the square box at the bottom of the fifth column.

4. Right above the dividing line, begin numbering the first column from the bottom up 1, 2, 3, 4, 5, 6, and 7. Keep the spacing of the numerals fairly equal.

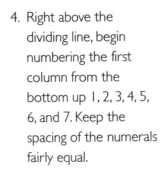

■ Do the activity

1. Fill the sand and water table with water and add the different containers.

2. Ask the children to predict how many cups it will take to fill each container.

3. Have the children take turns pouring cups of water into one container.

4. After the children have counted the number of cups it took to fill one container, have them glue the same number of paper cutouts in the appropriate column.

PAPER CUTOUTS

5. Continue predicting and filling the other containers. Glue the appropriate number of cup cutouts to the chart for each item.

6. Extend the activity by adding different sizes of measuring cups to the sand and water table. Ask the children to predict how many of each type it will take to fill one cup. For example, how many half cups fill a cup? Quarter cups? Let the children experiment with the cups to prove or disprove their prediction.

✚ *Virgina Jean Herrod, Columbia, SC*

Fill It Up

measurement, volume

Materials

sand and water table
measuring cups
4 large plastic tumblers of equal size and shape
water

What to do

1. Line up the tumblers in a row in the sand and water table.
2. Fill each with water as follows: ⅓ cup, ½ cup, ¾ cup, and 1 cup.
3. Ask the children questions that encourage them to compare, estimate, and think about measurement. For example, "Which tumbler has more water? Which has less?"
4. Pour more water into one of the tumblers to make it equal to the amount of water in another tumbler. Move the tumblers around so that the tumblers with the same amount of water are not next to each other.
5. Ask the children to find the tumblers that have the same amount of water.
6. Keep the measuring cups and several larger containers in the sand and water table for the children to explore. Notice if they use the measuring cups to fill up the larger containers. Encourage them to count how many cups it takes to fill up the container. Remember to use the proper names of the measuring cups, for example, "It took three half cups to fill the yellow bucket."

✚ *Virgina Jean Herrod, Columbia, SC*

Foam Hunt and Match

matching, shapes

Materials

chart paper
marker
bucket of foam pieces
sand and water table filled with sand

What to do

1. Before the activity, make a large grid on chart paper by drawing squares large enough to fit the foam shapes. Trace all the foam pieces on the squares of the grid.
2. Hide a few foam pieces in the sand.
3. Invite one child at a time to hunt for the pieces.
4. When the child finds a piece, help her put the piece on the grid in the proper square.
5. After the child finds all the pieces, ask her to hide the pieces in the sand for another child to find.

✚ *Sue Fleischmann, Sussex, WI*

Frogs and Lily Pads

counting

Materials

sand and water table
foam cut lily pads
marker
small rubber frogs

What to do

1. Number the lily pads, and then place them and the frogs in the water table.
2. Invite the children to put the correct number of frogs on the lily pads.

✚ *Wanda Guidroz, Santa Fe, TX*

Ocean Animal Grouping

grouping, sorting

Materials
sand and water table
large number of small ocean animal toys
fish net

What to do
1. Put the ocean animal toys in the water table.
2. Show the children how to fish out the animals from the water table and sort them by type of animal.

✚ *Wanda Guidroz, Santa Fe, TX*

Ping Pong Float

counting, matching, one-to-one correspondence

Materials
sand and water table
12 Ping Pong balls
foam egg carton (washed and rinsed in bleach water)
permanent marker
small fishing net

What to do
1. Number the Ping Pong balls 1–12 with the permanent marker.
2. Number the sections of the egg cartons (1–12).
3. Fill the water table with water and add the Ping Pong balls.
4. Invite the children to fish the balls out and put them in the correct section of the egg carton.

More to do
Language and Literacy: This is a fun way to practice letter matching as well. Label the balls and egg carton sections with letters, for example, a set of uppercase letters and a set of lowercase.

✚ *Bev Schumacher, Racine, WI*

Pot of Gold

counting, number sense

Materials
10 rainbow patterns
marker
sand and water table
gold-colored tokens
10 small black pots or bowls
index cards

What to do
1. In advance, write a numeral on each rainbow pattern (1–5 or 1–10). Attach a rainbow inside each black pot or bowl.
2. Fill the empty sand and water table with gold tokens.
3. The children count out tokens and place them in a pot according to the numeral on the rainbow. For example, if the rainbow has a 4 on it, the child puts four tokens in the pot.
4. Draw tokens on index cards (1–5 or 1–10). Attach the cards to the outside of the pots as a way for children to check their counting. For example, if the rainbow has a 5 written on it, draw five tokens on the card for that pot.

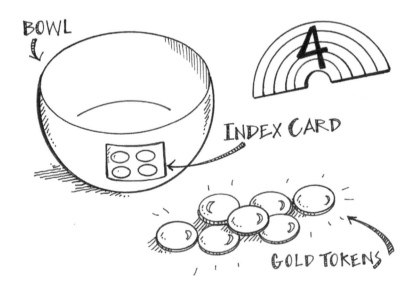

BOWL

INDEX CARD

4

GOLD TOKENS

✚ *Quazonia J. Quarles, Newark, DE*

Prehistoric Islands

counting, numeral recognition, sorting

Materials
foam sheets (in one color or variety of colors)
scissors
marker
sand and water table
small dinosaurs

What to do
1. Cut out island shapes from foam sheets. If the concept is counting numbers, write numerals on each island shape (same color). If the concept is sorting by color, cut out the island shapes in a variety of colors.
2. Place the dinosaurs in the sand and water table.
3. Ask the children to sort the dinosaurs by color onto the islands, or to place the correct number of dinosaurs on the islands.

✚ *Wanda Guidroz, Santa Fe, TX*

Sand Comparisons

comparison, measurement, sequencing

Materials
variety of measuring cups (⅓ cup, ¼ cup, ½ cup, 1 cup)
sand and water table
wet sand

What to do
1. Ask the children to pack wet sand in each cup and turn them over to release the sand, making a line of cups of sand.
2. Talk about the cups of sand and compare their sizes.
3. Experiment with using the smaller measuring cups to fill the larger ones and discuss.

✚ *Jean Potter, Charleston, WV*

Sand Counting

counting

Materials   sand and water table
sand
small items (coins, small plastic jewels, buttons, beads)

What to do   1. Hide similar small items in the sand table. Add small containers and tools for digging, if desired.
2. Ask the children to find a specific number of an item (10 coins, for example) and then bring them to you and count them out.
3. At first, put only the amount of items that you are asking for. When children are ready, add a few extra items.
4. Add items that correspond to your theme or letter of the week.

✚ *Gail Morris, Kemah, TX*

Sand Table Measurement

measurement

Materials   measuring cups and spoons
sand and water table
sand
containers in a variety of sizes

What to do   1. Use only one type of measuring device at the sand table each day. For example, provide tablespoons one day, teaspoons another day, ⅓ cup measuring cups another day, and so on.
2. Invite the children to use the measuring devices to measure sand into containers.
3. After children have explored using one measurement device at a time, provide all of them for children to explore.

✚ *Jean Potter, Charleston, WV*

Scoop and Pour

measurement, measurement vocabulary, volume

Materials
sand and water table
many containers of different sizes (bottles, cups, bowls, milk cartons, empty clean juice cans)
boxes (for use with dry materials)
spoons, scoops, funnels, strainers, beaters
water, sand, seeds, or anything that can be poured

What to do

1. Fill the sand and water table with any type of material you choose: water, sand, seeds, and so on. (As an example for this activity, we'll use water.)
2. Place several different containers in the sand and water table. Let the children explore the materials before starting the activity.
3. Fill one container with water with the children's help.
4. Pick out another container. Ask, "If I pour the water from this bottle into this other bottle, will the second bottle be able to hold all the water?"
5. Let each child make a prediction, then pour the water from the first container into the second as the children observe.
6. Ask a child to describe what happened. Were their predictions correct?
7. Continue with several other containers, following the same procedure.
8. Ask the children to line up the bottles from the one that held the most to the one that held the least.
9. Pick out a standard container, such as a measuring cup. Point out one of the larger containers in the table. Say, "If I want to fill the big bowl with water and use this measuring cup, how many times will I have to fill the cup and pour water into the bowl?"
10. Write down the children's predictions.
11. Let each child take turns using the cup to fill the large bowl. Record the number of cups by making a slash on a piece of paper for each cup.
12. When the bowl is full, help the children count the number of slashes. Compare that amount with the predictions the children made.

More to do
This activity can be done with a variety of materials. Use different sizes of containers and common objects. For example, in the dramatic play center, ask which of three different size boxes would make the best bed for a baby doll.

✚ *Virgina Jean Herrod, Columbia, SC*

Searching for Buried Treasure

counting

Materials   sandbox or sand and water table
shovels
several small objects to hide

What to do   1. Bury several groups of small objects (for example, five blocks, four toy cars, and eight pencils) in a sandbox or sand and water table.
2. Then, call out the buried items, and ask the children to find them.
3. Once all the items have been found, count them as a group to make sure everything is accounted for.

✚ *Erin Huffstetler, Maryville, TN*

Shoveling Sand

counting, volume

Materials   plastic tub filled with sand
large plastic sheeting or plastic swimming pool
large number of 2" paper triangles
transparent tape
plastic drinking straws or stir sticks
assortment of plastic sand pails or containers
plastic sand shovel or scoop
marker

What to do   1. Place the tub of sand and the other materials on the plastic sheeting or in the swimming pool. This makes cleanup easier.
2. Create a large number of "flags" by taping paper triangles to drinking straws.

3. Put the flags and marker in a box near the sand tub.
4. Invite one or two children to do this activity at a time.
5. The child chooses a pail and scoops sand into it. Have her count the scoops as she works.
6. Help the child write the number of scoops on the flag and stand the flag in the bucket full of sand.
7. Let the child repeat the activity by filling several other pails and counting the scoops.
8. When all the pails are full, or the child tires of the activity, have her remove the flags from each pail and dump the sand back into the tub.

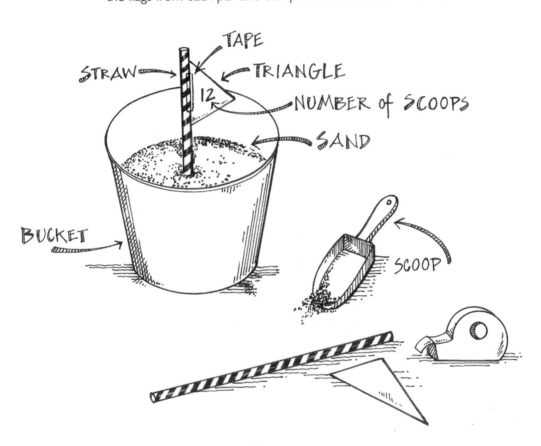

TAPE
STRAW
TRIANGLE
12
NUMBER of SCOOPS
SAND
BUCKET
SCOOP

More to do   **Art:** Invite the children to cut and paste several sand pails on a sheet of paper and then tape their flags to the paper to show how many scoops they counted. If desired, let them glue real sand at the top of each bucket!

✚ *Mary J. Murray, Mazomanie, WI*

Are You Well Balanced?

measurement, weight

Materials
child's balance scale
small objects, such as 1" snapping cubes, rubber insects, crayons,
  buttons, and so on
chart paper

What to do
1. Put the balance scale and small objects in a learning center and invite the children to experiment with balancing the scale to determine which objects are the heaviest, which are lightest, and how many objects it takes to balance both sides of the scale.
2. Encourage the children to keep track of the results, and chart them as a class.

➕ *Barbara Saul, Eureka, CA*

Baby Goes with Mommy

pairs

Materials
pictures of mother and baby animals
construction paper
scissors
glue

What to do
1. Glue pictures of a variety of baby animals on one piece of paper and matching mother animals on another piece of paper. Make copies of the sheets, so that each child has one of each.
2. Ask the children to cut out all of the animals.
3. Invite them to match each mother animal to its baby, and glue the pairs onto a piece of construction paper.

More to do **Art:** Explain to the children that every animal has a unique color and texture. Talk about these characteristics and then ask the children to color in the animals on their paper.

Related book *A Pair of Socks* by Stuart J. Murphy

✚ *Erin Huffstetler, Maryville, TN*

Balancing Act

comparison, weight

Materials

empty 2-liter soda bottle
spring-type clothespin
thin dowel or skewer
hole punch
2 paper cups
string
scissors
2 packing peanuts
various items to weigh, such as
    paperclips, coins, cotton balls, blocks,
    erasers, and so on
paper and pencil

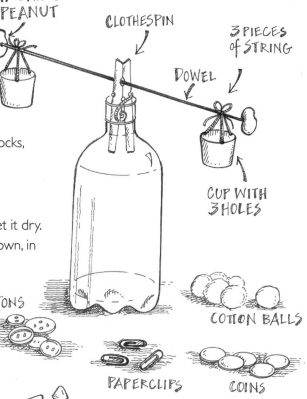

What to do

1. Rinse out the soda bottle and let it dry.
2. Put the clothespin, pinch-side down, in the mouth of the bottle.
3. Push the dowel through the hole in the clothespin to its mid-point.
4. Punch three holes around the top of each cup, spacing the punches evenly.
5. Cut six pieces of string into equal lengths.

6. Insert one end of the string through the hole of one cup and tie a knot. Insert the other two strings into the other two holes and do the same thing.

7. Tie the other ends of the three strings together in a knot. Do this for both cups.

8. Hang the cups on opposite sides of the dowel.

9. Put a packing peanut on each end of the dowel to hold the cups onto the dowel.

10. Encourage the children to experiment with weighing various items. *What weighs more? Less? The same?*

11. The children can chart their results on paper.

✚ *Monica Hay Cook, Tucson, AZ*

Big and Small Animals

matching, comparison

Materials

magazines and catalogs
scissors
copy machine
several pieces of poster board
glue
file folders

What to do

1. Cut out pictures of animals from magazines and catalogs. Enlarge each picture so that you have two of each kind of animal, one small and one large.

2. Glue the large animal cutouts to a file folder, and laminate or cover with contact paper. Glue each small animal picture to a piece of poster board, laminate, and cut out.

3. Hand out the small animal cutouts to the children and encourage them to match the small versions of the animals to the large versions, and then put them in their folders.

4. If desired, store the animal cutouts in animal cracker boxes.

Related books

Are You My Mother? by P.D. Eastman
If You Were My Bunny by Kate McMullan

✚ *Jason Verdone, Woodbury, NJ*

Caterpillar Crawl

estimation, measurement

Materials
green construction paper
thick yarn
scissors
clean plastic bug catcher

What to do
This is a fun math activity to do when studying caterpillars or insects.

1. Prepare beforehand by cutting a variety of symmetrical leaf shapes from green paper. Make each leaf a different length. Fold each leaf in half down the center, unfold the leaves, and place them in a stack.

2. Cut thick yarn into 2″ segments to make "caterpillars" and put them in the bug catcher.

3. Open the bug catcher and pour out the caterpillars. Pick up a leaf shape and lay it flat.

4. Ask the children to guess how many caterpillars will fit on the center line of the leaf.

5. Have them put caterpillars on the fold and count them as you go.

6. Repeat the activity with several other leaves, estimating how many will fit along the fold and then counting to find out.

7. Continue until all the leaves have a line of caterpillars in the center.

PLASTIC BUG CATCHER

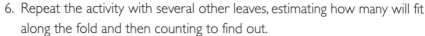

FOLDED LEAVES

CATERPILLARS

OPEN LEAF

More to do
Help the children trace around their hand or arm on paper. Invite them to see how many "caterpillars" will fit down the length of their hand or arm.

✚ *Mary J. Murray, Mazomanie, WI*

Chart the Rain

comparison, measurement

Materials
rain gauge, or a plastic container with straight sides and a ruler
calendar

What to do
1. When it rains, collect rainwater in the rain gauge. If you do not have a rain gauge, use a plastic container with straight sides.
2. After the rain, read the rain gauge with the children, or use a ruler to measure the amount of water in the container.
3. Empty the water and leave the container out for another rainy day.
4. Record the amounts of rain on the calendar every time it rains. Discuss the results with the children.

More to do
Cut strips of ribbon to represent the quantity of rainfall during a week or month. Discuss the total rainfall by lining the ribbons up end to end and measuring the total length of the ribbons.

✚ *Barb Lindsay, Mason City, IA*

Farm Animals and Numerals

counting, numeral recognition

Materials
pictures (or stickers) of farm animals
scissors
copy machine
tagboard
laminator
rubber cement
felt
flannel board

What to do

1. Locate pictures of farm animals and cut them out, or use stickers from a farm animal sticker book. Copy the pictures to make sets of different numbers of animals (for example, one horse, two cows, three sheep, four goats, five pigs, six geese, seven hens, eight rabbits, nine cats, and 10 chicks).
2. Glue the sets of animals to tagboard. Laminate for durability, and cut out.
3. Prepare for flannel board use by using rubber cement to glue felt to the backs of the pictures.
4. Cut out the numerals 1–10 from felt.
5. Place the animal sets on the flannel board. Invite one child at a time to count the number of animals in each set and place the correct numeral next to the picture.

Related books
Old MacDonald Had a Farm by Carol Jones
Spots, Feathers, and Curly Tails by Nancy Tafuri
This Is the Farmer by Nancy Tafuri

✚ *Jackie Wright, Enid, OK*

Feed the Frogs

one-to-one correspondence

Materials

small plastic, felt, or paper cutout frogs
small plastic, felt, or paper cutout flies
flannel board (if using felt frogs and flies)
small bowls or cups

What to do

1. Hand out a few frogs and flies to several of the children. Ask them to count how many of each they are holding. Discuss and decide whether there are enough flies for each frog to eat.
2. Ask a child to place his frogs on the table or flannel board. Then have him place a fly next to each frog. Ask the children questions: "Are there enough flies for the frogs to eat? If not, how many more are needed so each frog will get a fly? If there are more flies than frogs, how many more flies are there?"
3. After practicing several times with one frog gets one fly (one-to-one correspondence), change the directions to: one frog gets two flies.
4. Continue practicing with different numbers of frogs and flies.

More to do   You can do this same type of activity using other animals and foods, such as panda bears and bamboo stalks, dogs and dog bones, or butterflies and flowers.
Language and Literacy: Read *The Doorbell Rang* by Pat Hutchins and do the activity using flannel board children and cookies!

✚ *Sandra Nagel, White Lake, MI*

Gardening

measurement

Materials   small outdoor garden area, or shallow trays and organic potting soil
rake or shovel
grass seed, or real herbs or small flower seedlings
small watering can
measuring stick

What to do   1. Invite the children to fill the trays with the potting soil, or rake the designated outdoor gardening space.
2. Demonstrate how to plant a seed by digging a small hole, putting a couple of seeds in it, and covering it with soil. If you are using herb or flower seedlings, show them how to dig a small hole, insert the seedling, and put soil around it.
3. Every day, choose a different child to water the garden.
4. As the plants grow, encourage the children to carefully measure the plants' progress. Invite them to monitor how long it takes different plants to sprout.
5. At the end of the year, or when the garden needs it, let the children use scissors to "mow" the garden (if they planted grass) or prune the flowers (if they planted flowers).

More to do   **Language and Literacy:** Invite the children to keep a journal of drawings, pictures, and notes about the garden's growth.

✚ *Barb Lindsay, Mason City, IA*

Habitat Math

sorting

Materials small animals (stuffed or plastic)
carpet squares
colored tape or masking tape
pictures of animal habitats
(for example, animals that
live in a house or on a farm;
or rainforest, desert, and
arctic animals)
clear tape

What to do 1. Use tape to divide a carpet square into three equal sections.
2. Decide on three habitats that match a group of small animals that you have collected.
3. Find (or draw) pictures of the three habitats and attach each picture to one section of the carpet square with clear tape for durability.
4. Put the animals and the carpet square in the science center and ask the children to sort the animals according to which habitat they belong in.

 Gail Morris, Kemah, TX

How Heavy, How Light?

comparison, measurement, weight

Materials   a variety of classroom items such as paper clips, pennies, marbles, markers,
                  pencils, feathers, and small blocks
                  balance scale

What to do   1. Talk about weighing items on a balance scale.
                  2. Ask the children to choose two items to compare in weight.
                  3. Encourage them to predict which will be heavier.
                  4. Let the children take turns weighing the items to check their predictions.
                  5. Do this with a variety of classroom items.
                  6. Invite them to add two things to each side of the scale and compare.
                  7. This is a great hands-on comparison of weights.

✚ *Sandy L. Scott, Meridian, ID*

How Large Is a Whale?

measurement

Materials   books about whales and other large fish
                  pictures of whales
                  chalk or masking tape
                  100' tape measure (or longest you can find)

What to do   1. Read about whales and other large fish. Show the children pictures of whales.
                  Explain that the blue whale is the largest type of whale, and may reach a
                  length of 98 feet. Find out the sizes of other whales and record their lengths.

2. Help the children measure the length and width of different whales in the school gym or a long hallway. Use chalk or masking tape to draw the whale. **Note:** If you do not have a 100' tape measure, use a shorter tape measure and mark the end of each length and start over at the mark until you reach the length of the whale.

3. See how many children can stand, sit, and/or lie down inside the different whales.

Related book *The Whales' Song* by Dylan Sheldon

✚ *Sandy L. Scott, Meridian, ID*

How Many Animals Do You See Hibernating?

counting, printing numerals

Materials
pictures of 10 animals hibernating in different places
large paper
tape
pencil

What to do

1. Talk about the animals that find sheltered places and hibernate during the cold winter months.

2. Find and cut out pictures of 10 (more or less) animals hibernating in different places. For example: a turtle or a frog buried in mud, a snake in a hole, a bear in a cave, or a fox asleep in a den. Tape these pictures at the top of a large piece of paper or chart paper.

3. Underneath the pictures, list each child's name with a line next to the name.

4. Tape the paper on a wall within the children's reach.

5. Ask the children to count the animals that are hibernating in the pictures and write their answers on the line next to their name. If the child does not have the correct answer, help him to arrive at the right answer before writing it down.

✚ *Jackie Wright, Enid, OK*

Leaf Sorting

sorting

Materials
leaves in a variety of sizes
paper
old unwrapped crayons

What to do

1. Invite the children to put the leaves in order by size.
2. Show the children how to make leaf rubbings. Place a piece of paper over a leaf and rub with an unwrapped crayon.
3. Encourage the children to make a variety of leaf rubbings and then match them to the leaves.

UNWRAPPED CRAYON

PAPER

LEAF GOES UNDERNEATH PAPER

Related song

Autumn Leaves (tune: "London Bridge")
Autumn leaves are falling down,
Falling down, falling down.
Autumn leaves are falling down
All through the town.

Red, brown, yellow, and orange,
Yellow and orange, yellow, and orange.
Red, brown, yellow, and orange
All through the town.

Related books
Red Leaf, Yellow Leaf by Lois Ehlert
Why Do Leaves Change Color? by Betsy Maestro

✚ *Sandy L. Scott, Meridian, ID*

Make It Heavy

measurement, weight

Materials
bucket
12 dry sponges
kitchen scale
blocks of ice or ice cubes

What to do
1. Fill the bucket with 12 dry sponges. Ask the children to lift the bucket to see how heavy it feels.
2. Weigh the bucket of sponges on a kitchen scale.
3. Discuss how to make the sponges heavier (by adding water). Add water to the sponges and weigh the bucket again. Talk about the difference in weight.
4. Remove the sponges and put a small block of ice or ice cubes in the bucket. Ask the children if they think the weight of an object changes if it changes state (for example, ice to water, or a melted candle).
5. Weigh the bucket of ice and record the result. Let the ice melt and weigh the bucket again.

✚ *Shyamala Shanmugasundaram, Nerul, Navi Mumbai, India*

Making Playdough

measurement

Materials
measuring cups and spoons
½ cup salt
1 cup flour
1 tablespoon cream of tartar
1 tablespoon oil
1 cup water
food coloring
saucepan

What to do

1. Show the children the measuring cup and measuring spoons and demonstrate how to level off the ingredients to get the measurements exactly right.
2. It's a good idea to make a pictorial representation (rebus) of the recipe, so that young children can follow it easily.
3. Before adding each ingredient, ask the children to look at the rebus picture and say what they think should be added next.
4. Let each child take a turn measuring an ingredient, adding it to the pan, and stirring it in.
5. Cook the mixture on low heat (adult only), stirring continuously, and remove from the heat when the dough seems to be the correct consistency.
6. Let the dough cool before use.
7. Use the playdough to make numerals.

More to do

Literacy: Read stories that involve measuring and cooking.
Snack: Make something else using similar measurement techniques, such as cupcakes.

✚ *Anne Adeney, Plymouth, United Kingdom*

Nature Walk

· ·

classification, counting, shapes, sorting

Materials

colorful paper plates
1" or wider 2-sided tape
markers

What to do

1. Attach two or more strips of the two-sided tape to each plate.
2. Give each child a "sticky plate" and take them outdoors for a nature walk.
3. Invite children to collect a variety of interesting objects on the walk. Children may collect seeds, leaves, pebbles, blades of grass, and so on.

LEAVES
FLOWERS
BIRD NEST
PINECONE
STICKY PLATE

4. The children "stick" each item to their plate.

5. After children have collected an assortment of items, invite them to sit in a circle and "show and tell" what they collected.

6. Encourage children to identify the shape of each item, how many items they have, and how certain items could be grouped together.

7. Back in the classroom, let the children record what they found by drawing each item on another paper plate. Help them write words for each of the objects or shapes.

✚ *Mary J. Murray, Mazomanie, WI*

Planting Bulbs and Flower Seeds

counting

Materials

flower bulbs and seeds
dirt
small planting pots
small shovels
large paper
calendar

What to do

1. Explain to the children that they are going to plant both flower bulbs and flower seeds indoors. (Amaryllis or hyacinth bulbs are good to use for this activity.)

2. Count both the bulbs and seeds and record the number of each.

3. Ask the children which they believe will sprout first—the seeds or the bulbs. Ask them if they think all the seeds and bulbs will turn into plants.

4. Let the children help plant the seeds and bulbs in small pots area. Make sure to mark where the bulbs are planted and where the seeds are planted.

5. Water the pots each day.

6. Record which sprouts first—a bulb or seed.

7. Record how many of the bulbs turned into plants and then record how many of the seeds turned into plants.

8. Point out to the children that more bulbs sprout than seeds. For every 10 bulbs, about nine usually sprout. Flower seed packets, on the other hand, contain many seeds because it takes more seeds to actually develop into plants.

Related book   *Flower Garden* by Eve Bunting

✚ *Sandy L. Scott, Meridian, ID*

Pump a Number

counting, estimation

Materials   beach balls in different sizes
bicycle pump

What to do
1. Show the children a deflated beach ball. Explain that you are going to use a bicycle pump to push air into the ball.
2. Demonstrate pumping air into the ball, counting each time you pump.
3. Ask the children to guess how many pumps it will take to fill the ball. Fill the ball and see how close the children's guesses were.
4. Pump air into beach balls of differing sizes. Ask the children to guess which balls will need the most and least number of pumps.

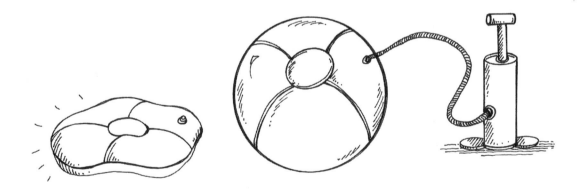

✚ *Karyn F. Everham, Fort Myers, FL*

Recipe for Mud

counting, measurement

Materials

small buckets or containers
dirt
measuring cup
water
spoons (optional)
paper
marker

What to do

1. Provide a variety of small buckets and containers.
2. Help the children measure one cup of dirt and put it into a bucket. Have them add one cup of water to the dirt.
3. The children mix the dirt and water with a spoon or their hands. After mixing, the children can decide if the mud is the right consistency, or if it is too thin or too thick.
4. If the mud is too thin (or too thick), ask them what they can do to make it thicker (or thinner). Let them add another cup of dirt if it is too thin, or a cup of water if it is too thick.
5. When the mud is "just right," help each child write down his recipe for mud. They might write the numerals and you can write the words (for example, 2 cups dirt + 1 cup water = mud).

Related books

Mud by Mary Lyn Ray
Mud Puddle by Robert N. Munsch
Preschool to the Rescue by Judy Sierra

✚ *Kristi Larson, Spirit Lake, IA*

Rock Patterns

patterns

Materials
tiny rocks and small pebbles
basket or container
glue
cardboard
paint

What to do
1. Ask the children to bring rocks to school or collect rocks around the school.
2. Place the rocks in a basket or a container, and let each child choose 10 rocks from the rock assortment.
3. Invite the children to place their rocks on a piece of cardboard. Explain that they will make a pattern by painting the rocks (for example, green rock, blue rock, green rock, blue rock).
4. Let the rocks dry and then invite the children to glue the rocks to the paper in the same pattern.
5. Ask the children to talk about their patterns.

✚ *Lily Erlic, Victoria, BC, Canada*

Seed Matching

matching

Materials
packets of seeds
pictures of the seeds' resulting flowers, vegetable, and fruits
trays
small planting pots and soil

What to do
1. Have the children work in pairs for this activity. Put each type of seed on a tray (make one tray of seeds for each pair).
2. Give the children the pictures of the plants and seeds of that plant and ask if they can choose the correct seed for each picture. This is a difficult activity so make sure the picture of the seeds look like the seeds on the trays.

3. The children will probably find it easier to match some of the seeds, such as watermelon, sunflower, and apple, because they may have seen the seeds before.

4. Tape one of the matching seeds to the back of each plant picture so the children can check their match.

5. When finished with this activity, plant some of the seeds and watch them grow.

Related books
The Carrot Seed by Ruth Krauss
Planting a Rainbow by Lois Ehlert
The Very Hungry Caterpillar by Eric Carle

✚ *Sandy L. Scott, Meridian, ID*

They Go Together

• •

matching, recognizing ways to analyze data

Materials
magazines and catalogs with a variety of pictures (people doing jobs, various objects, different animals, and so on)
scissors
4" x 7" unlined tagboard index cards
laminator or clear adhesive paper

What to do
Math skills and science skills are interrelated. Developing math skills means more than number sense and counting. Children must be able to discern things that go together in order to develop higher level math skills.

■ Prepare the activity:
1. Find and cut out pictures of people doing their jobs and the things they use in those jobs. Older children can help with this task. Some sample workers and their tools are:

   ■ Mail carrier: letters, mailbox, stamps, hat, mailbag, mail truck
   ■ Airplane pilot: airplane, uniform, hat, wings
   ■ Doctor: stethoscope, thermometer, bandages
   ■ Grocer: variety of foods, bags, shopping cart

2. Find pictures of things that go together by use, for example:
   - ◼ Glass tumbler: carton of milk, pitcher of juice, can of soda
   - ◼ Cup and saucer: coffee pot, teabag, spoon
   - ◼ Paper: pencil, crayon, pen

3. Find and cut out pictures of other things that are related, such as animals and their babies.
4. Attach the pictures to different colors of index cards (the workers and their tools on one color, things that go together by use on another, and animals and animal babies on a third color). This helps keep the sets separated.
5. Laminate everything or cover with clear adhesive paper for durability.

◼ Do the activity:
(Start with three sets and add more as the children's skills increase.)

1. Show a small group of children the clue pictures, such as a mail carrier, one at a time, and ask, "Who is this?"

2. When all the initial clue pictures have been named, show the "goes with" pictures one at time and ask, "Whom does this belong to?"

3. Give each child a clue picture. Hold each "goes with" picture up in turn and say, "Who has the person (or thing) this belongs with? What do you call this?"

4. Continue until all the pictures have been matched.

✚ *Virgina Jean Herrod, Columbia, SC*

Visiting the Produce Department

comparison, measurement, weight

Materials
fruit
kitchen scale
pen and paper

What to do
1. If possible, take the children on a field trip to a grocery store and go to the produce department. If it is not possible, do this activity in your science center.

2. Pick up a piece of fruit, such as an orange or a banana, and weigh it. Then pick up another piece of the same fruit and ask the children what they think it will weigh.

3. Weigh the fruit and record its weight on a piece of paper. Ask the children what they think two pieces of fruit will weigh.

4. Weigh and record the data for two pieces of fruit.

5. Ask the children if they think an apple will weigh more or less than an orange.

6. Weigh and record the data, and do so with other produce.

7. When you return to class, make a chart of the results and compare them to each other, asking the children which fruits were heaviest and lightest.

Related books
Grandpa's Corner Store by Dyanne DiSalvo-Ryan
Math at the Store by William Amato

✚ *Kristi Larson, Spirit Lake, IA*

What's the Temperature Today?

measurement, temperature

Materials

chart paper
marker
thermometer

What to do

1. Make a temperature chart. Write the name of each month at the top of a piece of chart paper. Write the dates on the left hand side of the paper.
2. With the children, check the outside temperature at the same time every day.
3. Compare the temperatures each month. Discuss which month is coldest, hottest, and so on.

Related book

Oh Say Can You Say What's the Weather Today? by Tish Rabe

	Jan.	Feb.	Mar.	Apr. ⟶
1	29°	40°		
2	28°	40°		
3	40°	30°		
4	41°	30°		
5	35°	35°		
6				
7				
8				
9				
10	↓	↓		
11				
12				
↓				

✚ *Monica Hay Cook, Tucson, AZ*

Winter Temperatures

comparison, measurement, temperature

Materials

large pan or plastic tub
snow
plastic sheet or vinyl shower curtain
thermometer
large calendar

THERMOMETER

PLASTIC PAN WITH SNOW

PLASTIC SHEET

What to do

1. Fill a large pan or plastic tub with snow and place it on a plastic sheet or vinyl shower curtain. Use a thermometer to measure the temperature of the snow and record it on a sheet of paper.

2. Let the snow melt, and then measure the temperature of the melted snow. Write the temperature next to the temperature of the snow, and talk with the children about the difference in temperatures.

3. For more practice with thermometers, check the temperature on a thermometer placed outside the classroom window. Record it on the calendar.

4. At the end of each week, compare the high and low temperatures for the week by creating a bar graph out of the information on the calendar.

CALENDAR

February

TEMPERATURE

					28° 1	30° 2
3	40° 4	40° 5	30° 6	26° 7	28° 8	9
10	11	12	13	14	15	16
17	18	19	20	21	22	23
24	25	26	27	28		

✚ *Barb Lindsay, Mason City, IA*

Feely Numbers

numeral recognition

Materials
sets of numerals made of different hard materials (wood, plastic, clay)
opaque drawstring bag

What to do
1. Fill the drawstring bag with the wooden or plastic numerals (0–9). If the children are just beginning to learn numbers, use only two or three numerals at a time, but have lots of them. Make sure the bag is large enough for two hands to fit in.
2. Sit in a circle with the children. Demonstrate how to do the activity by sticking your hand inside the bag and picking out a numeral. Then, with the numeral still hidden inside the bag, feel it with both hands, tell everyone what numeral you think it is, then pull it out and show everyone.
3. Pass the bag around the circle and give each child several turns to pick out a numeral and feel it and try to identify it.

Note: If the children in your class are very young and/or just beginning to learn numbers, let them take the numeral out of the bag to identify it.

✚ *Anne Adeney, Plymouth, United Kingdom*

The How Many? Jar

counting, estimation, numeral recognition

Materials
clear plastic jar with screw-on lid
objects to fill the jar
pencils
paper
number chart
graphing pocket chart
set of number cards

What to do
1. The first time you do this activity, fill the jar with a small number of objects (between three and seven). Be sure to fill the jar before the children arrive.

2. Ask the children how many items they think are in the jar. (Don't worry if their first answers are as large as 100. Eventually they will get closer to the right number.)

3. Help the children write their answers on a small 2" x 2" piece of paper, or use a 0–20 number chart and invite them to write down their own estimations.

4. When ready to count the objects, use a two-column graphing pocket chart, putting the number cards 0–20 in one set of pockets, and the children's guesses in the second set of pockets.

5. Take each item out of the jar, say the number it represents aloud, and put the item in the appropriate number chart pocket.

✚ *Linda Ford, Sacramento, CA*

Let Your Fingers Do the Counting

counting, shape identification

Materials
10 small objects with different shapes (different sizes of balls, various blocks— rectangle, oval, square)
dark cloth
tray
number cards

What to do
1. Ahead of time, place a set of objects (five or fewer to start with) on a tray. Cover the shapes with a dark cloth.
2. Invite a child to come and press her fingers over the cloth, feeling the number of objects in the set. You can also ask the child to identify the shape.
3. Ask her to count the number of objects out loud. Then ask her to choose the matching number card for that set of objects. For example, if she counts four hidden objects, she would choose the numeral 4 card.
4. Uncover the items and count them together as a group.
5. Ask the children to identify the shapes.
6. When the children are counting well up to sets of 5, increase the number of objects to sets of 6 through 10.

Related books   *26 Letters and 99 Cents* by Tana Hoban
Count and See by Tana Hoban
Moja Means One by Muriel Feelings

✛ *Susan Oldham Hill, Lakeland, FL*

Making Touch-and-Feel Numerals and Shapes

numeral recognition, shapes

Materials   card stock
markers
glue
containers of various items, such as beads, sand, feathers, cotton balls, sequins

What to do
1. Depending on your focus (numeral recognition or shape recognition), write or draw different numerals or shapes on card stock.
2. Show the children a couple of the cards. Invite them to feel the cards, pointing out how smooth the card stock feels when they rub their finger or hand over the printed lines.
3. Give the children a number shape card, or let each child choose her own.
4. Show them how to put glue on the lines of the numeral or shape.
5. Invite the children to choose a material to put on the glue. Have them shake off the excess material over a trashcan.
6. Let the number or shape cards dry overnight.
7. The next day, have the children share their cards with the rest of the children. The children will enjoy feeling the different textures.

✛ *Sandra Nagel, White Lake, MI*

Math Bottles

counting, sequencing

Materials   10 empty water bottles
water
55 small objects (to fit through the opening in the water bottle)
glue

What to do   1. Place one object in a water bottle.
2. Fill with water and glue the lid on the bottle.
3. Place two objects in another water bottle, fill with water, and glue the lid on.
4. Follow the same procedure with the rest of the bottles, adding one more item each time (three objects in one bottle, four in the next, and so on up to 10).
5. Invite the children to put them in order from one to 10.

✚ *Jean Potter, Charleston, WV*

Mittens, Hats, and Gloves

numeral recognition

Materials   plastic numerals
20 or more adult-size mittens, gloves, or winter hats

What to do   1. Place a plastic numeral inside each hat, glove, or mitten.
   Note: If you do not have plastic numerals, make textured number cards (1–10) by gluing a variety of textured materials such as sandpaper and yarn on cards small enough to fit inside a child's hand.
2. Arrange the garments along the length of several tables.
3. Have the children line up at the tables so that everyone has a mitten, glove, or hat to work with.

4. The children put their hand inside the glove, mitten, or hat and try to guess what the numeral is by feeling it. Remind them not to peek inside and not to take the numeral out until after they guess.

5. After they feel and guess their first numeral, invite them to move along the table to a new mitten, hat, or glove.

6. Ask the children to verbalize each numeral as they recognize it and then move along to the next numeral. If they do not recognize the numeral, they may peek inside the hat or mitten to see what it is.

7. If the children are learning about shapes, do the activity using shapes instead of numerals.

✚ *Mary J. Murray, Mazomanie, WI*

Mystery Blocks

shape identification

Materials
bag
small geometric blocks

What to do
1. Put the geometric blocks inside the bag to make a "feely bag."
2. Invite one child to close her eyes, put her hand inside the bag, and pull out a shape. With her eyes still closed, ask the child to talk about the shape and try to figure out what it is.
3. When the child figures it out, have the child keep the shape, and choose another child to take a turn.
4. When all of the children have a shape in their hand, invite them to look around the room for things that are a similar shape to theirs.

✚ *Kaethe Lewandowski, Centreville, VA*

Number Memory

numeral recognition

Materials
tray
wooden or plastic numerals (0–9)
cloth

What to do
1. Put all 10 numerals on the tray and show the tray to the children.
2. Cover the tray with the cloth and secretly remove one of the numerals.
3. Show the tray to the children again and have them figure out which numeral is missing.
4. If they are guessing randomly, ask them to count out loud and check if each numeral is on the tray.

✚ *Anne Adeney, Plymouth, United Kingdom*

Playdough Shapes

geometry, shape recognition

Materials
playdough

What to do
1. Give each child a lump of playdough. Invite the children to make shapes and figures out of playdough (circles, squares, lines).
2. After they have a chance to explore different shapes, ask each child to make one particular shape.
3. Divide the children into pairs or groups of three, and ask them to put their shapes together to make a new shape. Demonstrate ways they can do this, for example: "When I put my circle with

2 CIRCLES

SNOWMAN

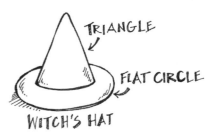
TRIANGLE

FLAT CIRCLE

WITCH'S HAT

Owen's line, we have a hat." "If Claire and Julio put their circles together, they could make a snowman."

4. Remind the children that this is a sharing activity so they may not take their partner's shape. Each child puts her own shape on the table and adjusts it as needed.

5. The children might wish to combine their playdough shapes together into one lump. Help them create two shapes and see what they can make with the new shapes.

6. Ask questions, "How many sides does your shape have?" "How else could you put these pieces together?"

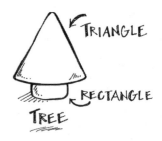

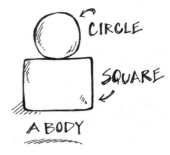

✚ *Cassandra Reigel Whetstone, Folsom, CA*

Rub a Numeral

numeral recognition

Materials

sandpaper
old crayons
copy paper
tape

What to do

1. Trace and cut numerals out of sandpaper. Tape them onto the table.
2. Peel the paper off the crayons.
3. Give each child a piece of paper and demonstrate how to put the paper directly on top of a numeral and rub with a crayon.
4. The numeral will appear "magically" on their paper.
5. Talk about the numerals. Ask them what else they could rub, such as leaves, coins, or fabric. Try out a few materials (if desired) to see what works.

More to do

Cut out a large set of numerals (0–9) from sandpaper. Place them on a wall at eye level. Let the children feel the curves and bumps of the numerals.

✚ *Shelley F. Hoster, Norcross, GA*

Scoop It!

estimation, counting

Materials

3 empty baby food jars
3 metal pie plates
3 spoons
1 cup of bird seed
1 cup of sand
1 cup of walnuts in a shell

What to do

1. Put one jar and one spoon next to each pie plate. Pour sand into one plate, walnuts into another, and bird seed into the third plate.
   Safety Note: If any of the children have nut allergies, do not use walnuts for this activity.
2. Ask the children to estimate how many spoonfuls of sand it will take to fill the jar.
3. Have a child spoon sand into the jar as the rest of the children count.
4. When the first jar is full, ask the children to guess how many spoonfuls of walnuts it will take to fill the next jar. "Will it take more or less than the sand?"
5. Have a child spoon walnuts into the jar as the rest of the children count.
6. Do the same thing with the third jar and the bird seed.

More to do

Outdoor Play: Provide a variety of buckets, scoops, shovels, and so on for children to experiment with in the sandbox.

 Cassandra Reigel Whetstone, Folsom, CA

Sensory Alphabet

numeral recognition

Materials

scissors
light card stock
markers
glue
textured materials (pipe cleaners, craft sticks, Q-tips, toothpicks, yarn)

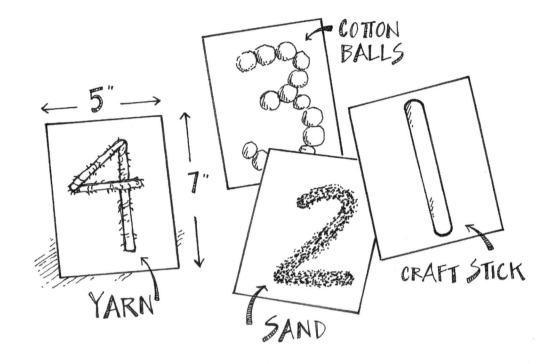

What to do

1. Pre-cut cardstock to about 5" x 7". With a marker, write a numeral on each card.
2. Each child picks a number card.
3. Have textured materials available, such as yarn, cotton balls, toothpicks, Q-tips, pipe cleaners, sand, colored salt, cornmeal, sandpaper, and craft sticks.
4. Children select one type of the textured items to glue onto their numeral.
5. When the cards have dried, the children can trace each other's numerals with their fingers.
6. Have the children describe their number card to the other children. Ask the children to describe how their numerals feel. "Do they feel soft? Rough?"

Related books   *In the Rain Forest* by Maurice Pledger
Pat the Bunny by Dorothy Kunhardt

✚ *Monica Hay Cook, Tucson, AZ*

Slime Time

counting, measurement

Materials
cornstarch
food coloring
measuring cups
plastic tub
10 plastic animals

What to do

1. Make slime by mixing together the following ingredients:

   1 cup cornstarch
   ½ cup water
   food coloring

2. Hide 10 plastic animals in the slime.
3. Have the children take turns finding all 10 animals, counting out loud each time they discover an animal.
4. Let the children make their own slime, measuring their own ingredients.

Related books
Counting Little Geckos by Charline Profiri
Over in the Garden by Jennifer Ward
Somewhere in the Ocean by Jennifer Ward and T.J. Marsh
Ten Dirty Pigs/Ten Clean Pigs by Carol Roth
Way Out in the Desert by T.J. Marsh and Jennifer Ward

✚ *Monica Hay Cook, Tucson, AZ*

Swirly Shapes

representing numbers, shapes

Materials   shaving cream or fingerpaint

What to do
1. Pour some fingerpaint or shaving cream onto the table top.
2. Model drawing numerals and shapes in the shaving cream with your finger.
3. Invite the children to imitate the numerals and shapes you draw.
4. Next, have the children take turns drawing numerals and shapes and ask the other children to guess what they drew.

Related book   *Harold and the Purple Crayon* by Crockett Johnson

✚ *Monica Hay Cook, Tucson, AZ*

Tactile Numerals

numeral recognition

Materials   plywood or heavy card stock
fabric scraps with different textures (satin, velvet, corduroy, lace, plastic, suede, denim, and so on)
numeral templates or stencils
glue

What to do   Engaging more than one sense makes learning more effective. This activity gives the child tactile memories of the numbers, as well as auditory and visual ones, so the numbers are mastered more thoroughly.
1. Cut out several sets of numerals from card stock or thin plywood. At least one set for each child is the ideal number. (Use 1–5 or 0–9, depending on the children's age and ability.)
2. Choose a different fabric for each numeral. Cut out matching numerals from the fabric, and glue them onto the plywood or card stock.

3. Introduce the textured numerals to the children and invite them to trace the shape of the numeral with their fingers.

4. Ask them to close their eyes and feel the numerals. Encourage them to describe the way the numerals feel. For example, "Two has bumpy lines on it" (corduroy) or "Five is really smooth" (satin).

5. Provide scraps of the material to look at and feel. See if they can identify which numeral was made from which fabric.

✚ *Anne Adeney, Plymouth, United Kingdom*

Texture Math Book

numeral recognition

Materials

numeral stencils
markers
textured materials (velvet, fine sandpaper, fake fur, sheets of acetate, seersucker fabric, dotted Swiss fabric, suede, craft foam, screening material)
scissors
8 ½" × 11" poster board or card stock in bright colors
glue
hole punch
3-ring binder

What to do

1. To make a book for the children, trace each numeral on the several different textured materials and cut them out.

2. Glue the cutouts on 8 ½" × 11" sheets of poster board or card stock.

3. Label each page with the name of the numeral and draw a corresponding number of dots. Allow to dry.

4. Punch holes in the pages and place them in a 3-ring binder. Encourage the children to trace the numerals and say the names out loud when they read the book.

Related books

Hand Rhymes by Marc Brown
My Five Senses by Aliki

✚ *Susan Oldham Hill, Lakeland, FL*

Water Glass Math

sequencing

Materials
several drinking glasses (same size)
water
food coloring

What to do
1. Fill several drinking glasses with water, increasing the amount in each glass.
2. Add food coloring to each glass of water.
3. Mix up the glasses so that they are in no particular order.
4. Ask the children to arrange the glasses in order according to the amount of water in each.

More to do
Music: Once the glasses have been arranged in order, demonstrate how to tap the glasses with a spoon to make music. This will only work with glass, not plastic, so supervise carefully.

✚ *Erin Huffstetler, Maryville, TN*

What Number Am I?

numeral recognition

Materials
scissors
shoeboxes
pairs of wooden numerals (0–9)
heavy duty rubber bands (2 per shoebox)

What to do
1. Cut a 3" circle out of the center of the lid of each shoebox.
2. Put two pairs of wooden numerals into each shoebox, for example, a pair of twos and a pair of threes.
3. Put the lids on the shoeboxes. Secure with two rubber bands.
4. Instruct the children to put one hand into the box (without looking) and touch the wooden numerals.
5. Challenge the child to match and remove each pair of numerals using their sense of touch only.

✚ *Karyn F. Everham, Fort Myers, FL*

1- 2- 3- 4 for You to Eat

counting, measurement, subtraction

Materials
teaspoons for each child
maraschino cherry juice (cherries removed)
powdered sugar
softened cream cheese
graham crackers
bowls for each child
knife or tablespoon

What to do

1. Each child places 1 teaspoon of cherry juice in a bowl.
2. The children measure 2 teaspoons of powdered sugar and 3 teaspoons of cream cheese and add it to their bowls.
3. They blend all of the ingredients until the mixture is smooth.
4. Give each child four graham crackers and invite them to spread the cream cheese mixture on top.
5. Teach the children subtraction as they eat their snack. Ask them to count the number of graham crackers that are left when one graham cracker is eaten, and so on.

Safety Note: Some children may be sensitive to red food dye. You may want to do this activity without the maraschino cherry juice.

Related books
Cooking Art: Easy Edible Art for Young Children by MaryAnn Kohl and Jean Potter
Pretend Soup and Other Real Recipes: A Cookbook for Preschoolers and Up by Mollie Katzen and Ann Henderson

✚ *Randi Lynn Mrvos, Lexington, KY*

Animal Cracker Math

counting, sorting

Materials   animal crackers

What to do
1. Pass out animal crackers to the children. Make sure each child gets the same number.
2. Encourage the children to sort the animals by type, and count how many different kinds of animals there are.
3. After they have counted each type of animal, help the children add all of their animals together to get a total.

✚ *Wanda Guidroz, Santa Fe, TX*

Apple Preference Chart

comparison, counting

Materials   pictures of different apple products or markers
chart paper
name card for each child

What to do
1. Discuss various ways apples may be eaten, such as whole apples, sliced apples, apple juice, apple pie, applesauce, apple muffins, and so on.
2. Create a chart titled, "Which do you like best?"
3. At the bottom of the chart, draw or cut out a picture of the different ways to prepare and eat apples.
4. Have each child, in turn, come forward and vote to show his preference by placing his name card next to his choice.
5. Discuss the chart with the children. What is the class favorite?

Related books   *Apple Picking Time* by Michele B. Slawson
Rain Makes Applesauce by Julian Scheer

✚ *Jackie Wright, Enid, OK*

Cereal Math

counting

Materials
die
small, unsweetened cereal pieces
a small container for each child

What to do
1. Show the children how to take turns rolling the die and counting the number of dots on the top of the die.
2. Explain to them that they may eat the same number of pieces of cereal as the number of dots on the top of the die. For example, if a child rolls a five, each child can eat five cereal pieces.
3. Continue rolling the die until snack time is over.

✚ *Susan Oldham Hill, Lakeland, FL*

Chart It!

charting, counting

Materials
large paper
markers
goldfish crackers
teddy bear graham crackers

What to do
1. Divide a large piece of paper three sections. Draw a goldfish at the top of the first section, a teddy bear at the top of the second section, and a face with a frown on it in the third section along with the words: "I don't like these crackers."
2. Have the children wash their hands and get ready for a snack.
3. Provide goldfish crackers and teddy bear graham crackers. Let the children taste one of each.
4. Ask each child which cracker he likes best. Help the child write his name in the section under the item he named. Give the children some of their favorite item to eat.

5. If a child says he doesn't like either cracker, help him write his name in the last section. Provide an alternate snack.

6. After the children finish their snack, count how many names are in each section and write the number at the bottom of each column.

7. Talk about which column has more and which has the least.

More to do

Chart everything, including snack preferences; Velcro vs. laces; bus riders, walkers, and car riders; favorite colors; long hair, short hair, or medium hair; and so on. Let the children suggest categories to chart.

General Tips: Make reusable charts by drawing columns on paper and laminating. Use wipe-off markers to do the charting. You could also use a small wipe-off board, chalkboard, or magnet board. If using a magnet board, put the children's names on magnetic tape.

✚ *Sandra Nagel, White Lake, MI*

Circle Squares

addition, counting, shapes

Materials

3 tablespoons margarine
1 bag of miniature marshmallows
4 ½ cups of "O"-shaped cereal (such as Cheerios™)
microwave-safe bowl
13" x 9" pan

What to do

1. Let the children help measure by counting the tablespoons of margarine and cups of marshmallows (use the whole bag but let children add them using measuring cups to practice counting) into a microwave-safe bowl and microwave on high until puffed up (1–2 minutes).

2. Show them the cereal and discuss how the pieces are shaped like circles.

3. Show the children a clean 1-cup measuring cup. Explain that they will need 4 ½ cups of cereal for the recipe, which means they will need to fill the cup four times. Show them what half means. Add ½ cup of cereal to the bowl.

4. Spoon the mixture into a greased 13" x 9" pan. Press down gently. The mixture will still be hot from the microwave. Cool slightly before cutting.

5. Cut the circle-shaped treats into squares and serve "circle squares" as a yummy snack! (You can also cut the squares into halves to explain the concept of "half" again.)

More to do   **Art:** Encourage the children to cut out objects that are circles and squares from old magazines and make a circle-square mural.

✚ *Susan Grenfell, Cedar Park, TX*

Count a Rainbow Salad

counting

Materials
large recipe card
strawberries (1 per child)
oranges (2 segments per child)
bananas (3 slices per child)
green apples or pears (4 slices per child)
blueberries (5 per child)
purple grape halves (6 per child)
bowls and spoons

What to do
1. Prior to the activity, put each type of fruit in a different bowl. Write the following recipe on a large recipe card:

   Count a Rainbow Salad
   1 red strawberry
   2 orange oranges
   3 yellow bananas
   4 green apples
   5 blueberries
   6 purple grapes

2. Tell the children they are going to make a rainbow fruit salad. To make it, each child will need to count six colors of the rainbow.
3. Point to each type of fruit and name the color. Ask, "How many different types of fruit do we have?" Help them count to six.
4. Read the recipe card together. You might want to add a picture of each fruit next to the words (for example, draw one strawberry, two oranges, and so on).
5. Encourage the children to count out the correct number of each piece of fruit and add it to their bowls.

6. As a variation, make a Count a Rainbow Salad with vegetables. Substitute one cherry tomato, two carrot slices, three yellow pepper slices, four slices of cucumber, five blue taro chips or blue corn chips, and six slices of purple cabbage.

✚ *Cassandra Reigel Whetstone, Folsom, CA*

Cracker Shapes

fractions, shapes

Materials crackers of various shapes and sizes

What to do
1. Provide a variety of crackers for snack.
2. Look at the crackers with the children and talk about the shapes and sizes.
3. Break a graham cracker rectangle in half and then into quarters. Try this with other crackers as well. Discuss the fractions with the children.
4. Pass out the crackers and encourage the children to break their crackers into halves or quarters before eating them.

✚ *Sandra Nagel, White Lake, MI*

Creamy or Crunchy Peanut Butter?

comparison, counting

Materials chart paper
markers
jar of creamy peanut butter
jar of crunchy peanut butter

What to do

Safety Note: Do not do this activity if any of the children have peanut allergies. If anyone is allergic to peanuts, substitute a different food item, such as jelly or jam in two different flavors.

1. Make two columns on a piece of chart paper. Write "Creamy Peanut Butter" at the top of one column and write "Crunchy Peanut Butter" at the top of the other column.
2. Discuss the possibilities on the chart and have the children talk about which peanut butter they prefer.
3. Have both types of peanut butter available for tasting.
4. Place each child's name in the appropriate column.
5. Have the class count the total in each column and discuss the results.

✚ *Jackie Wright, Enid, OK*

Eating Numbers

counting, number relationships

Materials

bite-size snacks (pretzel sticks, animal crackers, goldfish crackers, mini pretzels)
small cups
napkins

What to do

1. Put snacks in cups for each child.
2. Call out a number and the children make one pile on their napkin with that number of snack items (for example, if you call out three, they put three snack items on the napkin).
3. Call out a larger or smaller number and have the children make another pile next to the first pile.
4. Compare the sizes of the two piles and compare the numbers. Talk about which pile has less and which has more.
5. Ask the children to eat the pile that has the fewest number and put the other pile back in the cup.
6. Continue to call numbers so that the children have a variety of piles. Compare the piles using words such as *more, less, fewer,* and *greater.*
7. Continue until the children have finished eating their snack.

✚ *Sandy Scott, Meridian, ID*

Fishing

counting, subtraction

Materials   goldfish or whale-shaped crackers

What to do
1. Give each child 10 goldfish or whale-shaped crackers.
2. Invite the children to pretend that they are whales.
3. Tell the children that their whales are swimming in the ocean and eat two fish, and encourage them to eat two fish.
4. Have everyone count how many fish they have left.
5. Continue doing this, using different numbers, until all the fish are eaten.

Related book   *One Fish, Two Fish, Red Fish, Blue Fish* by Dr. Seuss

✚ *Barbara Saul, Eureka, CA*

Five Fat Peas Salad

addition, counting

Materials   fresh young pea pods (5 per child)
cherry tomatoes (4 per child)
sliced cucumbers (3 slices per child)
pieces of sweet yellow or orange peppers (2 pieces per child)
lettuce (1 piece per child)
small bowls

What to do
1. Place all of the ingredients in separate large bowls. Give each child a small bowl.
2. Do the following fingerplay with the children:

   Five Fat Peas
   Five fat peas in a pea pod pressed. (hold hand in a fist)
   One grew, two grew, and so did all the rest. (put fingers up, one by one)

They grew and grew (raise hand in the air slowly)
And did not stop,
Until one day the pod went POP! (clap hands together)

3. Ask each child to take five pea pods. Show them how to split open a pea pod and count the peas inside. Are there five, like in the song, or even more?
4. Invite them to open their pea pods and put all the tiny peas into their bowl and count them.
5. Ask the children to add four tomatoes, three cucumbers, two peppers, and one piece of lettuce to their bowls. See if any of the children notice that each time there is one less of each ingredient.
6. Talk about the textures and colors of their salads.
7. Let the children eat their bowls of salad with their fingers.

✚ *Anne Adeney, Plymouth, United Kingdom*

Food Patterns

patterns

Materials
variety of snack items (apple slices, orange wedges, dried fruit, raisins, pretzel sticks, cereal, goldfish crackers)
paper napkins
sentence strips

What to do
1. Place each type of snack in a separate bowl and give each child a sentence strip.
2. Invite the children to make patterns on their sentence strips with the food (for example, pretzel, raisin, raisin; pretzel, raisin, raisin).
3. As the children are making the patterns, go around the classroom and ask them to talk about the patterns.
4. When each child finishes his pattern, invite him to eat it.

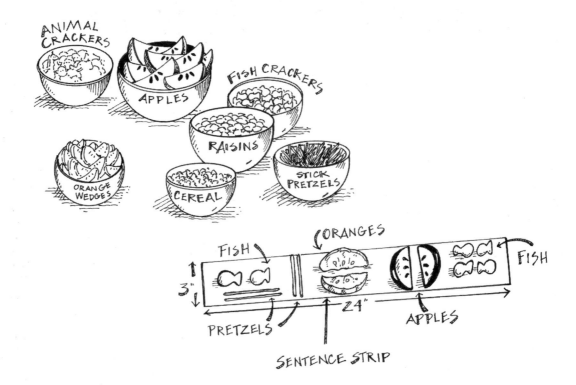

Related books *The Gingerbread Boy* by Richard Egielski
Stone Soup by Marcia Brown

✚ *Barbara Saul, Eureka, CA*

Fraction Cheese Sticks

basic fractions

Materials string cheese

What to do
1. At snack time, provide string cheese.
2. Cut the string cheese in half and tell the children, "This is one half of a string cheese stick."
3. Show them ¼ and ⅓ of a string cheese stick.
4. Ask them which piece they would prefer.

✚ *Lily Erlic, Victoria, BC, Canada*

Fruit Kabob Patterns

patterns

Materials   various fruits cut into chunks
bamboo skewers
picture cards of fruits (optional)

What to do
1. Give each child a bamboo skewer.
2. Demonstrate a fruit pattern on a skewer, for example, orange, apple, grape; orange, apple, grape. If desired, provide picture cards in a pattern for them to duplicate.
3. After the children make their patterns, invite them to eat the kabobs.

Related book   *The Very Hungry Caterpillar* by Eric Carle

✚ *Kristi Larson, Spirit Lake, IA*

Fruit Smoothies

counting, fractions, measurement

Materials   vanilla frozen yogurt
large spoon
bananas
plastic knives
1 cup and ½ cup measuring cups
milk
berries
blender
cups

What to do
1. Help one child at a time make a smoothie.
2. Have the child put a large scoop of frozen yogurt in a blender.
3. Help the child cut a banana in half, peel it, and place ½ of the banana into blender. Save the other half for another child.
4. Invite the child to measure ½ cup of milk and ½ cup of berries and add to the blender.
5. Put the lid on and turn on the blender until thoroughly blended (adult only).
6. Pour into a glass and drink.
7. If desired, make a rebus recipe card for children to follow.

Related books   *Good Enough to Eat: A Kid's Guide to Nutrition* by Lizzy Rockwell
Gregory the Terrible Eater by Mitchell Sharmat

✚ *Kristi Larson, Spirit Lake, IA*

Gingerbread Men

fractions, geometry, shapes

Materials   gingerbread dough (see recipe on page 477)
dried currants or raisins cut in halves or fourths
individual baking sheets (3" x 6" pieces of tagboard covered with aluminum foil)
plastic knife (1 per child)
oven

What to do
1. Make the gingerbread dough with the children. Make sure everyone washes their hands. Let them help measure the ingredients.
2. Demonstrate the following steps before distributing materials to the children. You might want to practice using playdough before making the cookies.
3. Start with a lump of dough about the size of a walnut.
4. Cut the lump of dough in half, noting that both pieces are equal in size.
5. Cut each of the two pieces in half. You now have four equal pieces.
6. With a forward/backward motion, roll two of the pieces to make cylinders.
7. Cut each cylinder in half. Now you have four short cylinders.
8. With a circular motion, make two round spheres.
9. Arrange the spheres on the cookie sheet so they touch. These make the head and body of the gingerbread man.

10. Using two of the cylinders, place them on either side of the body to make arms. Use the other two cylinders to make legs the same way.

11. Press with your thumb so the dough is flattened evenly.

12. Make eyes and mouth with the currants or raisins. You may use bits of dried cranberries for the mouth if you wish.

13. Give each child a baking sheet with his name on it, a small lump of dough, and a plastic knife. Help them make their cookies.

14. Arrange the individual cookie sheets on a large cookie sheet and bake at 350°.

Gingerbread Man Recipe

1 teaspoon ginger

¼ teaspoon cloves

½ teaspoon salt

¼ cup butter

½ cup sugar

½ cup molasses

3 ½ cups flour

½ teaspoon cinnamon

1 teaspoon baking soda

5 teaspoon water

Mix together butter, sugar, and molasses. Sift flour with spices and soda. Add dry ingredients to butter mix alternately with water. Knead until smooth. Mold gingerbread men and bake at 350° until lightly browned.

✦ *Mary Jo Shannon, Roanoke, VA*

Graham Cracker Fun

fractions, parts and whole, shapes

Materials
small plates
graham crackers

What to do
1. Ask the children to wash their hands for snack time.
2. Give each child a small plate with a large rectangle graham cracker.
3. Show the children the perforations in the cracker.

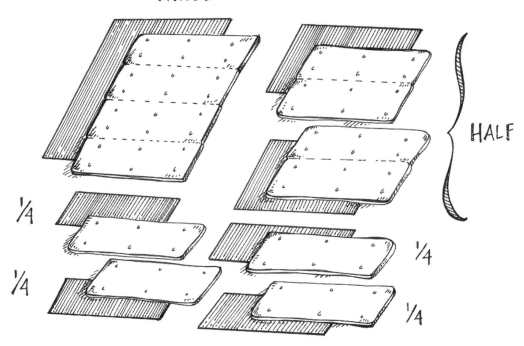

WHOLE

HALF

¼   ¼   ¼   ¼

4. Demonstrate how to break the cracker into halves and fourths.

More to do
Vary the activity by cutting other foods into fractional parts: slices of toast, apples, and bananas.

✚ *Susan Oldham Hill, Lakeland, FL*